OTHERS
KNOWING
OTHERS

To Gamal and Mavis with affection and hope of happiness.

Dad

5-2-94
Bloomington, IN

SMITHSONIAN SERIES IN ETHNOGRAPHIC INQUIRY
William L. Merrill and Ivan Karp, series editors

Ethnography as fieldwork, analysis, and literary form is the distinguishing feature of modern anthropology. Guided by the assumption that anthropological theory and ethnography are inextricably linked, this series is devoted to exploring the ethnographic enterprise.

ADVISORY BOARD

OTHERS
KNOWING
OTHERS

PERSPECTIVES ON ETHNOGRAPHIC CAREERS

EDITED BY DON D. FOWLER AND DONALD L. HARDESTY

SMITHSONIAN INSTITUTION PRESS
Washington and London

Edited by Robin Gould.
Production editing by Rebecca Browning.
Designed by Janice Wheeler.

Library of Congress Cataloging-in-Publication Data
Others knowing others : perspectives on ethnographic careers / edited by Don D.
    Fowler and Donald L. Hardesty.
        p.   cm. — (Smithsonian series in ethnographic inquiry)
    Includes bibliographical references.
    ISBN 1-56098-336-1
        1. Ethnology—Field work. 2. Ethnology—Philosophy. 3. Ethnology—
Methodology. 4. D'Azevedo, Warren L.   I. Fowler, Don D., 1936– .   II. Hard-
esty, Donald L., 1941– .   III. Series.
GN346.084   1994
305.8'001—dc20   93-29354

British Library Cataloguing-in-Publication-Data is available.

Manufactured in the United States of America.

10 9 8 7 6 5 4 3 2 1
03 02 01 00 99 98 97 96 95 94

Contents

Preface

This book contains essays by seven anthropologists about their long-term quests to record other cultures and what they learned about those cultures and themselves in the process. The essays were originally presented as "town-gown" lectures at the University of Nevada, Reno, during the 1989–90 academic year. Although fleshed out with footnotes and references, they retain the sense of personal immediacy and retrospective thoughtfulness of the spoken offerings. They are presented as contributions to the necessary and ongoing tradition of self-reflection within anthropology.

The occasion of the lecture series was to recognize the transition of Warren L. d'Azevedo to the status of Professor of Anthropology Emeritus. Professor d'Azevedo was brought to the university in 1963 to found a department of anthropology, which came into formal existence in 1966. The department, so ably begun, continues in good fettle under Warren's benevolent but watchful eye to the present.

For Warren, achieving emeritus status simply means cessation of formal classroom teaching. He remains as active as ever, working with graduate students, writing, and lecturing. We decided to mark the transition by a public lecture series, each lecture followed by a seminar in which the speaker, colleagues, and students would review the issues raised in the public presentation. The series, entitled *Another Look: Perspectives on Long-Term*

Anthropological Field Work, was funded by the Nevada Humanities Committee and the University of Nevada, Reno Graduate School. We owe special thanks to Judith Winzeler, executive director of the Nevada Humanities Committee, and Kenneth W. Hunter, vice-president for research and dean of the graduate school, for their interest and support. We also deeply appreciate the work of Cleda Burney, Jan Douglass, Ava Hahn, Susan Hardesty, and Susan Rodriguez in helping to make the lecture series and the book successful realities. Our special thanks to Rebecca Browning and Robin A. Gould, whose combined editorial acumen has greatly improved the volume. After the lectures were given and the papers revised in light of the seminars, it seemed clear that *Others Knowing Others* (suggested by Catherine S. Fowler) was a more appropriate title for the collected papers.

We invited friends and colleagues of Warren's who, like him, have engaged in long-term ethnographic fieldwork and who, like him, share in the tradition of concerned humanism within anthropology. We asked the speakers to provide personal assessments of their careers as ethnographers. What does it mean for ethnographers and for the people(s) they know and work with to "grow up" together, to move together from novice to senior scholar and, in some cases, tribal elderhood? How do one's perceptions of self, of one's profession, of the people one knows, change and mature over time?

Three participants are colleagues of Warren's at the University of Nevada, Reno—William Douglass, Catherine Fowler, and Robert Winzeler. Indeed, Warren played central roles in bringing them, as well us, to the university. Nazif Shahrani was a vital and gracious member of our faculty before moving first to the University of California, Los Angeles, and then to Indiana University. Joan Ablon, James Fernandez, and Simon Ottenberg have been colleagues and friends of Warren's since student days.

Warren L. d'Azevedo was born in Oakland, California, in 1920 and grew up in central California. He attended the University of California, Berkeley, where he took courses with A. L. Kroeber, Robert H. Lowie, and others in anthropology and a number of savants in literature. He graduated in 1942 with a B.A. in anthropology and english and signed on with various merchant vessels for the duration of World War II. (He was later declared to be a veteran of the U.S. Coast Guard by the government.) One seabag was always full of anthropology books—at first Benedict's *Patterns of*

Culture, Malinowski's *Argonauts of the Western Pacific,* and Frazer's *Golden Bough* filled his spare shipboard hours. But he soon became increasingly interested in contemporary social issues, and his reading turned to Herbert Aptheker, Eric Williams, W. E. B. DuBois, and Melville Herskovits's *The Myth of the Negro Past,* which, as he says, "became for a time a kind of scripture."

His newly acquired social awareness ultimately led to confrontations with the conservative Sailors' Union of the Pacific, and his joining the militant National Maritime Union. This group actively pursued a policy of desegregation in its hiring halls and on ships, almost an anomaly at that time, and Warren's education in the politics of race and labor relations proceeded at a rapid pace as a result. Warren married Kathleen Addison during the war, and they had two children, Anya and Erik. For a half century, Kathleen has been partner to Warren, her wondrous insights into people, their foibles, follies, and innate humanity equalled by none.

After the war, Warren worked as a sailor and at other odd jobs in the Bay area, continuing his involvement in seamens' union activities. In 1950 he was able to return to school at Berkeley. He took course work in anthropology with Theodore McCown, David Mandelbaum, and John Rowe, and with Wolfram Eberhard in sociology, Kenneth Stamp in history, and John Carter in literature. His interest in race relations and current social issues increased. He was among those who sought out the charismatic Paul Radin, whose star-crossed career is legendary in anthropology (Diamond 1981). In the early 1950s, Radin was teaching in the extension division at Berkeley. According to Warren,

Radin instilled in us an awareness of the links between anthropology, history and literature, insisting always that the role of ethnographer as ostensibly objective observer must be tempered by a disposition to enter as fully as possible into the ways of thinking of individuals in other cultures. He saw fieldwork as an art requiring special qualities and motivations on the part of those who chose to undertake it. (d'Azevedo 1993:7)

Encouraged by Radin, Warren and Kathy made their first visits to the Washoe Indians, who traditionally lived along the eastern slopes of the Sierra Nevada from about Bridgeport, California, on the south to Susanville, California, on the north, their territory centering on Lake Tahoe. There was a group of peyotists among the Washoe, and Warren became an advocate for their religious rights, an advocacy he continues to pursue.

Warren's study of Washoe history and culture convinced him that ethnography was his calling. His interests, however, were turning increasingly toward Africa. In 1953 he applied for and received a fellowship to go to Northwestern University to work with the inimitable Melville J. Herskovits, an already legendary figure. Herskovits's work on Africans and African Americans was outstanding. His breadth of knowledge, his acerbic wit, his militant humanism, and willingness to stand and fight on intellectual and social issues were his hallmarks. For the following two years, Warren and his fellow graduate students were immersed in studies with William Bascom, David Apter, the much-admired Edward Dozier, Francis L. K. Hsu—and of course with Herskovits.

In 1955 Warren passed his doctoral exams and received a grant from the Ford Foundation to study the Gola of Liberia. But 1955 was the era of rampant McCarthyism. Warren's application for a passport was denied on the grounds that he was an active member of the Communist Party. His explanation, that he was no longer a member, was meaningless in the context of the times, especially his refusal to name former associates. Herskovits gave unstinting and courageous support and helped secure a Washington, D.C., law firm to resolve the problem. Meanwhile Warren, Kathy, and children returned to western Nevada to work for eight months among the Washoe until the passport was finally issued.

There was a flurry of activity to get ready to go. The d'Azevedos embarked on a ship from New Orleans. Once in Liberia, there were many delays, but Warren was finally granted an interview with President W. V. S. Tubman. President Tubman grudgingly granted permission for the family to go upcountry among the "troublesome" Gola. Thus began what is now (1993) a nearly four-decade involvement with the Gola, their culture, and their art. It is not appropriate here to review Warren d'Azevedo's scholarly career, which is still very actively underway. We can only say that our lives, and those of multitudes of colleagues and students at Utah, Pittsburgh, Nevada, Indiana, Princeton, and elsewhere, and those of their many friends worldwide, would have been far, far poorer had Warren and Kathy d'Azevedo not come among us.

After teaching at the universities of California, Utah, and Pittsburgh,

Warren came in 1963 to the University of Nevada, Reno, to found an anthropology department, as noted previously. From Nevada, Warren has made periodic major trips back to the Gola in Liberia and continued to work with the Washoe people just down the road—work and relationships that have continued over forty years. His long-term involvements are the inspiration for the present book.

Don D. Fowler
Donald L. Hardesty
April 23, 1993

OTHERS
KNOWING
OTHERS

Introduction

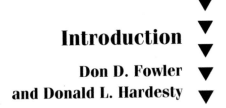

Don D. Fowler
and Donald L. Hardesty

A central problem for scholars, whether anthropologists, linguists, political scientists, or students of literature, is how to achieve accurate knowledge and understanding of different lifeways, and how these are properly conveyed within the scholar's own culture. Anthropology's special province, as a scholarly discipline, was originally the study, description, understanding, and interpretation of exotic peoples and cultures. Until after World War II, the primary focus was on tribal, or traditional cultures. Since then anthropological study has broadened to include the detailed study of nation states, and ethnic and minority groups within them.

The educated public has long been fascinated by "exotic, other" peoples and cultures. Most of the information about other peoples and cultures that is conveyed through the popular scientific press or documentary television derives from anthropological research and writing. This imposes an obligation on anthropologists to insure that the data they present are as culturally accurate as they can be. How one gains accurate and valid knowledge about another culture, and how that knowledge is conveyed to the scholarly world and the public has been, over the past decade, a major debate within anthropology. The recent (sometimes acrimonious) public discussion of the late Margaret Mead's interpretation of Samoan culture is a case in point (Freeman 1983; Holmes 1987). She initially studied the Samoan people for about a year in the 1920s. In the 1970s, scholar-critics and some Samoan people charged that her depiction of traditional Samoan culture was inaccurate. Other scholars, and some Samoans, disagreed. The general issue, however, remains for further consideration: What is required if the anthropologist is to achieve an adequate and accurate understanding of very different, seemingly exotic, cultures? And, how does one properly interpret (or translate) that understanding to the scholarly world and the educated public in the anthropologist's own society?

Earlier in this century, the approach adopted was usually a "scientific" one. That is, world cultures were grouped into classes or types, often on the basis of an arbitrary scale of cultural complexity. Cultures of the same type then could be studied and compared in a manner somewhat analogous to the way species were studied and compared in biology. Or parts of cultures, for example, religions, kinship systems, technologies, and legends, could be separated out from several cultures, again to be studied in a comparative framework. In either instance, the aim was the formulation of scientific generalizations that would elucidate the commonalities of human cultural behavior. The approach grew out a central tenet of the scientific method: that all phenomena in the universe—physical, biological, or cultural—operate according to natural laws. The task of the physicist, biologist, or anthropologist, as scientist, is to delineate these laws by analysis and comparison of relevant data. The scientist in this approach stands outside as an objective, neutral observer.

Within this general framework, anthropologists went to the field and lived with and studied a group of people for six months to a year. A monograph or book on the culture of the group would be produced, usually with sets of data that could be used in the comparative framework outlined above. Often, the anthropologist would then move on to other groups for similar periods of study. Some anthropologists studied several different peoples over the course of their careers. To again use Margaret Mead as an example, she worked with Samoans, Balinese, three different New Guinea peoples, and an American Indian tribe during the course of her remarkable fifty-year career. Although her work was usually more humanistic than scientific in tone, it was still done within the general comparative, scientific framework noted above. Mead spent a period of a few months to a year with each group, often over two or more field trips.

But many anthropologists are concerned that short-term fieldwork, no matter how good the field worker, produces only a superficial understanding of the cultures studied. As humanist scholars have long known, languages and cultures are extraordinarily complex and subtle. Scholars struggle for a lifetime to achieve an adequate understanding of some portion of the Western tradition, of which they are a part. How much more difficult, then, is it to understand a very different, non-Western culture?

It is clear that tribal or traditional do not equal simple, as some earlier anthropologists had assumed by constructing their arbitrary scales of cultural complexity. Rather, we understand that all human languages are completely capable of communicating highly subtle and complex ideas and that all cultures are very complex; value systems, mores, and modes of behavior are as complex as those of the anthropologist's culture. But because the languages and cultures are so different, their apparent exoticism renders them even more difficult for an outside observer to comprehend and appreciate. How, then, do anthropologists achieve adequate understanding of another culture, so that they can properly interpret, or translate, as accurately and as fully as possible to their own society? Long-term involvement seems to be the most feasible approach.

Since the 1960s discussion of these issues has taken place in reflective and reflexive modes. The concept of the anthropologist as an outside, neutral observer is recognized as a myth. By the anthropologist's very intrusion on another people, by the process of attempting to properly and meaningfully communicate with them, and the potential impacts on the people of what is written about them, the anthropologist is anything but an outside, neutral observer. What then are the roles and obligations of the anthropologist in the study, short-term or long-term, of another people and their culture? A host of issues arise from this question.

First, one needs to study one's self in relation to the culture studied. How does one prepare to be a scholar, a recorder, an interpreter of another culture? How does the anthropologist change by immersion in the other culture? One is intellectually and emotionally honed by the experience. The initial apparent "exotic-ness" produces culture shock, a common phenomenon experienced by tourists visiting other societies. But the anthropologist is more than a visitor. The anthropologist learns the language, engages in extended discussions with the people, seeks understanding, and emerges with a very different kind of experience than that of the casual visitor. The well-known French anthropologist Claude Lévi-Strauss reflects on this often transforming experience in his book *Tristes Tropique* (1963), in which he chronicles his culture shock and his struggles to understand and interpret the hunter-gatherer peoples of the southern Amazon Basin during his work with them in the 1940s. The key is how the field experience changes one as an observer and as an interpreter of another culture. What new perspectives on oneself as scholar, and on the peoples one studies, are gained?

Second, as the anthropologist returns to a culture again and again, more is learned, and there is a constant reappraisal of one's own view of the culture. Seemingly opaque practices and ideas slowly become clear as more inter-relationships within the culture come to be understood. How do interpretations change as more is learned? Long-term study also affords the opportunity for the development of a truly ethnohistoric perspective—one that covers the observer's own life as well as those of the people studied. It becomes possible to see the direction of individuals' lives as they grow up and play out different life-roles. This, in turn, allows a better understanding of the central values and practices of the culture as they structure and influences the lives of individuals within it.

Long-term study provides a perspective on culture change. Earlier studies of tribal/traditional cultures were often couched in terms of an ethnographic present, a cultural baseline that was at best chimerical. The assumption was that traditional cultures were static and unchanging until impinged upon by "civilization." In fact, all cultures change over time. Especially since World War II, all world cultures have been subjected to increasingly rapid change, be they traditional, or First, Second, Third, or Fourth World cultures, however defined.

Anthropologists, during their first work with a group of people, observe culture at a particular point that is often taken as a baseline. When the anthropologist returns, there is apparent culture loss. But the loss may simply be illusory: the culture has continued to change and new practices have replaced the old. Core cultural features and values remain and influence how the culture does change. A long-term view allows the anthropologist to sort out the permanent from the transitory, and to better understand the directions of, and reasons for, change in that culture.

There is also the issue of the anthropologist creating the history of the people studied. The people have an oral (and sometimes written) tradition about their own past. Anthropologists use the tools of modern ethnohistory and historiography to produce their own written interpretation of that past. The anthropologist's history may be rejected as meaningless, or incorporated as fact, by the people themselves. In the latter case, it becomes part of the tradition of the culture. But, how accurate is the anthropologist's history?

A related issue is that of the anthropologist as the definer of "traditional" culture. For example, many twentieth-century Native American groups use the nineteenth-century anthropological publications of the Smithsonian Institution as guides to recover and interpret their own past cultures. But those reports were often based on very hasty fieldwork and are known to be inaccurate. How can contemporary anthropologists insure that their work will not do a disservice to future generations of the peoples they study?

The papers in this volume contribute to a growing literature on the issues outlined above: what are the personal, social, political, and intellectual complexities and meanings of doing anthropology in the field. Over the past two plus decades, especially since Hymes's *Reinventing Anthropology* (1969), discussions of the complexities and meanings of doing anthropology in general, and ethnographic fieldwork in particular, increasingly have been cast in a reflexive mode. A central issue is how do anthropologists relate to the people they study (Tedlock 1991, 1992); how do they relate to the images of "the other," which in some sense they create (Fabian 1983)? At the same time, as the present papers and many other essays attest, the people anthropologists study, especially the consultants with whom they are most closely associated, create their own "others," their own images of anthropologists and other "theys" and "thems." Such mutual creative perceptions gives us our title.

In his cogent and perceptive essay about becoming and being an anthropologist, Miles Richardson (1975) points out how different the meanings and contexts of anthropology were in the 1970s from earlier pre–World War II times. Many of the concerns of the 1970s he points to are still with us, some greatly magnified by the critical and reflexive examinations of anthropological selves and others in the intervening decades (Asad 1973; Clifford and Marcus 1986; Diamond 1974; Marcus and Fischer 1986; Ruby 1982; Vidich 1974).

Concurrent with these assessments have been a number of papers and books on being an anthropologist in the field. Some studies are of historical figures (for example, the ever-popular Bronislaw Malinowski), as in the papers by Cole, Hinsley, Clifford and Stocking in Stocking (1983) and by Stocking, Tomas, Feet, and Bashkow in Stocking (1991). Others are current and primarily autobiographical. All writers agree that ethnographic fieldwork is the *leitmotif* of cultural anthropology. All agree that it is a kind of rite of passage; not all agree that it is a strictly *necessary* rite. Most agree that fieldwork teaches anthropologists how they might better know others. Most agree that such self-knowledge makes one a more skilled interpreter of humanity.

In the 1920s and 1930s, some anthropologists took the "know thyself" dictum to mean psychoanalysis. Indeed, Clyde Kluckhohn, and perhaps others, underwent analysis so that they might be better, presumably more aware and perceptive field anthropologists. Modes of self-discovery changed in subsequent decades, although some (for example, Wengle 1988) still tend to see fieldwork as effecting some sort of psychotherapeutic change in anthropologists.

How neophyte fieldworkers are prepared for the field also has changed over time. Early workers, such as Frank Hamilton Cushing and Jesse Walter Fewkes, were entirely self-trained (Hinsley 1983). The Laboratory of Anthropology in Santa Fe, New Mexico, conducted the first ethnographic field schools in the United States from 1929 through 1934, led (successively) by A. L. Kroeber, Leslie Spier, Ruth Benedict, Leslie A. White, Ralph Linton, and Spier again in the final, 1934 season. Students included May Mandelbaum, Regina Flannery, John Gillin, Morris Opler, Sol Tax, Fred Eggan, Edward Kennard, Mischa Titiev, E. Adamson Hoebel, Earl Count, and Philleo Nash, among other luminaries (Nusbaum 1934). The instructors had all been through the "Throw 'em off the pier to sink or swim" school of ethnography. But after the Laboratory of Anthropology program ended in 1934, formal instruction became a rarity.

But, by 1960 things had begun to change. The universities of Nevada and Pittsburgh, together with Stanford University, held summer ethnographic field schools from 1964 through 1970 under National Science Foundation sponsorship. Warren d'Azevedo played a prominent role in that consortium. Various other field schools got underway about that time, or soon thereafter. Although ethnographic field manuals of one kind or another have a long history (Fowler 1975) dating to the 1500s, comprehensive instructions for the study of other cultures did not appear until Degérando's *The Observation of Savage Peoples* (1800) and the little known, but extremely thorough and insightful, *How to Observe Manners and Morals* by Harriet Martineau (1838). Aside from *Notes and Queries* (Royal Anthropological Institute 1964), which first appeared in the 1880s, no ethnographic field manuals more comprehensive than Degérando's and Martineau's appeared until the late 1960s. Since then students have had the advantage of several major works (Bernard 1988; Epstein 1967; Honigmann 1979; Narroll and Cohen 1970; Pelto 1970; Spradley 1980; Werner and Schoepfle 1987). In theory at least, modern students go off to exotic climes better prepared than their immediate professional ancestors. Once sociologists discovered real live fieldwork, euphemistically glossed as natural sociology (Schatzmann and Strauss 1973) or ethnomethodology (Bruyn 1966), a spate of how-to-do-it manuals appeared, some of use to anthropologists (see Hammersley and Atkinson [1983] for a critical assessment of a range of sociological and anthropological field manuals).

Several themes run through the autobiographical works on fieldwork. One is the aforementioned perception of it being a rite of passage, with the incumbent entering the field as a neophyte, no matter how many manuals on method they absorbed, and emerging in some sense reborn as anthropologist. A second theme is who goes into anthropology and why? Stanley Diamond (1974:401) says that "Anthropology, reified as the study of man, is the study of men in crisis by men in crisis." Elaborating on this, Bob Scholte (1977:5) writes:

The men and women in crisis were and are those conquered and oppressed by civilization. The men and women who seek to understand these peoples' indigenous lives are also in crisis. Their search is for alternative possibilities to the repression and alienating aspects of their own civilized lives.

Scholte echoes here Claude Lévi-Strauss's (1963:381–392) views about alienation and becoming an anthropologist. The present authors examine this matter from their own perspectives and come to various conclusions, as have nearly all those cited in the following paragraph.

A third theme is the matter of culture shock exacerbated by the sheer

complexities of learning to navigate, spatially as well as intellectually, socially, and politically, in a different culture (see Barley 1983, 1986; DeVita
1990, 1992; Freilich 1970; Honigmann 1976; Jongmans and Gutkind 1967;
Kimball and Watson 1972; Nash 1963; Spindler 1970; Wax 1971). As Watson (1972:301) puts it, anthropologists must struggle with the antinomies of
strange:familiar; outsider:insider; sojourner:resident; transient:one-of-us, or,
in Hortense Powdermaker's (1967) terms, the tension inherent in the
stranger:friend dyad. Part of this, as Vincent Crapanzano (1977:3) notes, is
that anthropologists must constantly struggle with and against "the illusion
of sensitivity to cultural differences." Laura Bohannan, under the pen name
of Eleanor Smith Bowen (1954), and Gerald Berreman (1962) provide classic and telling statements about these tensions and struggles and how one
learns to "navigate" in another culture in spite of and because of them.

A fourth theme centers on the relationships between anthropologists and
their consultants (formerly informants). Examples include Richardson
(1975), Magnarella (1986), Lawless (1986), and Sanjek (1990, 1993). Each
approaches this theme in a slightly different way. As Richardson (1975:520)
says, "In the field the relationship most critical to the ethnographer, the
one that actually changes him from tourist to ethnographer, is the relationship with his informant." Richardson (1975:520–521) goes on to ask,
"Who is this person who defines, even creates, the ethnographer?" and
then points out that conversely it also is "the ethnographer who defines the
informant. . . . The informant is not a subject . . . not an interviewee . . .
not necessarily a friend," but is "the teacher of the ethnographer." A close
teacher-pupil relationship has always been central in fieldwork. Frank
Hamilton Cushing (1990) in the 1880s was taken in hand by the Governor
of Zuni Pueblo so that Cushing might properly learn to be a Zuni. Nearly
all the anthropologists in the works we have surveyed at some point find,
work with, and cherish such a teacher. Certainly that is echoed in the present papers.

There is also the obverse relationship, in which the consultant becomes
the ethnographer, asking about and interpreting the culture of the anthropologist. Laura Bohannan (1966) has a wonderful story about how her consultants questioned her about and reinterpreted her rendition of Shakespeare's *Hamlet*. Lawless (1986:71) notes that this obverse relationship is in
itself heuristically useful:

With the proper perspective, it can be liberating to realize how irrational one's own cultural beliefs and behaviors are when viewed through the prisms of another folk model.

Another aspect of the relationship between anthropologist and consultant has to do with cross-gender relationships in the field. Picchi (1989) discusses the complexities arising when the anthropologist becomes perceived, in some senses, as a member of the group and then is expected to act in appropriate gendered fashion. Other complexities due to gender considerations in differing cultural contexts are raised by Cesara (1982) and the papers in Altorki and El-Solh (1988) and Golde (1970).

A fifth theme relates to individuals trained formally or informally as anthropologists who then work in their own cultures (Liberty 1978; Fahim 1982). *The Tewa World* by Alfonso Ortiz (1969), a native of San Juan Pueblo in New Mexico, is an excellent and sensitive example of studies that can emerge from this situation. But the complexities are many. Nita Kumar (1992) and Kirin Navayan (1993) provide us with a rich and insightful discussions of the dilemmas involved in returning to India to do fieldwork. Nesha Haniff (1985) describes a very different field situation in the Caribbean but also gives us useful insights on her work as an "insider" anthropologist. These studies complement the paper by Nazif Shahrani in the present volume, who examines not only the meanings and complexities of returning to his own country to do anthropology, but also what it means to then have his country engulfed in revolution.

Finally, there is the theme of the present book: long-term fieldwork. In the late 1970s a group of anthropologists gathered at a Wenner-Gren conference (Foster et al. 1979) to discuss methodological and theoretical implications of such work and the value of the information derived from a commitment to such studies. While there are personal insights in the papers in the volume, it is generally objectively focused. As such, it provides a neat complement to the papers in the present volume.

As one reads the papers herein, one will find the basic themes discussed in ways both similar and different than they are in the papers reviewed above. Most importantly, one will find very personal expositions about the meanings and complexities of *Others Knowing Others* over the courses of professional lifetimes. The collective papers are, we feel, an appropriate way to celebrate and honor the more than four decades of work of Warren L.

d'Azevedo. In his own quest, Warren has gained wisdom and insight from his Washoe and Gola colleagues, has combined that knowledge with his own, and has enriched all of us with the results. He adds to the gift with thoughts on his own career and the papers herein in Afterthoughts at the end of the volume.

References Cited

Altorki, Soraya, and Camillia Fawzi El-Solh (editors)
1988   *Arab Women in the Field. Studying Your Own Society.* Syracuse University Press, Syracuse, New York.

Asad, Talal (editor)
1973   *Anthropology and the Colonial Encounter.* Humanities Press, New York.

Barley, Nigel
1983   *The Innocent Anthropologist. Notes from a Mud Hut.* Henry Holt, New York.
1986   *Ceremony. An Anthropologist's Misadventures in the African Bush.* Henry Holt, New York.

Bernard, H. Russell
1988   *Research Methods in Cultural Anthropology.* Sage Publications, Newbury Park, California.

Berreman, Gerald
1962   *Behind Many Masks: Ethnography and Impression Management in a Himalayan Village.* Society for Applied Anthropology Monograph no. 4. Ithaca, New York.

Bohannan, Laura
1966   Shakespeare in the Bush. *Natural History* 75(7):28–33.

Bowen, Eleanor Smith [Laura Bohannan]
1954   *Return to Laughter.* Anchor Books, Garden City, New Jersey.

Bruyn, S. T.
1966   *The Human Perspective: The Methodology of Participant Observation.* Prentice-Hall, Englewood Cliffs, New Jersey.

Cesara, Marta
1982   *Reflections of a Woman Anthropologist: No Hiding Place.* Academic Press, New York.

Clifford, James, and George E. Marcus (editors)
1986   *Writing Cultures: The Poetics and Politics of Ethnography.* University of California Press, Berkeley.

Crapanzano, Vincent
1977   The Life History in Anthropological Fieldwork. *Anthropology and Humanism Quarterly* 2(2–3):3–11.

Cushing, Frank H.

1990   *Cushing at Zuni. The Correspondence and Journals of Frank Hamilton Cushing, 1879–1884,* edited by Jesse Green. University of New Mexico Press, Albuquerque.

d'Azevedo, Warren L.

1993   *Rebel Destinies: Remembering Herskovits.* Hans Wolff Lecture Series, African Studies Program, Indiana University, in press.

Degérando, Joseph-Marie

1800   *Considérations sur les diverses méthodes à suivre dans l'observation des peuples sauvages.* Paris. (Translated and edited by F. C. T. Moore as *The Observation of Savage Peoples.* University of California Press, Berkeley, 1969.)

DeVita, Philip R. (editor)

1990   *The Humbled Anthropologist: Tales from the Pacific.* Wadsworth Publishing Company, Belmont, California.

1992   *The Naked Anthropologist. Tales from Around the World.* Wadsworth Publishing Company, Belmont, California.

Diamond, Stanley

1974   *In Search of the Primitive: a Critique of Civilization.* E. P. Dutton, New York.

1981   Paul Radin. In *Totems and Teachers. Perspectives on the History of Anthropology,* edited by Sydel Silverman, pp. 67–99. Columbia University Press, New York.

Epstein, A. L. (editor)

1967   *The Craft of Social Anthropology.* Tavistock, London.

Fabian, Hohannes

1983   *Time and the Other: How Anthropology Makes its Object.* Columbia University Press, New York.

Fahim, Hussein (editor)

1982   *Indigenous Anthropology in Non-Western Countries: Proceedings of a Burg Wartenstein Symposium.* Carolina Academic Press, Durham.

Foster, George M., Thayer Scudder, Elizabeth Colson, and Robert V. Kemper (editors)

1979   *Long-Term Field Research in Social Anthropology.* Academic Press, New York.

Fowler, Don D.

1975   Notes on Inquiries in Anthropology: A Bibliographic Essay. In *Toward a Science of Man. Essays in the History of Anthropology,* edited by T. H. Thoresen, pp. 15–32. Mouton, The Hague.

Freeman, Derek

1983   *Margaret Mead and Samoa: The Making and Unmaking of an Anthropological Myth.* Harvard University Press, Cambridge.

Freilich, Morris

1970   *Marginal Natives: Anthropologists at Work.* Harper and Row, New York.

Golde, Peggy (editor)

1970　*Women in the Field: Anthropological Experiences.* Aldine, Chicago.

Hammersley, Martin, and Paul Atkinson

1983　*Ethnography. Principles in Practice.* Tavistock, London and New York.

Haniff, Nesha Z.

1985　Toward a Native Anthropology: Methodological Notes on a Study of Successful Caribbean Women by an Insider. *Anthropology and Humanism Quarterly* 10(4):106–113.

Hinsley, Curtis

1983　Ethnographic Charisma and Scientific Routine: Cushing and Fewkes in the American Southwest, 1879–1893. In *Observers Observed. Essays on Ethnographic Fieldwork,* edited by George W. Stocking, Jr., pp. 53–69. History of Anthropology, vol. 1. University of Wisconsin Press, Madison.

Holmes, Lowell D.

1987　*Quest for the Real Samoa: The Mead/Freeman Controversy.* Bergin and Garvey, South Hadley, Massachusetts.

Honigmann, John J.

1976　The Personal Approach in Cultural Anthropological Research. *Current Anthropology* 17(2):243–261.

Honigmann, John J. (editor)

1979　*Handbook of Social and Cultural Anthropology.* Rand McNally, Chicago.

Hymes, Dell (editor)

1969　*Reinventing Anthropology.* Random House, New York.

Jongmans, D. G. and P. C. W. Gutkind (editors)

1967　*Anthropologists in the Field.* Van Gorcum, Assen.

Kimball, Solon T., and James B. Watson (editors)

1972　*Crossing Cultural Boundaries. The Anthropological Experience.* Chandler Publishing, San Franciso.

Kumar, Nita

1992　*Friends, Brothers and Informants. Fieldwork Memoirs of Banaras.* University of California Press, Berkeley.

Lawless, Robert

1986　Ethnoethnographers and the Anthropologist. *Anthropology* 10(1):55–74.

Lévi-Strauss, Claude

1963　*Tristes Tropiques.* Criterion Books, New York.

Liberty, Margot (editor)

1978　*American Indian Intellectuals.* West Publishing Company, St. Paul, Minnesota.

Magnarella, Paul J.

1986　Anthropological Fieldwork, Key Informants and Human Bonds. *Anthropology and Humanism Quarterly* 11(2):33–37.

Marcus, George E., and Michael M. J. Fischer
1986   *Anthropology as Cultural Critique.* University of Chicago Press, Chicago.
Martineau, Harriett
1838   *How to Observe Manners and Morals.* Lea and Blanchard, Philadelphia. (Reprinted 1989 by Transaction Publishers, New Brunswick.)
Narayan, Kirin
1993   How Native is a "Native" Anthropologist? *American Anthropologist* 95 (3):671–686.
Narroll, Raoul, and Ronald Cohen (editors)
1970   *A Handbook of Method in Cultural Anthropology.* Columbia University Press, New York.
Nash, Dennison
1963   The Ethnologist as Stranger: An Essay in the Sociology of Knowledge. *Southwestern Journal of Anthropology* 19:149–167.
Nusbaum, Jesse
1934   A Review of the Development of the Laboratory of Anthropology. Manuscript on file, Archives, Laboratory of Anthropology, Museum of New Mexico, Santa Fe.
Ortiz, Alfonso
1969   *The Tewa World. Space, Time and Becoming in a Pueblo Society.* University of Chicago Press, Chicago.
Pelto, Pertti
1970   *Anthropological Research: the Structure of Inquiry.* Harper and Row, New York.
Picchi, Debra
1989   Yare's Anger: Conformity and Rage in the Field. *Anthropology and Humanism Quarterly* 14(2):65–72.
Powdermaker, Hortense
1967   *Stranger and Friend: The Way of an Anthropologist.* Norton, New York.
Richardson, Miles
1975   Anthropologist—the Myth Teller. *American Ethnologist* 2(3):517–533.
Royal Anthropological Institute of Great Britain and Ireland
1964   *Notes and Queries on Anthropology.* 6th revised edition. Routledge and Kegan Paul, London.
Ruby, Jay (editor)
1982   *A Crack in the Mirror. Reflexive Perspectives in Anthropology.* University of Pennsylvania Press, Philadelphia.
Sanjek, Roger
1993   Anthropology's Hidden Colonialism. Assistants and Their Ethnographers. *Anthropology Today* 9(2):13–17.
Sanjek, Roger (editor)
1990   *Fieldnotes: The Makings of Anthropology.* Cornell University Press, Ithaca, New York.

Schatzman, L., and A. Strauss
1973   *Field Research: Strategies in Natural Sociology.* Prentice-Hall, Englewood Cliffs, New Jersey.

Sholte, Bob
1977   Critical Anthropology Since its Reincarnation: On the Convergence between the Concept of Paradigm, the Rationality of Debate and Critical Anthropology. *Anthropology and Humanism Quarterly* 2(4):4–17.

Spindler, George D. (editor)
1970   *Being an Anthropologist: Fieldwork in Eleven Cultures.* Holt, Rinehart and Winston, New York.

Spradley, James P.
1980   *Participant Observation.* Holt, Rinehart & Winston, New York.

Stocking George W., Jr. (editor)
1983   *Observers Observed. Essays on Ethnographic Fieldwork.* History of Anthropology, vol. 1. University of Wisconsin Press, Madison.
1991   *Colonial Situations. Essays on the Contextualization of Ethnographic Knowledge.* History of Anthropology, vol. 7. University of Wisconsin Press, Madison.

Tedlock, Barbara
1991   From Participant Observation to Observations of Participants: The Emergence of Narrative Ethnography. *Journal of Anthropological Research* 46:69–94.
1992   *The Beautiful and the Dangerous: Encounters with the Zuni Indians.* Viking Press, New York.

Vidich, Arthur J.
1974   Ideological Theses in American Anthropology. *Social Research* 41(4):719–745.

Watson, James B.
1972   Epilogue: In Search of Intimacy. In *Crossing Cultural Boundaries. The Anthropological Experience,* edited by Solon T. Kimball and James B. Watson, pp. 299–302. Chandler Publishing, San Francisco.

Wax, Rosalie H.
1971   *Doing Fieldwork: Warnings and Advice.* University of Chicago Press, Chicago.

Wengle, John L.
1988   *Ethnographers in the Field. The Psychology of Research.* University of Alabama Press, Tuscaloosa and London.

Werner, Oswald, and G. Mark Schoepfle
1987   *Systematic Fieldwork,* vol. 1, *Foundations of Ethnography and Interviewing;* vol. 2, *Ethnographic Analysis and Data Management.* Sage Publishers, Newbury Park.

Honored Guest and Marginal Man: Long-Term Field Research and Predicaments of a Native Anthropologist

M. Nazif Shahrani

The *ideal ethnographer* studies *another culture* by bringing external and internal diversity to bear upon an ethnographic problem. Playing this role can make him or her an interesting pupil for the natives—one who is fun to teach and who therefore learns more. [emphasis added]
—Werner and Schoepfle, *Systematic Fieldwork*

So-called natives do not "inhabit" a world fully separate from the one ethnographers "live in." When people play "ethnographers and natives," it is ever more difficult to predict who will put on the loincloth and who will pick up the pencil and paper. More people are doing both, and more so-called natives are among . . . those who read and write ethnographies.
—Renato Rosaldo, *Culture and Truth*

Anthropology . . . is a worthwhile endeavor in as much as it enables us to understand ourselves in relations to others: the old definition of it as the study of "other cultures"—whether an honest confession or an expression of cultural arrogance— is no longer acceptable.
—Triloki N. Madan, "Anthropology as Mutual Interpretation of Cultures: Indian Perspective"

Ethnographic research carried out in one's own society may be the sine qua non for anthropology itself.
—Harry F. Wolcott, "Home and Away: Personal Contrasts in Ethnographic Style"

When I was invited by colleagues at the University of Nevada to take part in a lecture series celebrating the career of Professor Warren d'Azevedo, I agreed without hesitation. To me it seemed quite natural to honor our chief, one of anthropology's senior tribesmen. During my eighteen years of personal relations and professional association with my other tribe, the Kirghiz of Afghanistan,[1] in my role as an anthropologist I frequently participated in their cultural performances of hospitality honoring their Chief, the Kirghiz *Khan*. I also knew, both from my "fieldwork" among the Kirghiz and my working "in the field" as a student and a practitioner in the discipline of anthropology in United States academic institutions, that an invitation to participate in the rites of honoring an elder professional tribal member is a rare privilege. It is an occasion in which the invitee assumes a dual role, taking part in honoring the chief, and enjoying treatment as an honored guest.[2] My understanding of the Kirghiz ceremonial feasts cautioned me, however, that participation in such public performances in any capacity necessarily renders one vulnerable to the possibilities of public self-exposure. Among the Kirghiz, the constitution or reconstitution of the Khan's honor and prestige in the community is, at least in part, attained and sustained over time through the considerable self-exposure of the host's affairs (personal, familial, social, economic, and political—whether actual, potential, or hoped for), and at least a partial public exposure of the affairs of honored guests present at the feasts.[3] Not surprisingly, on this particular occasion, it appeared to me that the cultural norms for honoring our anthropological elder tribesman also called for some public exposure of our anthropological "self" or "selves."

The principal issues we were asked to reflect upon were the effects of long-term fieldwork upon the anthropologist as a scholar, as an observer, as a recorder, and as an interpreter of another culture, and the need to study one's self in relation to the culture one studies—and in my case, perhaps also the culture one studies *in*. Serious and sustained examinations of the effects of long-term field research upon ethnographers, their ethnographic products, and especially upon the communities they study, are sorely lacking, with the one important exception of a 1975 Burg Wartenstein conference that examined aspects of this subject (see Foster et al. 1979). Reasons for the scarcity of studies of our anthropological self (selves) in relation to communities and societies we study are surely many and complex. Fundamental among them has been the naive adherence to empiricism and positivism in the social sciences, which enjoined anthropologists to assume a posture currently labeled as the fictions of "objectivity, neutrality, and impartiality" (Rosaldo 1989:21). The required professional stance also discouraged expressions of the personal and experiential dimensions of fieldwork activities because of prevailing "'scientific' conventions of ethnographic presentation" (Babcock 1980:10). As a result, the anthropological fieldworker, native and Western alike, has long been rendered "a self-effacing creature without any reactions other than a recording machine" (Nash and Wintrob 1972:527; also see Sass 1986:53–54).

Only since the last decade, and more recently with the self-conscious claims and self-indulgent practices of post-modernist anthropology, are we told that the "Lone Ethnographer's guiding fiction of cultural compartments has crumbled," and that "a sea change in cultural studies has eroded once-dominant conceptions of truth and objectivity" (Rosaldo 1989:45, 21). This "sea change" appears to have not only introduced but to have made quite fashionable a reflexive, self-conscious, self-aware, and self-critical approach in anthropological writing, at least for the moment (see, among others, Manganaro 1990; Whitehead and Conaway 1986; Cesara 1982; Marcus and Fischer 1986:69; Geertz 1988; Clifford and Marcus 1986; and Sass 1986). It is, at least in part, in the spirit of wishing to contribute a ripple in this new sea change (even if it turns out to be just another passing academic fad) that I welcomed the opportunity to address the impact of my long-term fieldwork at "home" and my own studies in another culture as a native anthropologist, from a reflexive, self-conscious, and self-critical perspective.

At the same time, I could not but wonder whether and how, or to what extent, questions and concerns raised by and for Western anthropologists regarding the impact of long-term field research, might be relevant to my experiences as a native anthropologist—one who has done fieldwork in his own country of origin and culture of orientation and who does not appear to fit the widely held and accepted view that "the *ideal ethnographer* studies *another culture*" (Werner and Schoepfle 1986:24; for earlier statements on this issue see Nash 1963; Paul 1953:442; Simmel 1950:405; Schuetz 1944). The professional concerns and personal predicaments of "native,"[4] "local," or "indigenous" anthropologists and their place in the field (in both senses of the word) remain for the most part unexplored either by them or their Western colleagues.[5] Much of the anthropological preoccupation with the natives, so far at least, has focused on a number of patently methodological issues of interest only to the so-called ideal ethnographers. The natives are examined in their role as objects of ethnographic research by foreign (primarily European and American) anthropologists and other social scientists; as key informants; and as the "sidekick of the Lone Ethnographer" (Rosaldo 1989), who helps the ethnographer obtain the native cultural knowledge. Such knowledge is said to be "rarely if ever, made fully explicit [by the natives themselves]" because, it is contended, "the *natives*, by definition, do not engage in systematic acquisition of knowledge" (Werner and Schoepfle 1986:23, emphasis added). Given this curious epistemological supposition, the ideal ethnographer is said to make an "interesting pupil for the natives—one who is fun to teach and who therefore learns more" (Werner and Schoepfle 1986:24). By living with the natives, conversing, observing, and participating in their activities during the mystical experiences of doing fieldwork, the ideal pupil ethnographer is expected to gain the "internal or native" view, and his or her ethnography "must represent its host culture with fidelity" so that "the natives are able to recognize in it the familiar features of their own culture" (Werner and Schoepfle 1986:24). Systematic fieldwork as a scientific exercise is supposed to provide the anthropologist with the "'stereo' vision of the ethnographer" and unusual "binocular depth perception," enabling him or her to write "in the interface between the native culture and the culture of the users of the ethnographic product" (Werner and Schoepfle 1986:24, also see Aguilar 1981:20). Furthermore, it is also in the context of systematic fieldwork among the natives that anthropologists have come to claim the role of "marginal native at work" for themselves (Freilich 1977). Werner and Schoepfle's (1986) rather rosy picture of the lot of the systematic field worker aside, the role of marginal native, as Morris Freilich points out, "is not an easy one to play, for the *real natives* are often suspicious of the anthropologists" (1977:2). Apart from the traditional reasons for native suspicion of foreign anthropologists, the methodological and epistemological assumptions expressed in the discourse of *Systematic Fieldwork* (Werner and Schoepfle 1986) seem to invite further suspicion. One gets the clear impression that the ideal ethnographer's native is a lot like the "oriental" in Edward Said's *Orientalism,* who must be represented and spoken for by the ethnographer (Said 1978:6).

The persistence of such an impression in the anthropology of the 1980s is especially troubling in view of the fact that Said, at least initially, regarded anthropological research and writings as a possible corrective alternative to Orientalism (Said 1978:326), although in his more recent writings he appears to have revised his views on the matter (see Said 1985, 1989). Still, following the publication of Said's *Orientalism* the current rise in the popularity of reflexivity, the emergence (rediscovery?) of modernist anthropology, and the realization that the natives may be inhabiting the same world as the ethnographer and that these natives number increasingly among those who "read and write ethnographies" (Rosaldo 1989:45; see Hymes 1972:4), may not be entirely coincidental. Awareness of the presence and participation of the natives amidst anthropologists in Western metropolitan culture has surely heightened concerns and added new anxieties for the anthropological community over the accuracy and fidelity of ethnographic representations of other cultures. These new developments appear to have cast into doubt the veracity of ethnographic writings, long held sacrosanct by the anthropological enterprise (Clifford 1988; Clifford and Marcus 1986; Marcus and Fischer 1986; Fabian 1983). The present self-doubt and the impending malaise in anthropology might worsen in time if, as the Indian native anthropologist Triloki N. Madan states, anthropology, whether reflexive and self-critical or not, continues to operate on the basis of the Western dominated "old definition" of anthropology "as the study of 'other cultures,'" instead of adhering to a broader concept of anthropology as a discipline that "enables us to understand ourselves in relation to others" (1982).

It is not my aim, however, to address the nature of the construction of the self identity of anthropology and anthropologists (Western, non-Western, or native) in relation to the choice of more or less exotic research subjects. Nor is it my aim to examine the nature of the self-doubt currently being expressed about ethnographic writings. Rather my aim is very limited: It is to draw attention to, and to discuss, critically if and when possible, the dilemmas and predicaments—personal, professional, moral, and political—facing a native anthropologist as a long-term field researcher and a practitioner of a self-consciously defined Western social science discipline (as it has been briefly outlined above), both at home in the field, and in the field—that is, the discipline of anthropology at places of work and study in the institutions of higher education and research in the West. It is to the discussion of these issues that I now turn.

I use the dichotomy between native, indigenous insider or non-Western and foreign or Western anthropologists to highlight difficulties facing native anthropologists that may not confront the Western or foreign anthropologists in the field,[6] at least not in the same manner and with the same intensity (for a discussion of some aspects of these issues, see Fahim and Helmer 1982:xxii and Altorki and El-Solh 1988:1–23). Although occasional voices have been raised by some non-Western anthropologists both for and against (see Ahmed 1986, and Asad 1986, respectively)[7] the need, and possibilities, for the development of distinct national, ethnic, religious-sectarian, or regional anthropologies, I tend to believe that anthropology is likely to remain one discipline in spite of its many producers and practitioners. Diversity within the discipline has been a function of the critical role of the ethnographer as the principal "instrument of data generation" (Ruby 1980:153); as the intellectually, sociopolitically, and historically "positioned subject" (Rosaldo 1989:19); and as the "perspectivist" investigator and analyst (Maquet 1964:50). In this context it is worth raising the question of what difference being a native anthropologist might, or might not, make in systematic ethnographic data generation, descriptive representation, and interpretation and explanation. To address these issues calls for critical reflection and elaboration on my part about a number of related matters: Why and how does a native become an anthropologist? What is it like for a native to study anthropology and to join a professional "tribe" in a strange and exotic, dominant and hegemonic, Western society and academy and to do anthropological fieldwork in the familiar surroundings of one's own dependent, underdeveloped, Third World and Muslim culture of orientation? What is it like for a native anthropologist to study, live and work as Stonequist has termed the "Marginal Man"[8] in Western society and culture, that is, a society and culture that is "not merely different, but antagonistic" to one's own society and culture of orientation and field research? Ultimately, for the purposes of this volume, I want to look at what effect, if any, all of these experiences might have had upon my long-term field research activities, my relationship with my compatriots among whom I have conducted fieldwork, and my collective personal and professional roles and moral and political commitments and outlook toward the discipline and the communities I have studied and researched over the last decade and a half.

Frankly, I find this undertaking challenging, complex and difficult for several reasons. First, as Barbara Babcock (1980:1) points out, writing about oneself "does not have a good press" in the Western cultural tradition because "it smacks of narcissism, solipsism, and subjectivism." Second, Central Asian Muslim communities abide by a particularly strong injunction against divulging information about oneself, one's relatives, friends, or community to strangers. Guarding such information often is considered a matter of personal and collective security in that it creates a zone of control and exclusivity for the sake of community welfare. In fact, despite the presence of a strong literary tradition and historiography in the region, the art of writing autobiographies, biographies, and memoirs, so common in the West, is lacking, even today. Exceptions such as the *Babur Nama,* the memoirs of Zahiruddin Muhammad Babur Padshah, the sixteenth-century founder of the Moghul Empire in India, are very rare indeed (see Babur 1921). As a result of these influences, I have neither written about nor discussed at any length the personal dimensions of my experiences as a native anthropologist. Yet, for the sake of a better contexualization and, perhaps, a more accurate understanding of the processes that produce anthropological knowledge, we need to begin to reveal our anthropological self (selves). The immediate problem we face in this endeavor appears to be the fact that, as with most academic fads, especially in the social and humanistic sciences, the conventions of reflexivity are not yet clearly articulated. What, for example, are the limits of decency in exposing our anthropological self (selves)? Where should one begin? How and to what extent should one resist or avoid the temptation to produce autobiography or "personal anthropology" rather than ethnography and social and cultural analysis?

The general epistemological significance of such an approach and its methodological complexities are, however, well known. For example, Gramsci in his *From Prison Notebooks* states,

The starting-point of critical elaboration is the consciousness of what one really is, and is 'knowing thyself' as a product of the historical process to date, which has deposited in you an infinity of traces, without leaving an inventory . . . . therefore it is imperative at the outset to compile such an inventory. (quoted in Said 1978:25)

Any attempt to compile a detailed inventory of all the traces, or even a systematic accounting and examination of limited aspects of my "existential situation"—the relevant biographical, social, economic, educational, political, and historical factors that have influenced my own activities as native student and practitioner of anthropology—is beyond the scope of this work. Therefore, the inventory presented here will be by necessity limited and highly selective. As such it may not approximate the desired expectations, but it is hoped it will provide some ground on which to build.

Let us begin with motives—both ours and others—something anthropologists have managed to avoid discussing in general. Yet motivation and commitments are the driving forces behind all actions. Indeed, we all invest our lives with meaning through commitments to causes, often deemed greater than our mortal selves. Motives undoubtedly change and commitments waiver and evolve through time, thus providing the distinctive contours of our personal and professional self (selves). Hence my choice for a starting point.

My wish to pursue a career in anthropology, which emerged in the mid-1960s during my first year at Kabul University, Afghanistan, where no anthropology courses were taught, was propelled by my own very strong motivation, determination and commitment to become Afghanistan's first trained anthropologist. Viewed as a simple statement of a college student's choice of a major, there is hardly anything unusual about my decision. Although I did not think of it as unusual at the time, my particular background, in contrast with those of other students who made similar decisions in Western universities at the same time, may have made it so. The clearest indication of how uncommon my actions were has been the consistent stream of queries directed to me, always mixed with a degree of surprise: But why and how did you become . . .? My answer almost always begins with a sigh, and, "Ah well! That is a long story." But I will spare you the not so relevant details.

I was born and raised in a small village located in a relatively remote high valley (a little over 7,000 feet above sea level, ringed by ranges towering in places up to 15,000 feet high), in the central part of the mountainous Badakhshan province of northeastern Afghanistan. The second son born into an Uzbek-speaking, nonliterate, peasant family, I grew up bilingual in

Uzbek and Persian. The latter language, spoken in some of the neighboring villages, was also the dominant literary and spoken language in the country. At my father's urging, and sometimes firm insistence, my elder brother and I, like most other children in our village, began taking lessons in the traditional Islamic teachings in the mosque school, the *maktab,* during the long, cold winter months. These lessons began a year or two before we had to attend the then recently established government secular elementary school in the village, which encompassed grades one through six and which was in session during the warmer months of the year. In the mosque school I learned to read the Qur'an (Koran) in Arabic and how to read the popular Islamic didactic texts available in the local vernaculars, Turki (Uzbek) and Persian, including the works of some of the classical Persian poets. The medium of instruction in the government primary school at that time alternated between Persian and Pashtu (the language of the politically dominant ethnic group in the country) since government policy regarding language of instruction in non–Persian-speaking minority communities such as ours was apparently in a state of flux. Although I was unaware of the political significance of the choice of language of instruction at my village school at the time, my studies in Persian and Pashtu marked for me the beginning of a long experience with the pervasive influence of the so-called institutions of modern nation-state upon my life and the lives of the peoples of my village and ultimately upon the whole country, Afghanistan. During these early years of my life in the village, year-round schooling, religious and secular, was also fully complemented by participation in all the common chores that young boys in peasant communities are expected to do.

Upon finishing the sixth grade in the village school, I was chosen, along with six other children in my class, by education department officials of the government in Badakhshan province to be sent to a boarding school in Kabul, the capital city of Afghanistan, in order to pursue further education.[9] There were no middle schools or high schools with boarding facilities for rural children except in Kabul. With my father's permission, I went. My tearful departure (for the very first time) from the safe, secure, and all too familiar environment of my family and the village community when I was only fourteen, confronted me with mixed emotions. Breaking out of the confines of that high valley on that cold, crisp winter morning, being filled with youthful anticipations, traveling on foot to the provincial town,

Faizabad, marked without a doubt one of the turning points in my life. I rode in the backs of trucks from Faizabad to distant larger commercial towns of northern Afghanistan on the way to the capital city. Within a few days I found myself some six hundred miles from home, bewildered, terribly homesick and disoriented, treading the muddy streets of the noisy, dirty, crowded, colorful, and exotic Kabul bazaars.

In boarding school I came for the first time face to face with what Afghanistan really meant: my new school was a microcosm of the nation. That is, my several thousand new schoolmates had been recruited, like me, from among the best and brightest graduates of rural provincial elementary schools all over the country. We were a very diverse group indeed, representing the enormous linguistic, regional, ethnic, and sectarian variety of rural communities in Afghanistan. For the first few days, until Western-style school uniforms were handed out to homogenize us, the newcomers, the full pageantry of ethnic and regional clothing for young boys was on display in and around the school. Shortly thereafter, wearing of such traditional garments in school was regarded as evidence of rural backwardness. Self-respecting, prospective modern citizens of the state wore Western-style suits in Kabul. In this highly heterogeneous educational establishment, the familial, neighborhood, kinship, and village communal identities and loyalties, which informed and guided social interaction in our respective villages, had but little relevance to our new lives. We had to learn, discover, construct, and understand the social and cultural norms more appropriate to the city. Soon, broader ethnolinguistic, provincial, regional, and sectarian identities and loyalties assumed greater significance and relevance in our much widened area of social experience. As is often the case with first-time fieldwork in a strange and exotic educational, social, and cultural environment, my first year as a seventh-grade student in the Ibn-Nisina (Avicina) boarding school in Kabul was as exciting and pleasurable as it was challenging and traumatic. When I returned to my own home village for winter vacation at the end of the nine-month school year, which had felt inordinately long, I was welcomed by my anxious parents and relatives and treated like an honored guest. I promised myself and my parents that I was going to return home to the village, permanently, as a school teacher as soon as I completed my high school education in Kabul. This was not to be, but for a few years the thought of returning home to my village as a wage-earning teacher comforted me and my parents and made the separation bearable, at least for me.

The boarding school that I attended was one of several educational establishments in the capital specially designed for rural boys by the planners for the "modernizing Afghan nation-state." Their aim was to help train the necessary vocational cadre from the provinces to meet the Afghan government's anticipated manpower needs in the countryside (educational, administrative, agricultural, technological, and professional) because the graduates of the more urban elite schools in Kabul were unwilling to serve in remote, primitive areas of rural Afghanistan. My personal plans seemed to conform well with that of the Afghan state's declared goals. After completing ninth grade, I happily enrolled in Kabul Teachers' Training High School *(Daru Mu'alimin-i Kabul)*, one of the less desirable vocational schools, especially for the more ambitious or studious kids, unless of course their ambition in life was to become a teacher in their village school.

My fourth year away from the village, also my first year in teachers' training (only two years away from reaching my goal of going home triumphantly as a school teacher), proved to be tumultuous and fateful. An older maternal first cousin, who acted as my mentor and protector, had just graduated from the same high school. Instead of becoming a teacher and returning to the village, he had decided to enroll in the newly established Faculty of Education at Kabul University. This new department was organized and partially staffed by American scholars from Columbia University Teachers' College in New York, and it promised new opportunities for further study abroad. The rumor circulating at the time was that for at least the next five years the top three students from the freshmen class would, at the end of their first year, be sent on scholarships to the American University in Beirut (AUB) to continue their studies in Lebanon. Indeed, three students *were* sent to AUB at the end of that year.

My school performance in the previous three years in Kabul had not been exceptional, especially compared to my cousin's expectations based on my earlier records in the village school. So a month or two into the school year during my tenth grade, my cousin began to persuade me to take my studies more seriously and to consider taking advantage of educational opportunities beyond high school and college. I complied and finished the tenth grade exceptionally well. Having proven to myself, many of my doubting classmates, and my mentor that I could do well, even in Kabul schools, I set aside my plans for returning to the village as a schoolteacher. I was now determined to go on to the Faculty of Education at Kabul University and from there to pursue higher education overseas. I returned home that year as usual for winter vacation but did not disclose my revised future plans to the family. I feared it would worry my parents, especially my father, who had recently joined a sufi order and was inclined to think that higher education in government schools might turn me into an atheist or secularist. More important, I was not certain that my goal of entering college was feasible despite my confidence in my own school performance. I was by then a bicultural youth, knowing both the operative norms and values of my village and those of the workings of the urban educational establishment as it functioned within the Afghan state apparatus. It was clear to me by then that as an Uzbek, a member of a linguistic minority, from a distant province, in a country where ethnolinguistic and regional identities played a considerable role in the distribution of limited strategic resources, one's personal determination, commitment, and hard work were not always sufficient to assure success. All important resources, educational and otherwise, were at the disposal of the state, and the operation of state bureaucracy, especially involving certain minorities, was highly arbitrary and unpredictable, to say the least. I was not, however, discouraged by these realizations; instead my commitment to work towards the achievement of my new and revised educational objectives remained firm through the last years of high school. Upon graduation from Kabul Teachers' Training High School I was admitted to the Faculty of Education at Kabul University, and, through the persuasive intervention of one of my high school teachers, who was from a village close to mine and had recently returned from spending a few years at AUB in Lebanon, I was permitted by my family to attend college.

Once in college my pressing desire, undoubtedly shared by most of my now coeducational and mixed urban and rural-provincial classmates, was to get an overseas scholarship, preferably, but by no means exclusively, to a Western country. College was an entirely new and fascinating venture since only at the university was educational segregation of rural and urban students and boys and girls lifted. This meant a whole new set of understanding for social discourse, both in and outside the classrooms, had to be acquired, often constructed through subtle but firm negotiations concerning identities, loyalties, rights and responsibilities. For me, the other pressing issue was, now that I was in college, and if I were to be given a scholarship, what was I going to study? My dissatisfaction with the rote learning and memorization of endless strings of facts that bore no relevance to my life had grown steadily. I was particularly concerned about the preoccupation of the entire educational system with totally irrelevant matters, that is, an almost fanatical search for the glories of some remote historical past combined with total disregard for present social and demographic realities as part of a dismal effort by nation-state builders to construct an Afghan national identity that could unite the diverse peoples of the country. The exercise served to divide and alienate the populace more than it integrated them (see Shahrani 1986a). Another major fascination of the Afghan educational system was, as elsewhere in the post-colonial Third World, with things Western, especially Western technology and technical education. The best and the brightest students wanted to become engineers, scientists and technocrats to help bring Afghanistan out of the Dark Ages and into the twentieth century by ridding the society of all that was deemed traditional and primitive and imitating what they regarded to be Western, progressive, and modern. The national gaze in Afghanistan was fixed entirely upon the remote historical past and equally glorified West, where the future of the modern Afghan nation-state could be envisaged. There was no evidence of any real interest in inquiry into or systematic study of the present social, cultural, economic, and political realities of the country, and this indifference did not change substantially even during later years.

It was in this broader social and educational context in my home country that I began my freshman year at Kabul University. As fate, and a good bit of fortune, would have it, Introduction to the Social Sciences, a course offered during the first semester at the Faculty of Education was taught by Canadian anthropologist, A. Richard King,[10] at the time a member of the Columbia University Teachers' College team in Kabul. He began the course with lectures on anthropology, perhaps the first ever given to college students in Afghanistan. It was then that I heard about the strange kula ring exchange systems of the distant Melanesians and the apparently wasteful potlatches of the Kwakiutls in North America. Hearing such exotic facts made no real impression on me until Dr. King began to talk about the potential relevance of anthropological knowledge to the planning and implementation of social and economic development programs in a country like Afghanistan. The positivist tone of his arguments persuaded me.

The first half of the 1960s, when I went through high school and entered the university, was a time of unusual and promising socioeconomic and political change in Afghanistan. The country had just completed its first five-year development plan, showing some visible signs, here and there, of technological modernity in the fields of road construction, power plants, and other so-called infrastructural development. The second five-year plan, placing a high priority on the expansion of schools, especially in rural areas, was launched with even greater anticipation of progress. Developments came courtesy of the infusion of a substantial amount of foreign aid, from the United States and the U.S.S.R., due to the Cold War competition in the region. Thus, the traditionally extractive and punitive state apparatus in Afghanistan was beginning to act as the national development corporation and welfare state. The government's power and prestige were on the rise, and its bureaucratic reach expanded slowly into the remoter regions of rural Afghanistan. Distribution of economic development funds and allocation of resources by the state, however, seemed to favor, as in the past, certain ethnolinguistic and tribal groups and certain local or regional areas over others. Much of the money was being spent on a few large-scale, showcase, white elephant-type development projects in a few politically desirable areas. Successes were reported in terms of figures, the larger the better, but they appeared to promote economic and political inequities, noticeably along ethnolinguistic, regional, and sectarian lines, giving rise to growing resentment towards the state, especially among segments of the educated youth. The public reaction to these national development efforts seemed ominous and, as it turned out, their consequences lived up to that promise.

Anthropology, particularly sociocultural anthropology, as a discipline interested in the study, analyses, and remedy of contemporary social realities—problems of poverty, injustice, inequality, socioeconomic and technological development—in a country such as Afghanistan, seemed most relevant indeed. So before the end of my first semester in college, I had chosen my discipline. Anthropology, I thought to myself at the time, could help show us the way out of the agonizing problems of underdevelopment in Afghanistan. Yet, there were no trained Afghan anthropologists in the country and, as far as anyone could tell me, no one was studying it either. It was, therefore, my new mission in life to study anthropology, to become Afghanistan's first anthropologist, and to help my country, no longer just my village or family, in addressing national development problems and processes. My interest in anthropology, while exhibiting all the naive idealism, humanism, and scientism, which I learned later to be associated with all students of anthropology, Western and non-Western (see Freilich 1977:30), had nevertheless a certain urgency and immediacy about it. I was determined to pursue my studies in anthropology. The quickest way, it seemed then, was to earn the highest marks in my freshman class of 177 students in order to get a scholarship to AUB. I made it to the top of the class, but the scholarship program to AUB for freshmen was canceled in favor of sending new college graduates to earn the M.A. degree. I was, however, nominated by the university for a scholarship to Banaras Hindu University (BHU), in India. I happily applied and declared my intention to study anthropology at BHU. Despite an inordinate amount of paperwork, and regular trips to the Indian Embassy in Kabul, no admission from BHU surfaced during my sophomore year at Kabul University. In the meantime, after some hard negotiations with Kabul university officials, I was allowed to compete in an examination, along with two hundred other sophomores in the university, for one of five East-West Center scholarships offered to Afghanistan by the United States government, in cooperation with the University of Hawaii. After a long selection process my name appeared on a short list of seven students who were given University of Hawaii admissions applications, which were then forwarded, during autumn of 1966, to Honolulu. Again, I declared my intention to study anthropology. As I completed the many application forms, which asked for a variety of names, I became concerned that I might be forsaking my earlier commitment to my village by wishing to go abroad, so I chose my village name as my family name: Shahran(i), from Shahran (the name of my village in central Badakhshan), as if to assure myself permanently of my primordial connection with my real home. Uncertain of the outcome, I returned to my village for winter recess, and said nothing about the possibility of going abroad in the spring. Upon my return to Kabul, in mid-March 1967, I was surprised to learn that I had been awarded one of the scholarships to work towards my B.A. degree in anthropology at the University of Hawaii in Honolulu.

Euphoric, yet anxious about what lay ahead, I prepared to begin my mystical journey into the "field" to become an anthropologist. As had always been the case, up to that point in my life, I felt that I made the choice of what I wanted to do, but where and how it had to be done was decided for me by the invisible hands of the state. This time the place was an island paradise in the Pacific, which I did not even know existed, let alone as a part of the United States, until the scholarship announcement declared it so.

As with most first expeditions into the field, my initial departure in pursuit of the "Science of Man" was most memorable—filled with excitement, a sense of adventure, feelings of misgivings, doubts, and sometimes shocking surprise, and persistent cultural disorientation and distress. Most anthropologists heading out for some remote part of the globe have been trained intellectually and methodologically to explore the lifeways of a primitive band, tribe, or peasant community. My situation was the reverse. I began my journey long ago in a peasant village, and now I was on my way to begin learning first hand the intellectual and methodological fundamentals of anthropology in the academies of the powerful "civilized" Western World, without even knowing the language. Despite my eight years of English classes in school, in which I earned relatively good grades, my comprehension of English was extremely poor, and I could not speak it well at all.

My first airplane flight was from Kabul to Hong Kong via New Delhi, India. After three days of suffocating heat, intolerable humidity, and the ghastly smell of decaying fish and sea in the air, I boarded an American ocean liner in Hong Kong harbor, along with several dozen other East-West Center grantees (our new collective and meaningful identity for the duration of our grants) from South Asia, Southeast Asia, and South Pacific island nations. After several hours of noisy farewell rituals on the dock (with a musical band, a jungle of colorful unfurled paper ribbons, flowers, and many tearful relatives and well-wishers), our ship ceremoniously set sail on June 2, 1967, only days before the start of the third Arab-Israeli war, which ended in the devastating defeat of the Arab (Muslim) armies by Israel. Our two-week-long cruise to Honolulu by way of Yokohama, Japan, was planned by the East-West Center officials to be the time for our orientation to American culture and university life (teaching us the proper use of knives and forks, table manners, and all) and the time for our English language competency placement tests. It seemed then, and it became even clearer to me in later years, that American natives were not willing to take the chance of leaving us foreigners to learn such critical matters the hard way! We had to be taught, tested, and certified in civilized ways. Thus, hour after hour, day after day, through incredibly rough seas, nauseating seasickness, and frightening claustrophobia from the tiny, musty cabins down below, we were subjected to lectures, demonstrations, movies, exams, and oral interrogations, during which I was asked, among other things, whether I dreamed in English or in Afghani. The answer was, of course, not in English. I always dreamed in Uzbek or Persian. I thought the question puzzling at the time, and its significance only became apparent to me months later when I began to dream in English. Our arrival in Honolulu harbor—the sight of land, the end of orientation trials (I thought!), and the welcoming party of half-clad hula dancers who placed fragrant leis around our necks—caused me to heave a genuine sigh of relief.

Within hours after arrival at the East-West Center facilities on the Manoa campus of the University of Hawaii in Honolulu, a new round of interminable welcoming and orientation meetings began. We were told that we were the ambassadors of our countries through our participation in this unique program founded by the late President John F. Kennedy and funded by the U.S. Congress, the East-West Center: Center for Inter-Cultural Exchange. Several hundred students, one-third chosen on a competitive basis from the United States and the rest from Asia (as far west as Afghanistan) and the Pacific, were brought to live together (sharing rooms in special dormitories) and to learn from and with each other. The assumption was, of course, that we were bound to develop lasting friendships and, as future leaders of our respective nations, would ensure the emergence of a more peaceful regional and world order. Given the fact that the war in Vietnam was raging and an Arab-Israeli war had only days earlier been fought, the thought of imagining a peaceful world order, with or without our leadership, was comforting indeed. Today, twenty-five years and many more devastating wars later (including the ongoing [1989–94] war in Afghanistan), we hear talk of a "new world order" from Washington, but the means most recently employed by the United States and its allies to achieve it has been warfare. The possibilities for a new, peaceful world order, especially outside America and Europe, seem remoter than ever, yet the East-West Center is still in operation.

When I had time to reflect outside orientation meetings, I realized I was again facing a major environmental shift. Having left the microcosm of Afghan society at my Kabul boarding school, I had to try to come to grips with a totally new situation at the East-West Center, what appeared to me to be a microcosm of at least half the world's societies. Hardly any of my earlier identities—kin-based, local, linguistic, sectarian, regional—were relevant to the new context. All of a sudden, I was an alien, a foreign student, an Afghan (sharing the honor with certain kinds of blankets and a highly desirable breed of hound), a Muslim, a Middle Easterner, at times even an Arab, an Asian, or an Oriental, depending on the situation. My three years of intensive experience within the Center's forced international educational environment were in my mind valuable beyond measure as an anthropological rite of passage in cross-cultural and comparative awareness.

The East-West Center was a good provider of minimal comforts to its grantees, so I was free from the worry about money or visa problems that would later be the major preoccupation of my graduate studies. The Center had found me a host family, a wonderful, burly Irish American sculptor and his wife. The couple came periodically to collect me from the dorms, together with my new host family sister, Gloria, a very smart, and beautiful young lady from the Philippines who was doing graduate work in journalism. Our family treated us to expensive Sunday brunches at Waikiki hotels and even on occasion took us to Sunday church services so that we could learn how the real natives lived in paradise.

Thus, in these strangely comfortable surroundings, began my struggle to learn the English language and the fundamentals of anthropology. My English language competency tests were found to be very poor, as I had already anticipated. I was assigned to take a full year of classes in English as a second language and pass the required competency assessment tests. I began the task in earnest, enrolling in English classes as well as Introduction to Anthropology. Attending my first real anthropology lecture in a huge lecture hall, without an instant Persian translation to follow, was a sobering experience. I could not understand most of what the professor was saying. In my room at the dorm, which I shared with a Malaysian Chinese chemical engineering student, I tried desperately to decipher Adamson Hoebel's introductory text, line by line, with dictionary in hand. In contrast to most fieldwork encounters in other cultures, hand signals and other kinds of facial and body gestures do not reveal much meaning in the American academic culture. Frustrated and very worried about the possibility of failing the course, thus jeopardizing my entire mission at the outset, I felt increasingly dumb and became very quiet and withdrawn. With the passing of time and long hours of looking up words in the dictionary, lectures and text books began to make some sense. I began to wonder silently to myself what my tribe, clan, and lineage was and whether my village and most of my compatriots back home qualified as savages or barbarians in the evolutionary scheme of things, or whether we were merely primitives and natives waiting to be studied by some adventurous Western ethnographer. It was soon clear to me that the natives of academic culture in the United States, unlike the natives of most cultures studied by anthropologists elsewhere, did not tolerate the presence of marginal natives in their midst. The system is truly hegemonic, bent on making a real native out of all foreign students (culturally at least, but not necessarily politically) who wish to be certified as successful. In order to fulfill my goals, I was ready to imbibe the language of discourse and the culture of anthropology and to go native, as best I could, to earn the necessary certificates.

During my undergraduate education I learned much about the "island civilizations" in the Pacific and read and heard a lot about anthropological approaches, concepts, and ethnographic methods; but hardly anything was ever mentioned about the relevance of anthropology to societal problems either in the United States or elsewhere. This did not bother me much because I had already convinced myself that it was relevant to solving my own country's mounting socioeconomic problems. How, specifically, I did not care to ask since I did not know the answer yet. Nevertheless, forward and onward I continued. After earning my B.A. in anthropology from the University of Hawaii, I was offered a teaching assistantship and admission to the Ph.D. program in anthropology at the University of Washington in Seattle. My other option for graduate school was the University of Kentucky at Lexington, which I declined.

My initial interest in the University of Washington began during the summer of 1969, at the height of student demonstrations against the Vietnam War, while I was still at the East-West Center. Asian students were given the opportunity during the last year of their grants to attend a mainland institution to see and experience what life in real America was like. The Center's American grantees were sent to Asian countries for their field study tour. I wished to go to one of the major universities with a strong Middle East studies program, such as Harvard, Chicago, Columbia, or the University of California, Berkeley, but they were closed, I was informed, due to campus unrest. My advisor at the Center asked me to look for another place for my field study, so I suggested the University of Washington, whose catalogue listed a course entitled Cultures of the Iranian Plateau and Afghanistan. On arriving in Seattle, I inquired eagerly for Professor Fairservice, who was identified in the catalogue as the instructor for the desired course. A senior member of the office staff in the anthropology department, a charming and most gracious lady who became one of my guardian angels throughout graduate school, told me with a puzzled look that he had left the university for Egypt at least two years earlier. I was comforted to find that another professor, an applied anthropologist who had done fieldwork in Afghanistan, was teaching in another department at the university. So I spent the summer and autumn quarters of 1969 in Seattle, getting to know the department elders, the natives. A few of the friendly elders of the community showed interest in me as a pupil; thus was I invited to begin my graduate studies there in the fall of 1970.

By this time, I was beginning to feel comfortable in the academic culture of university life. In fact, sometime during the second year of my residence among the natives in Hawaii I noticed that I was experiencing some kind of fundamental cognitive reorientation, a transformation, brought about by long-term immersion, though I could not be certain of the true nature or causes of the feelings. As a result, I was willing and able to engage in dialogue and debate inside and outside the classroom from my first days in Washington, quite unlike the period shortly after my arrival in Hawaii. Becoming a teaching assistant, and thereby earning my keep for the first time in my life, eased the process even more. At that point I realized that I had been literally a ward of the institutions of the Afghan State (directly or indirectly) since I left my village at the age of fourteen. Now through a defiant act of delaying my immediate return to Afghanistan at the termination of my East-West Center grant, as I was obligated to do, I was beginning to overcome my own earlier image of myself as an utterly powerless, dependent, inarticulate alien, a foreign student, a grantee. I was now a teaching assistant and a graduate student in anthropology!

The first two years of graduate life were trying and challenging to say the least. However, my progress in the program went smoothly and it was for the most part uneventful. I completed the required courses and passed the necessary exams for the candidacy to the Ph.D. degree by June 1972, without ever taking a single course (lecture or seminar) focusing on Islam, pastoral nomadism, the Middle East or Central Asia—the areas of my ethnographic interest—because none was offered. I had been, however, sufficiently drilled in the principles of ethnographic objectivity and impartiality (both matters of serious concern to me since I had decided to return home to Afghanistan to do my dissertation fieldwork) and had been taught all the appropriate conventional methods of data collection in the field. I was made fully aware of the inherent dangers of bias in research conducted in one's own society. My proposal to study the ecological adaptation to cold and high altitude conditions of a Turkic-speaking Kirghiz pastoral nomadic group, in Badakhshan, my own home province in the extreme northeastern part of Afghanistan, received funding from two national funding agencies (the Social Science Research Council—American Council of Learned Societies and the Wenner-Gren Foundation) in the United States. I was much gratified and very happy at the prospect of returning home after five years of studying anthropology in the United States. I was on my way, expectantly, to discover what had been represented to me as the mysteries of doing fieldwork for my final certification, the Ph.D. degree in anthropology.

My decision to study the Kirghiz was not entirely arbitrary. My determination to do fieldwork in my home country, Afghanistan, in spite of my awareness of the considerable methodological dogma in the field against it, persisted and prevailed, but only after substantial personal and scientific soul searching and rationalization over my choice of group to study. I could have chosen any number of communities in which to do my research in Afghanistan, including my own village or other villages in the same valley. After all, I told myself, I had become a scientist! Western social scientists, even a few anthropologists, had studied their own societies scientifically, that is, impartially and objectively, so I was going to try to do the same.

My choice also was influenced by my theoretical fancy at the time. Although never having taken a course in cultural ecology, because none was offered then, I had been impressed by the writings of Fredrik Barth on Iran and Pakistan and by the works of other cultural-ecologically oriented authors. Besides, studies of nomadic tribes in West Asia were in vogue at the time, and, as far as I knew, nomadic tribes in Afghanistan, especially the Turkic-speaking ones, had not yet been studied. The Kirghiz fit, in my imagination, the ideal ethnographic subjects. They were perhaps the most exotic nomadic pastoralist tribe in Afghanistan, located in the highest inhabited mountain valleys, in the most isolated and remote part of the country, and they were inaccessible to foreign anthropologists. They lived in a restricted area along Afghanistan's frontier with the Soviet Union and Communist China, but I would be permitted to enter the region as an Afghan. The Kirghiz were not members of my own Uzbek ethnolinguistic group, and they were pastoral nomads. Thus, they were a sufficiently different "other." My interest was to study their ecological adaptation to high altitude and severe cold climatic conditions, which lasted as long as nine months each year. The available estimates of their population ranged from 3,500 to 15,000 people, so I thought they would make a relatively manageable group for a proper ecological adaptation study. In fact, my own household economic and demographic survey later showed that they numbered only 1,825 souls, an even more manageable size. At this time the paramount issue on my mind was not the relevance of my research to Afghanistan's problems of underdevelopment, but rather the suitability of my project for a Ph.D. dissertation. To get my degree, fieldwork had to be done and the right mix of quantitative and qualitative data had to be collected, brought back, analyzed, and presented in accordance with the established norms for the issuance of that all important professional certificate. So in July 1972 I set out to experience the mystique of doing fieldwork at home, among the Kirghiz and Wakhi of Afghanistan.

In early July 1972 I returned home to Afghanistan after brief stops in London, Madrid, and Tehran, thus completing the first of my many trips around the world. During my five years of studying anthropology in the United States, absence from home (my village, my province, and my country, Afghanistan) had indeed made my heart grow fonder—and my mind more reflective and more aware of my primordial identities and loyalty. I felt I had relived, in thought and imagination, some of my earlier experiences in Afghanistan more intensely while in the United States than ever before. This was primarily because I found I could not read, hear, or think about anything in anthropology without somehow relating it to my life (i.e., the lenses of my own situated-self) at home. For me at least, while out of sight for five years, home and Afghanistan had by no means been out of mind. I did not expect any radical changes to have taken place in the country during my years of absence either, so there was little disappointment and no real sense of culture shock or social disorientation awaiting me upon arrival in Kabul.

To be sure there were visible changes in Kabul and other parts of the country, but these changes appeared incremental, not structural or radical. That the population of Kabul city, like other capitals of other developing countries, had grown appreciably was easily noticeable in the congested streets, crowded public transportation, and the sprawling new residential quarters on all sides of the city where there previously had been either fertile vegetable gardens, crop fields and orchards, or barren, dry mountain sides. There were further signs of the encroachment of what V. S. Naipaul (1990) has called "our universal civilization": scores of discotheques and dancing halls, pizza houses, Chinese restaurants, a Marks & Spencer department store, an Intercontinental Hotel, private or free printing presses, foreign tourists, antique and handicrafts shops and tour guides, together with throngs of half-dazed and poorly clad hippies, many of them begging for their keep on the streets of Kabul. There were also a few new tall buildings, city parks, even a Kabul zoo, more cinemas, some signs of greater wealth and prosperity, but also much evidence of an increased gap between the lifestyles of a small segment of the Westernized nouveau riche elite and the masses of urban and rural poor underclasses in the capital city and the country.

Student discontent was rampant, and politicization of the high school and college students had reached new heights compared to only seven years earlier in 1965, when I had participated in the first major student public political demonstration. Revolutionary rhetoric (of various shades of Marxist-Leninism, Maoism, Western-oriented secular nationalism, and revolutionary Islamism, among others) was the common language of political discourse on the Kabul University campus for students and faculty alike. Violent demonstrations against the government, as well as confrontations between ideologically opposed parties and groups, were rampant in the capital and provincial towns all over the country. In addition to the older and more traditional principles of ethnicity, language, regional and sectarian affinities, new sets of ideological and political identities and loyalties had become important in the management of social and political relations, especially among the educated Afghans.

The debate over the structure of national political authority and relations between state and society appeared to be intense, especially in view of the fact that a serious drought during 1970–1971 caused much suffering due to famine in the northern and northwestern regions of the country. Improvements in East-West relations, due to detente, had resulted in substantial reductions in foreign aid from both the United States and the U.S.S.R. This gave rise to a national economic crisis, increased political discontent, uncertainty and instability, which a year later (17 July 1973) resulted in the first Marxist-inspired military coup leading to the overthrow of the Afghan monarchy, under King Zahir Shah, and the establishment of a Royal Republic headed by the former King's brother-in-law and first paternal cousin, Muhammad Daoud. It was in this pre-coup environment of a heightened national sense of urgency for change and revolutionary expectancy in the country that I returned home to do fieldwork.

My proposed fieldwork, however, did not in any way reflect the urgent societal concerns of the early 1970s in any of the major cities and key socioeconomic regions of the country. My sole purpose in returning home to Afghanistan was to conduct anthropological research among the Kirghiz and Wakhi (see Shahrani 1979:xiii–xvi). After a short visit with my family, I was back in Kabul making preparations to spend the next twenty months in northeastern Afghanistan, in the Wakhan Corridor and the Pamirs. My research plans among the Kirghiz, who are high-altitude pastoral nomads, and their Wakhi agriculturalist neighbors, involved living among them for an extended period of time. This was most puzzling to my family, relatives, friends, colleagues, and government officials because no one from among the educated urban or urban-oriented individuals would voluntarily go to such a "backward, poor, distant and primitive" part of the country. Among even the lowest ranking clerks, school teachers, and government officials, an appointment to the Wakhan was considered a hardship post on the frontier. Assignment to the area was normally limited either to the politically undesirable or financially corrupt, and as such it was seen as a form of punishment. Generally, anyone having just returned from five years of study abroad, especially in the United States, would expect to be appointed to a relatively prestigious academic or administrative position in some government institution in Kabul. The fact that I was not interested in a government job or in marriage and settling down was virtually incomprehensible to my parents and family. My determination to leave for the distant Wakhan and Pamirs to do fieldwork for my Ph.D. dissertation seemed equally puzzling to my friends and colleagues. I tried to convince them that the requirements of anthropology as a scientific discipline were different and that fieldwork, preferably in small, isolated, primitive communities such as the Kirghiz and Wakhi, was an essential part of my training if I were to successfully complete my doctoral degree and earn the title of Doctor, by which I already was being addressed by my friends and acquaintances. In retrospect, I am not certain whether my explanation was entirely convincing, but this was my scientific project, and with the means to pursue it to fruition, I proceeded.

Accompanied by a young male cousin from my own village whom I asked to assist me with travel and housekeeping chores in the field and the necessary field gear, I set out for the Wakhan and Pamirs of Afghanistan. I had never been to this part of my home province before, but I had seen and spoken with a few Kirghiz and Wakhi individuals from the area on a number of occasions in my village, in the provincial capital, Faizabad, and in Kabul. I also had heard a great deal about the area from my father who had served his two years of compulsory military service some twenty-eight years earlier in an Afghan frontier post security detachment near the village of Qala-i-Panja, in Wakhan district. My father had visited Wakhan at least once or twice since that time and had been otherwise in contact with a few individuals, including an Uzbek trader originally from another village in our own valley who had settled in Khandud, the administrative center of Wakhan district.

The Uzbek trader, Mullah Muhammad Ismail, had apparently prospered not only economically but also politically in Wakhan. During the post-1965 liberal constitution and relatively free elections he had been elected by the Kirghiz and Wakhi as their deputy *(wakeel)* to the Afghan national parliament in Kabul.

Happily, my familial contacts proved immensely beneficial for my initial entry into the area. Upon arrival in Khandud, I was received very warmly by Wakeel Mullah Muhammad Ismail, who offered me hospitality and, more importantly, introductions to other local notables including the *khan* or chief of the Kirghiz, Haji Rahman Qul. I also discovered that the principal and several of the teachers in the local elementary school at Khandud, the only one of its kind in the entire district, were my former schoolmates in the Kabul boarding school. Even a few shopkeepers and itinerant traders in Khandud, originally from central parts of Badakhshan near my own village, turned out to know my family and relatives. It soon became clear to me that the notion of anthropological field worker as a marginal native in the field had no meaningful relevance to my fieldwork experiences. Indeed, I was a native and was being treated by everyone with whom I came into contact as an honored guest in accordance with the customary practices of rural Badakhshan.

The news of my presence in the area spread quickly throughout the tiny Wakhi hamlets up and down the Oxus and Wakhan river valleys and into the Kirghiz nomadic camps in the Pamirs long before I was able to visit them myself. The purpose of my presence in Wakhan was as enigmatic and incomprehensible to the local officials, the Wakhi farmers, and the Kirghiz pastoral nomads as it was to my parents and relatives in Shahran and my friends in Kabul. With my own outside sources of fellowship support for the fieldwork, I did not fit any of the familiar categories: I was not an appointed and salaried government official; nor was I accompanying any foreign dignitaries, mountain climbers, or Marco Polo sheep hunters; and although referred to and addressed by everyone as "Doctor Sahib," I was not a medical doctor.

Even more puzzling to the local people was the fact that, unlike all other educated visiting Afghans, I insisted upon compensating them for any goods and services I required. Like marginal natives in the field, as I had been taught, I claimed I was there because I wanted to collect information about their way of life so that I could write a book about them to earn my doctorate degree. It was then that the utterly self-centered nature of anthropology as the self-proclaimed science of describing and explaining "other" peoples and cultures, began to unfold. Questions of what relevance or utility my dissertation would have for them, either now or in the future, were not an issue, at least not until much later and then under radically altered sociopolitical conditions in the country.

The problem of explaining my presence among the natives, just like the predicaments of marginal natives in other fieldwork situations, was not a serious problem after all, but rather an artificial problem of anthropological self-indulgence in what Beidelman and Sahlins reportedly have called the "epistemological hypochondria" of the younger generation (quoted by Sass 1986:57). It mattered little to the local population what high-minded reasons lay behind my presence among them. All that mattered was that I was there, that they had to deal with my presence, that I was an educated son of a man some of them knew personally, and that my family lived in a specific village in Badakhshan. I encountered no significant interpersonal difficulties during my fieldwork, with one small exception: a young head of a Kirghiz family, during an interview for a household economic and demographic survey, showed considerable anxiety when I asked him about the size and composition of his herd. Agitated and angrily pointing at me, he blurted out "Bolshevik! Communist!" and he refused, at that time, to answer my questions. Respecting his wishes I told him that he did not have to tell me anything. A number of the young man's elderly camp mates who were present calmed him down, while apologizing to me for his ignorance and youth in making such accusations. They tried to assure him that what I was doing had nothing to do with Communism. The young man retorted that he had heard that the Bolsheviks also made lists of what people owned before they came and took their herds away from them. What I was doing, he asserted, seemed much the same. After being assured and urged by his older relatives and camp mates, I was later able to interview the young man. Apart from this episode I did not experience any serious difficulties in collecting the desired information. My command of the Badakhshan dialect of Afghan Persian (Dari), spoken as a second language by the Wakhi and understood by most adult Kirghiz males, together with my knowledge of Uzbek as my mother language, easily understood by all Kirghiz, made communication and comprehension easy. It also helped establish the necessary social rapport and understanding of reality on the basis of minimal clues, considered so unique to anthropological research by native or indigenous anthropologists (Messerschmidt 1981a; Altorki and El-Solh 1988:7).

In three separate trips during 1972–1973 from Kabul to the Wakhan and the Pamirs, including travels to Kabul with Haji Rahman Qul, the Kirghiz chief, and his entourage to observe his commercial and political activities in the capital, and back to the Pamir with him during the winter months of 1973, I tried, as meticulously as I could, to follow the anthropological lore and traditions of fieldwork. I made friends with a number of the Kirghiz and gained the confidence and support of the Kirghiz elders, including their Khan, for my research project. I was able to collect a considerable amount of data on their ecology, economy, demography, history, social organization, and culture to address the issues of Kirghiz and Wakhi adaptation, not only for my original research concerns pertaining to their adaptation to high altitude and severe climatic conditions, but also to the unanticipated constraints of the politically induced social and economic realities of closed frontier conditions imposed by Communist China and Soviet Russia in that region.

With substantial quantitative and qualitative field data in hand I returned to the University of Washington in March 1974 to begin writing my dissertation. My first experience as a student of anthropology in the field at home, treated as an honored guest rather than the expected marginal native, was remarkably stress-free and for the most part a pleasant learning experience. In fact, my major anxiety in the field was never over the quality or quantity of data I was seeking to collect, or worries about the confrontational nature of my encounters with the informants I was working with (see Crapanzano 1977, 1980). Instead, I worried about the nature and potential ill effects of hypoxia on my health and well being, heightened by the total absence of any kind of medical services in the area. Such anxieties, although never entirely removed, were considerably reduced after my first trip to the Pamirs. Confident that I had followed the proper ethnographic methods and obtained substantial information relevant to my research project, the next step was to present them in a coherent dissertation. This task was accomplished some two years later. I received my Ph.D. in the summer of 1976. My dissertation was then published with minor revisions three years later in book form (Shahrani 1979).

The book, *The Kirghiz and Wakhi of Afghanistan: Adaptation to Closed Frontiers,* although based on my research among the Kirghiz as an honored guest rather than a marginal native, was molded by my close adherence to all the conventions and traditions of scientific ethnographic presentation.

Highly detached, impersonal, composite, and abstract images of the Kirghiz and Wakhi societies were presented in the timeless and objective fashion of the ethnographic present. The Kirghiz and Wakhi were depicted primarily as rule bound, neatly integrated, well adapted, and exotic specimens of traditional Central Asian communities in a contemporary world of a nation-state. The value of my work, similar to numerous other ethnographies of its genre, I had argued, was that it documented a unique case study with significant theoretical implications for anthropological studies of pastoral nomadism in general and those of high-altitude pastoral nomads in particular. Its principal virtue was that it was different, unique, and exotic, and was presented in the familiar discourse of ethnographic science.

By the time my seemingly objective and impartial account of the Kirghiz and Wakhi was in print, illustrated with appropriate tables, charts, and figures showing, among other things, the numbers of sheep, goats, and yak owned and loaned, the new ethnography movement with its ultra reflexive and self-critical posture was beginning to question the dominant concepts and commonly held assumptions about ethnographic truth, objectivity, and impartiality, all of which I had so faithfully tried to adhere to in writing my ethnography of the Kirghiz and Wakhi communities. However, as it turned out, the apparent revolt within the discipline against the traditional conventions of ethnographic writing was but only one of a host of new predicaments I was about to face.

Another event, entirely external to anthropology, but with considerable impact upon me and my understanding of the purpose and relevance of anthropology, was unfolding in Afghanistan. It was the 1978 Soviet-inspired military coup and the subsequent establishment of a Communist government in Kabul, the rise of popular Islamist resistance, a *jihad*, the direct Russian military intervention, and perpetuation of an intense armed struggle in my homeland. This was a development that, by the time I had achieved my long-cherished desire to become a bona fide Afghan anthropologist, was effectively robbing me of the opportunity to return home to work or to do fieldwork. It was a totally unforeseen development (by international experts as well as native observers), which radically altered the trajectory of my personal and professional life, including the nature of my continuing long-term involvement with the Kirghiz and with Afghanistan.

Although in this "century of total war" (Smith 1983), punctuated by the "nationalist revolutionary wars," superpower military and political interventions, popular anti-colonial wars of resistance, economic devastation, ethnocide, genocide, and creation of large-scale internal and external refugees in the name of freedom and liberty, it seems that anthropology and anthropologists have historically managed to ignore researching and studying these painful and pervasive sociopolitical realities of our times. If wars and their devastations are studied at all, it has been always post facto and in the abstract, analytical, objective, and impartial mode of science, aimed at attempting to explain either its causes or consequence for the sake of theorizing about the nature of armed conflicts in human societies at a safe physical and social distance from the perpetrators and victims of such violence. Not surprisingly, most of my Western anthropologist colleagues working in Afghanistan before the outbreak of the war, following the April 1978 Communist coup, began quickly to look for new and safer research sites in other countries. Afghanistan was lost to anthropology because it was no longer safe for traditional ethnographic research. As a native anthropologist I shared the same intellectual predicaments as my Western colleagues, except that I could not, in good conscience, abandon research on my homeland because the war was so tragically tearing Afghanistan's body and soul asunder. Morally, emotionally, and intellectually I could no longer ignore the war in Afghanistan. My commitment to the study of the conflict in Afghanistan had an immediacy, urgency, and pertinence that I had not felt about my research before. My new interest in an issue generally avoided by anthropology and anthropologists strongly and unabashedly raised the prickly question of my own competence for such an undertaking. That is, what practical relevance did the kind of anthropology I had learned and practiced have when addressing the situation facing the Kirghiz and Wakhi, as well as the rest of the peoples of Afghanistan, including my own family and relatives in Shahran? Why was the future of these communities and the nation not a subject of anthropological enquiry? Why had I and other researchers only tried to deal with the present in terms of the past without considering the thoughts and imaginations of these people about their future? What was my moral responsibility as an individual, a native, an anthropologist, and a citizen toward the communities I had studied? The issue of the relevance of anthropological research and practice was no longer an abstract concept or theoretical notion; it was an eminently practical proposition, which I could not afford to ignore. I had to continue my long-term research on the Kirghiz, not simply as exotic tribal ethnographic specimens, but as an historically, socially, and culturally constituted community long embedded within the body politics of the Afghan nation-state, currently gripped by a complex, national, and international ideological-political-military conflict of major local, national, regional, and global proportions. In the present context, the examination of Kirghiz actions and experiences has proven invaluable for understanding and explicating the dynamics of the broader national popular response in the tragic, devastating war in Afghanistan.

The Kirghiz, twice displaced and forced to take refuge in the mountain ramparts of the Afghan Pamirs following the Bolshevik and Chinese Communist revolutions, were faced once again with another Communist revolution, this time in Kabul. Their collective decision, less than three months after the coup in Kabul, was to vote with their feet against the Communist regime and in favor of taking refuge across the border in the northern areas of Pakistan. The Kirghiz literally were the first among more than five million citizens of the country who ultimately chose flight out of the country into neighboring Iran and Pakistan as the preferred alternative. Indeed, their exodus so soon after the establishment of a Communist government in Kabul, especially from such a remote and inaccessible part of the country, was clearly indicative of the seriousness of the emergent tensions between the new revolutionary Marxist state and the Muslim society in Afghanistan, which the state wished not only to govern, but also to transform. The fact that initial reports of the Kirghiz decision to leave the Pamirs came from *Izvestiya* (15 September 1978), under the sensational headline of "The Bloody Paths of the 'Independent Khan'" (Akhmedziyanov 1978), was an important sign of Moscow's concern over the future course of events in Afghanistan. In this report the Kirghiz leader, the "Independent Khan," Haji Rahman Qul, was depicted as a cruel, ruthless, and oppressive feudal lord, "fearing punishment for his [past] crimes" at the hands of the revolutionary and "progressive forces," and incited and armed by the "Peking envoys." The Khan had turned "bandit," launching antigovernment activities before "ordering" his "fellow tribesmen to leave Afghanistan" (Akhmedziyanov 1978:J1). These same arguments were presented by Russians and Western experts sympathetic to the Kabul government in more elaborate form as popular opposition to the Russian puppet regimes in Kabul grew in later months and years (see Shahrani 1984a). The fact that the Kirghiz Khan and his tribesmen had left the Pamirs well in advance of any serious government actions threatening them also was puzzling to me, especially in view of the fact that the regime was incapable of sending any kind of credible force against the Kirghiz in the distant Pamirs. Therefore, in my view, at least during the early months after the coup, there was no imminent government threats to Kirghiz welfare that could have justified their speedy exodus into Pakistan. The critical question then was, why? What motivated the Kirghiz Khan and his followers, as well as millions of other Afghans, to leave the safety and security of their homes for the uncertain future of refugee life in Pakistan?

With these questions in mind, and my concern about the circumstances of the Kirghiz as refugees in a radically different environmental and sociopolitical situation in Pakistan, I went to Gilgit during the summer 1980. Gilgit is a town in the northern area of Pakistan, the area immediately south of the Afghan Pamirs, where the Kirghiz Khan and many of his some 1,200 followers were living.[11] Although the Kirghiz had been in Pakistan for nearly one and a half years, they were left without any meaningful support from the government of Pakistan or the international agencies concerned with Afghan refugees. The Kirghiz had suffered the loss of nearly one hundred members, mostly women and children, due to exposure to new illnesses, the extreme heat, and unsanitary living conditions. Depressed, disillusioned, and frightened, some 150 of them had returned to the Pamirs in late spring of 1980. The rest of them had sold their herds and were living in various scattered houses in Pakistani villages, separated from their relatives after depleting their resources. They were in desperate circumstances requiring assistance.

The news of my arrival was apparently greeted with the expectation that I might have brought some form of tangible economic assistance for them.[12] Much to my own personal dismay, and so true to the anthropological tradition, the only tangible gift I was able to offer them was a copy of my then recently published book detailing their former, happier lives in the Pamirs of Afghanistan—my salvage ethnography of the Afghan Kirghiz (Shahrani 1979). Under the circumstances, all I could promise to do was to prepare a written report about the seriousness of their situation and submit it to the office of the United Nations High Commission for Refugees (UNHCR) in Islamabad, Pakistan, urging them to assist the Kirghiz. This I fortunately was able to accomplish (Shahrani 1980), which resulted in the establishment of a single official Afghan refugee camp, located near Gilgit, bringing all the Kirghiz families together and providing them with the appropriate economic, medical, and educational services. During the summer of 1982 they were admitted by the government of Turkey for permanent resettlement in eastern Anatolia (Shahrani 1981, 1984c).

By the time I arrived in Gilgit in late June 1980, however, the Kirghiz presence in Pakistan was known to some Western journalists and a few brief reports about them were beginning to appear in the press. More significantly, a week before my arrival in Gilgit, a documentary film crew from Granada Television Limited, U.K., who had in 1975 produced an ethnographic film, *The Kirghiz of Afghanistan,* for their now well known *Disappearing World* series, had visited the Kirghiz Khan in Gilgit and interviewed him for another documentary film called *Afghan Exodus,* which was released in Britain and Europe in late 1980. The 1975 film, which depicts aspects of Kirghiz life in the Afghan Pamirs, was based on my earlier (1972–1974) research, and I had served as a consultant anthropologist in the field while the film was shot. My role as a consultant in the production of the Granada Television version of the film, however, was an entirely unsatisfactory experience. My main grievance was that my consultancy agreement with the producers stipulated my participation in the shooting process in the field as well as in the editing of the final product, but in reality my role was that of an inexpensive native tour guide, facilitator, interviewer, translator, and informant for the real ethnographer, the Western anthropologist filmmaker on their staff. Accompanying a team of seven outsiders, four of them foreign, to the Pamirs during the latter part of summer 1975, at the height of the Kirghiz seasonal work in preparation for the long winter, and intruding so rudely into their lives, gave me an entirely new perspective about what it is like to be in the field as a native with strangers and potential marginal natives. I asked my teammates about compensation for the Kirghiz. What will they get for the loss of their time, their efforts, knowledge, and hospitality? Precious little, as it turned out.

My disappointment grew stronger when a copy of the Granada film reached me during May 1976, some six months after its initial showing on British television. By then the film had won several awards, including an award for factual accuracy, and wide praise in the British media. I was denied any opportunity for input during the editing of the film. Focusing on the role of the Kirghiz Khan, Haji Rahman Qul, the film depicted him as an autocratic, exploitative, uncaring exemplar of a "paternalistic oppressor," as one reviewer of the film characterized him (N. Tapper 1976a). Indeed, the images of the Kirghiz Khan constructed in the Granada Television film, coming as it did on the heels of "Ongka's Big Moka," an extremely successful film about a New Guinea "Big Man" (by the same producer in the *Disappearing World* series) reflected the popular British image of the traditional Central Asian Khans and not the historically complex and textured realities of Haji Rahman Qul Khan's leadership role among the Afghan Kirghiz that it was supposed to represent. Frustrated by the film and utterly unable to do anything about altering the shape and content of a highly acclaimed, commercially and aesthetically successful product, I wrote a letter to the Royal Anthropological Institute News (Shahrani 1976) to question the ethical propriety of the film reviewer's characterization of the Kirghiz Khan as paternalistic oppressor on the basis of how he was represented in the Granada Television film. I was concerned that such characterization of a subject in a documentary film could be easily used by the Afghan government authorities to harm the Khan. Both the film reviewer and the staff anthropologist at Granada Television responded to my concern by casting strong doubts upon my impartiality and credibility, not only of my expressed sentiments in the letter but also of my future writings on the Kirghiz, presumably because of my close friendship with, and defense of, the Khan and my ethnic and national affinities with the Kirghiz, the subjects of my academic research (Tapper 1976b; Singer 1976). At the time, when I had just completed my dissertation, I had no viable defense against such baseless accusations, so I was much gratified when my academic advisor at the University of Washington, Professor Charles F. Keyes, wrote an unsolicited letter to RAIN (1977), assuring them that they did not have to be concerned about the quality of my future work on the Kirghiz. I thought then that such a public accusation of bias and impartiality against me as a native anthropologist might have been an aberration, and I was glad that it was over. Unfortunately, as I have learned in retrospect, it was just the beginning of the articulation of my status as a marginal man in a field where the concept of native anthropologist itself seems to be an aberration.

Fortunately in 1981, the story of the Kirghiz ethnographic film unexpectedly took a positive and, in the long run, rewarding turn. The Public Broadcasting Associates (PBA) in Boston, the producers of the anthropological series *Odyssey* on public television, decided to buy the rights for *The Kirghiz of Afghanistan* (along with several other ethnographic films) from Granada Television with the intention of re-editing and updating it with 1980 footage taken during their exile in Gilgit, Pakistan. Happily, I was invited to participate in the re-editing of the *Odyssey* version of the film, which still focused on Haji Rahman Qul and his family but reflected more adequately, in my view, the complex and intricate nature of his leadership role as the Kirghiz Khan. This new version of the film, which also raised the prospects for the future permanent resettlement of the Kirghiz community outside Pakistan, possibly in the state of Alaska—a topic of immense interest to the Kirghiz during 1980–1981—was widely shown on American television and generated considerable media coverage and interest about their plight. Indeed, the film may have played a part in their eventual resettlement in 1982 in Van province, in eastern Turkey.

My principal motive for going to Gilgit in the summer of 1980 was not advocacy on behalf of the Kirghiz (I had learned real anthropologists did not condone such involvements with natives), but to conduct further anthropological research—that is, to explore the motivations behind the Kirghiz exodus, so soon after the Communist coup and in the absence of any imminent danger to their well being. This relatively brief period of research among the Kirghiz refugees opened entirely new vistas and concerns for my future research interests. It raised new questions about the purpose and relevance of anthropological knowledge and the responsibilities of the anthropological researcher in the field. Much to my surprise, the Kirghiz readily agreed that they had not faced any imminent threat to their safety from the central government in Kabul. They did, however, report Russian action against them across the border, but only during the last day of their flight from the Pamirs after their intentions were discovered by the Soviets.

The Kirghiz decision to leave was, therefore, based entirely on their anticipation of future threats, which were based on their recollections of the past and not just the evaluation of the immediate circumstances. They told me that once they had convincingly established for themselves that the new revolutionary regime in Kabul was Communist, they were absolutely certain of the future dangers both from the Kabul regime as well as from direct Russian military intervention in Afghanistan, a development that they had correctly anticipated. Therefore, based on their considerable past experiences as victims of Communist revolutions, the fact that they were located in a small distant frontier community adjacent to the Soviet and Chinese borders, and lacking the possibility of effectively defending themselves by means of a credible, sustained resistance, they simply sought to safeguard the future integrity of their community as Muslims by taking refuge in the neighboring Muslim state of Pakistan. In essence, the single most dominant motivating force for the Kirghiz exodus was said to be Islam, that is, their desire to preserve the future continuity of their identity both as Muslims and Kirghiz. The centrality of Islam as the primary motivating force was consistent with their previous flights to Muslim Afghanistan in search of security from Soviet and Chinese Communist revolutions.

The suggestion that Islam was a cardinal motivating force for the Kirghiz, which justified their earlier historical decisions to leave their former homelands under Russian and Chinese control, was not new to me. They had mentioned it numerous times during my earlier research in the Pamirs in more peaceful and tranquil times while discussing the events of the relatively remote past. The invocation of Islam by the Kirghiz before the crisis in Afghanistan, it seemed to me, always was used to explain past events or the present circumstances and activities of members of the community. In Pakistan, under the uncertain conditions of refugee life, the invocation of Islam and Islamic religious and cultural symbols appeared to have gained a new focus, one intimately linked to the Kirghiz discourse about their future as a Muslim community. I soon realized that the phenomenon is equally pervasive among other Afghan communities, both those who sought refuge in Pakistan and Iran *(muhjireen)* as well as those who remained in Afghanistan and resisted *(mujahideen)*. Indeed, one of the most lasting impressions of my 1980 research among the Kirghiz in Gilgit, and later among other Afghan refugee communities in Pakistan, has been the overwhelming and forceful collective sense of loss (or the threat of impending loss) of personal, social, cultural, and national integrity as Muslims. The situation reflects the feelings of a people in a deep state of crisis, but yet without the usual accompanying sense of despair or despondency about their future. Their present actions, flight to a safe refuge or active armed resistance, was, and still is, understandable not solely in terms of past memories or in the assessment of present military and political realities. Rather, it is best explained in light of their powerful images of the future, both under Communism as well as in terms of its defeat and the establishment of an Islamic government.

As an anthropologist, a Muslim, and an Afghan, what has impressed me most in studying the situation in Afghanistan is the appeal of Islamic ideas and cultural capital as a charismatic motivating force to the believers, not only in helping shape and inform their present social and political behavior (see Shahrani 1987b) but also in providing the vocabulary for charting the trajectory of their discourse on their future and their political culture. My central research inquiries since 1980 have been, therefore, an understanding of the dialectics of the impact of Islam upon the social imagination of the Afghans concerning their future under the current prolonged situation of societal crisis in the country. Additionally, I have explored the impact of such images of the future upon the present actions and activities of the Kirghiz and other Afghan communities. My personal and professional desire as a native anthropologist to study these issues over the last decade, however, has resulted in a further articulation of my feelings as a marginal man, both within the discipline in the United States and at home among certain segments of my Afghan compatriots. It is to these specific issues which I now turn.

To the Kirghiz, especially to their leader, Haji Rahman Qul Khan, concern about the future was not just wishful thinking, a plan, or simply something to contemplate. It was an intense moral act aimed at finding ways and means to ensure the future continuity and integrity of their Muslim and Kirghiz community. Based on their historical experiences of repeated victimization and spatial displacement by Communist revolutions during this century, the Kirghiz wished to move as far away as possible from Communist Russia and China in their search for a new homeland. Regardless of the outcome of Islamist resistance in the country, they said, it would be unsafe for them to return to the Pamirs of Afghanistan. They imagined, therefore, that the United States would be the farthest away from their traditional enemies and thus the safest place for them to go. The idea of resettling in

Alaska, however, was the result of encounters with an Alaskan zoologist, a staff member of the United Nations Wildlife Federation, who had spent time in the Pamirs in the early 1970s while setting up a Marco Polo sheep reserve for the government of Afghanistan. Undoubtedly, they had heard much from him about the climatic and ecological similarities between the Pamirs and Alaska.

As one who was living in the United States and as their concerned anthropologist, I was asked by the Khan to give advice and assistance in this critical matter. I tried in vain during the summer of 1980 to dissuade him and other Kirghiz elders. I told them that the possibility of their admission as a community for resettlement anywhere in the United States seemed almost nil on the basis of U.S. immigration laws alone. Instead, I suggested that they consider resettlement in Turkey for historic, linguistic, cultural, religious, and ecological reasons and where their chances of admission would be much better. They told me that they wanted to go to the United States because I was there and I could help them. Besides, they argued, if the United States was good for me then it could not be bad for them. So the Khan and other Kirghiz elders asked me to assist them in their efforts to relocate and settle in the United States.

Respecting their wishes, but strongly against my own better judgment, I nevertheless worked with a number of interested individuals and small organized groups, especially in Alaska, to promote the Kirghiz cause. It soon became clear to me that such an effort was doomed to failure. I kept the Khan informed of the growing interest (by some people and the media) in their cause in the United States, especially following the airing of the Kirghiz film on public television in the fall of 1981. But I also let him know that he should not expect any positive results in the near future, thus urging him to consider other alternatives. The Kirghiz plight, and their expressed wish to immigrate to the United States as a community, had received considerable worldwide media coverage, much of it as a result of the ceaseless and effective public relations efforts of the Kirghiz Khan himself.

In early 1982, when the President of Turkey was on an official visit to Pakistan, the Kirghiz search for a new home to resettle was somehow brought to his attention. As a gesture of goodwill towards Afghan refugees, he immediately agreed to admit for resettlement in Turkey, with the help of UNHCR, all the Kirghiz, together with several thousand other Turkic-speaking Afghan refugees in Pakistan. Thus, exactly four years after their flight from the Pamirs, the Kirghiz were flown to Turkey in August 1982 and given a permanent home in eastern Turkey. In two subsequent research visits, in the summers of 1983 and 1986, among the Kirghiz in their new home, I found that while bemoaning the many new predicaments facing them and lamenting the loss of their real homeland in the Pamirs of Afghanistan, they were content that they had successfully, once again, ensured the future integrity and continuity of their Muslim community against what they considered to be the menacing Communist threat.

The Kirghiz, a demographically small and politically insignificant ethnolinguistic minority living in a remote frontier region of the country, were by no means a microcosm of Afghan society and polity. Nevertheless, my continued longitudinal research among this small community of Afghan Kirghiz proved to be extremely informative about the nature and dynamics of the prolonged conflict in Afghanistan. My growing personal and professional involvement with the Kirghiz concern about their future, following their tragic exodus from the Afghan Pamirs, for all intents and purposes was resolved with their successful resettlement as a community in Turkey. Nevertheless, I remain interested in further study of their readaptation to radically altered social, economic, political, ecological, and, to some extent, cultural conditions in their new homeland (see Shahrani 1988a).

The future of Afghan society and national polity, after twelve years of devastating war, unprecedented human suffering, and economic ruination of the country, still remains far from resolved. In the summer of 1980, after visiting the Kirghiz in Gilgit, I spent some time in Peshawar, Pakistan, looking into the larger issues of Afghan refugee problems and the nature and development of the popular armed resistance both in my own province of Badakhshan (Shahrani 1984b) and in the country as whole. By that time the conflict was nationwide, and, following the Soviet military intervention on December 1979, the war had begun to take the form of an Islamic *jihad,* not only against the Communist regime in Kabul, but also as an anti-Soviet and anti-colonial war of liberation. For me, at that juncture, the question of why there had been such a violent, armed response on such a national scale against a self-proclaimed revolutionary government, which promised to work towards improving the lives of what they considered to be the "poor, the oppressed, and the underprivileged masses" of Afghanistan, was impossible to ignore. The questions of revolution, war, rebellions, and foreign invasion were no longer abstract matters of heuristic concern to me. Rather, these were practical problems facing not only my anthropological tribe but also my real tribe, village, and nation, and these questions necessitated practical answers in the specific context of my own society and nation, Muslim Afghanistan. These, I realized, were not traditional questions addressed by anthropologists, but then, I wondered, how many real traditional ethnographers have faced the predicament and prospect of not only losing their research site to revolutions, wars, invasions, and rebellions but also their own real home and country to such a tragedy as well? As an Afghan and a student of Afghanistan studies, I felt I had no choice but to extend my research horizons beyond the study of the Kirghiz or other comparable units and to begin to investigate broader and more pressing problems at local, regional, national, and international levels in a systematic manner from my own perspective as a native anthropologist.

The need to broaden my research interests since the onset of the war in Afghanistan has been influenced by yet another unforeseen development. This complex, modern, political-military-ideological conflict is both a reflection and an embodiment of the partially congruent, often diverse, competing and conflicting domestic and international interests and forces that have converged temporarily, and for the most part incongruously, in the weakened and dependent political body of Afghanistan. As in most other conflicts during this century, the various internal and external participants, observers and "experts," have produced a considerable amount of literature on the conflict from a variety of national, ideological, political, and professional perspectives. Given what is at stake for the future of the peoples of Afghanistan in their struggle for cultural survival and political integrity, I have found myself inevitably engaged in debates and discussions of a wide range of issues either brought forth or ignored in this literature.

For example, after the Soviet invasion of Afghanistan and the transformation of the war into another geopolitical conflict between the U.S. and U.S.S.R. superpowers, the problem of addressing the domestic historical, socioeconomic, political, and ideological factors behind the Afghanistan tragedy became critical for at least two reasons. First, the most important issue for Western experts of all persuasions following the Soviet invasion revolved around speculation regarding the hidden Soviet ideological and geopolitical motives for direct military intervention in Afghanistan and its potential consequences for American interests in the region (see Shahrani 1987a). Second, those experts and observers who paid any attention to the domestic causes of the conflict in Afghanistan blamed the rise and development of armed resistance against the Marxist revolutionary government in Kabul upon the primitive, tribal, feudal, and backward nature of Afghan society and polity and upon the ignorance and fanaticism of the oppressive and self-interested tribal and religious leadership in Afghanistan. The pervasiveness of both of these views in the literature has seriously undermined the likelihood of a proper understanding of the Afghanistan crisis internally, and, as such, may have contributed to its perpetuation, either intentionally or unintentionally, on the part of the superpower patrons of the war.

The problem of the role of traditional local leaders in the current conflict, both in the armed resistance inside the country and in taking the initiative to lead communities into exile outside the country, as in the case of the Kirghiz Khan, was one of the earlier issues that I began to investigate. The general characterization of traditional local leaders by the so-called revolutionary governments in the Third World, as well as much of the social science literature, as oppressive, feudal, exploitative, paternalistic, and therefore opposed to positive social change, did not seem to make sense in the case of the current Afghan war of resistance in general and the Kirghiz refugee community in particular. So, during the summer of 1983 I went to eastern Turkey with the sole purpose of researching Kirghiz ideals, conceptions and practices of community leadership. I collected extensive biographical data on the Kirghiz Khans, including Haji Rahman Qul Khan. I also collected case histories of conflicts and other incidents taken by individuals to the Khan for resolution over the years and their feelings about, and evaluation of, the outcome of the cases. I also asked them to compare and evaluate the style and conduct of the various Kirghiz Khans they had either dealt with or knew by reputation in their community, stating the reasons for their judgment about the leadership quality of the specific Khans. In the case of Haji Rahman Qul Khan, they were asked why they came to Pakistan and eventually Turkey with him and whether they were satisfied with their current situation or not, and why. From these longitudinal life-history materials and evaluative data, there emerged a fairly complex three-fold typology of the Kirghiz notions of local leadership, only one of which approximated the usual conceptions of the traditional local leaders as tyrants and oppressors. Furthermore, the Kirghiz data revealed that while oppressive and exploitative local leaders exist, they were tolerated by the local community only because of the close ties and protection such leaders enjoyed with the oppressive state authorities. Such oppressive local leaders generally sided with the central government authorities (whether revolutionary or reactionary) and did not play any meaningful leadership role in the present conflict in Afghanistan in the resistance against the state. On the contrary, the traditional leaders who lead their people, either on the battlefields against the revolutionary government forces, or out of harm's way into the safety of the neighboring Muslim states of Iran and Pakistan, are those who have had a proven record of protecting their communities' common interests against external threats over a long period. Such leaders also are known for their Muslim piety, compassion, generosity, and courage in their community (Shahrani 1986b).

The current conflict in Afghanistan is claimed to be primarily a case of government failure to develop a strong centralized nation-state, because of the country's rugged topography, and because of a highly fragmentary, conflict-ridden, heterogeneous, independent-minded, ethnolinguistic, tribal and sectarian population that has consistently hindered state-building efforts. On the contrary, I have argued (Shahrani 1984a, 1986a) that the problem of state building in Afghanistan, as well as other multiethnic states, may be explicable less by topographic adversity or demographic heterogeneity than by the critical examination of the impact of discriminatory policies and practices of the governments themselves towards the different segments of their citizens. Indeed, in Afghanistan it is the socioeconomic, educational, and anti-Islamic cultural policies of the Afghan governments, past and present, that were responsible for the fragmentation of the heterogeneous society, alienation of the state from society, and growing economic, military, and political dependency of the state upon foreign powers, which culminated in the prolonged armed conflict (see Shahrani 1990b).

The Islamist revolutionary basis of the popular and at least partially successful Afghan resistance, expressed clearly in the idiom of Islamic *jihad,* against a self-styled and Soviet supported Marxist revolutionary state has been a unique and unexpected development in the history of revolutionary wars during this century. Not surprisingly, supporters as well as detractors of the Afghanistan resistance have emphasized primarily the emotional and reactionary anticommunist role of Islam in the mobilization of what they regard as the nonliterate and ignorant Afghan Muslim masses. These commentators ignored or denied the modernizing hopes and revolutionary aspirations of the largely middle class urban and educated youth who led the Islamist struggle to capture the powers of the state and establish an Islamic government in Afghanistan. I have tried to explore the nature and revolutionary character of the Islamist ideology of the Afghan resistance through fieldwork and critical reading of considerable vernacular literature produced by resistance groups both before and during the war. It has become clear to me that the *jihad* struggle in Afghanistan has been not only a resistance against Communism and Soviet invasion and occupation of the country. Rather it is, and has been, a moral and political struggle, waged primarily for the establishment of an Islamic government in Afghanistan (Shahrani 1988b, 1987a, 1986, 1985, 1984a). I have further argued, following extensive field research among the Kirghiz in Turkey in the summer of 1986, and in the Afghan refugee camps in Pakistan during the summer of 1988 and seven months in 1989, that the massive support extended by the ordinary nonliterate peoples of Afghanistan is not based on ignorance of either Islam or their self-interest, as some believe, but is rather a decision based on considerable knowledge of Islam and a commitment to the defense of Islamic religious and political values and way of life. I have examined the role of a substantial amount of didactic Islamic literature, in the local vernaculars of Afghanistan, in the processes of social production, and the transmission of local knowledge of Islam to the nonliterate Muslim masses. These investigations clearly are indicative of the fact that nonliteracy among Muslim masses, or lack of knowledge of Arabic, the language of Qur'an and the Prophetic traditions, does not necessarily mean that they are ignorant of the essential tenets and values of Islam. On the contrary, the existence and constant reading aloud of these popular didactic vernacular texts provides ready access to a wide range of nonliterate people in the rural areas of Afghanistan, as well as other Muslim societies. Indeed, it is knowledge gained through these textual sources that makes it possible for Islamic values to permeate the contemporary political culture and behavior of the Muslims both in Afghanistan and worldwide (Shahrani 1990b, 1987b).

Hostility towards Islam and Islamist political movements in Afghanistan, especially in the media and political circles, has been persistent during the entire *jihad* in Afghanistan. The true dimension of this hostility, however, has become more fully apparent since the military defeat and withdrawal of the Russian Red Army in 1989 from Afghanistan and the more recent collapse of the Communist ideological challenge to the West. This attitude is perhaps most poignantly expressed in a 1989 cartoon by Toles in *The Buffalo News* in which the caption under an image of a turbaned, gun-toting Afghan *mujahid* reads: "Before the Soviet pullout, heroic Afghan freedom fighter." In the next identical image the caption reads "After the Soviet pullout, backward, religion-crazed, sexist, infighting primitive, who now, likely as not, will turn on the U.S. or else cease to be of any interest whatsoever." This negative Western attitude towards Islamist resistance in Afghanistan was further confirmed during my close and extended observations (April–December 1989) while researching the political economy of international assistance for the Afghans in Pakistan. It appears that neither the Russians nor the U.S. and Western powers are willing to tolerate an Afghan *mujahideen* political victory over the Russian puppet Communist regime in Kabul, hence the continuation of the Afghanistan tragedy. This national tragedy of the Afghans, financially and politically supported and supervised by the so-called world superpowers, raises a new, and in my view more serious, question of whether the so-called revolutionary wars and wars of liberation fought in so many Third World countries during this century, and which have consumed so much of the meager resources of these nations, both human and material, have brought them freedom, liberty, and independence, or merely new and even more debilitating forms of bondage, dependency, and servitude to their former colonial masters. Indeed, as anthropologists and social scientists we may have to ask ourselves what does freedom, liberty, and independence mean today to the citizens and rulers of increasing numbers of small nations of the Third World, the objects of our scientific study?

Hostility towards Islam and Islamist political movements in Afghanistan and other parts of the Muslim world, however, is not limited to the media, politicians, and a few bigoted individuals on the streets. It is present in academia, albeit often but not always subtly expressed and conveyed. Since 1980, when I began researching and writing about contemporary national political issues in Afghanistan, especially when presenting an unconventional (i.e., positive) evaluation of the role of Islamist movements in the Afghan resistance, I have confronted a growing suspicion among some of my colleagues as to whether my recent work is as scientific and anthropological as my earlier ethnographic writings on the Kirghiz. A few have wondered, on occasions audibly, whether I have abandoned anthropological research, and whether what I have been doing more recently might not be akin to what political scientists should be doing. After all, they say, where are his data to support his claims about the positive role of Islam in the Afghanistan resistance? On at least one occasion I came across a letter in my personnel file (at my previous place of employment) saying that it would appear that I have become "susceptible to reaching conclusions based on an *insider's view* without supporting documentation to give it credence in a scholarly community. This possibility is very troubling." The same letter, as if to mitigate the criticism, adds "On the more positive side . . . [I appear] . . . committed to a full development of *the role of Islam in the more backward peoples of the near- and far-eastern regions*" [sic, emphasis added].

The concern about what constitutes data (or lack thereof) was very interesting to me. It seems that information not collected as part of ethnographic field recording similar to data presented in my writings on the Kirghiz is deemed less credible, even when my research unit has changed to encompass the whole nation, which calls for different methods of data gathering, analysis, and support. The problem obviously is further compounded when personal expertise and insider views of a native scholar about his own society and culture are concerned. It appears that in anthropology an insider's view is desirable only if and when it is gained by marginal natives, presumably by means of what Clifford Geertz had called "immaculate perception" during fieldwork (Sass 1986:52). But such a view when presented by a native anthropologist seems to be suspect in the eyes of marginal natives. The suspicion could easily turn into accusation if the native anthropologist should evince a commitment to the "full development of the role of Islam" among "backward peoples"! It is obvious that not only natives of other societies are suspicious of marginal natives, the Western anthropologists. In addition, Western natives seem to be equally prone to suspicions about other natives and native anthropologists.

One important consequence of my long-term research as a native anthropologist, especially during the last decade, has been to focus on the relevance of my research efforts to not only understand but also to work towards the resolution of the monumental problems confronting the peoples of Afghanistan. Ironically, the closer I have come to approaching this desired personal and professional goal, both in research and practice, the stronger I have felt the articulation of my sense of treatment as a marginal man both in anthropology and most recently at home among my Afghan compatriots. For example, in the spring of 1989, on the invitation of an anthropologist colleague working for the office of the UNHCR in Geneva, I joined a UNHCR technical mission team of ten experts for one month to carry out research among Afghan refugee and political organizations and to prepare a report on the feasibility of a proposed United Nations scheme for the repatriation and resettlement of Afghan refugees after Soviet troop withdrawal. I was the second anthropologist and the only Afghan in the team. The other anthropologist, an American teaching in a college on the East Coast at the time, had done research in East Africa, appeared not to know much about Muslim societies, and was blissfully ignorant not only of Afghan vernacular languages but even of the simplest facts about Afghanistan. Despite the fact that he might have benefitted from talking to Afghans for his portion of our research, he refused to talk to any Afghans during the entire month because, he said, "you can't trust the Afghans since they all belong to some political party or organization." Although he did not articulate further, I suspect that he meant "Muslim fundamentalist parties or organizations" about whom he assumed he knew enough to pass judgment. Thus, he only spoke to foreign officials of the various UNHCR and nongovernmental aid agencies (NGOs) in Pakistan while collecting his data.

Aside from this encounter with a marginal native in the field, I had high hopes of at last being able to make some kind of positive and practical contribution through my involvement with the United Nations to address problems of the Afghan refugees. Unfortunately, I found that the whole UNHCR establishment, which had no Afghan staff, apparently by design, was quite uncomfortable dealing with an Afghan in their midst who was not a dependent refugee but a professional anthropologist. So, for the entire month I was basically seen as an Afghan first and foremost, having, in their view, particular political and ideological commitments and loyalties with the Afghan refugee and resistance communities, and as such anything I said and did was suspect because I was an Afghan anthropologist. Naturally, natives are the only political animals in such contexts; all others are deemed impartial, objective, and, I might add, *indifferent* observers. Our reports were filed (Shahrani 1989), after considerable expense of time, energy, and resources, and as far as I can tell, they have not been put to any use.

Later the same year, I returned for six months to Pakistan, taking advantage of a sabbatical leave to work with the newly formed Islamic Interim Government of Afghanistan (IIGA), to help with planning for the reconstruction of Afghanistan. Until this time, much of my intensive research had been carried out among the ordinary Afghan refugees in the camps or with the Kirghiz whom I knew well because of my long association with them. I had some contact with the leadership of the various Afghan Mujahideen organizations, but these contacts were generally limited to interviews and short conversations. My feelings of being treated as an honored guest among the Kirghiz and other Afghan communities, both inside Afghanistan and in refugee contexts outside the country, especially in Pakistan and Turkey, have persisted and even further intensified over the years for at least two reasons: (1) my continued long-term personal and professional relationships with them; and (2) my maturing age, marriage, fatherhood, and professional and improved economic status. My continued treatment as an honored guest among the Kirghiz also exists because their greater familiarity with some members of my immediate as well as extended family and relatives. This long-held, comfortable and cherished feeling of being in the field at home, however, was shattered during my attempts to work with the emerging bureaucratic elite of the Afghan Mujahideen. To them, the fact that I have spent nearly half of my life in the United States studying, working, and now raising a family, makes my commitment and loyalties to Afghanistan (and, for some of them, to Islam) suspect. Thus, I realized, at last, as a native anthropologist doing long-term research at home in the field among Afghans and practicing my field primarily in the West, that is, becoming part of two not only different, but antagonistic, cultural traditions, that I have indeed become a marginal man, perhaps without the possibility of reaching a satisfactory resolution to this predicament.

Endnotes

1. My initial fieldwork among the Kirghiz of Afghanistan began during the summer of 1972 through the spring 1974. Subsequently I conducted further research during the summer of 1975 (in the Pamirs of Afghanistan), summer of 1980 (in Gilgit, Pakistan), summer of 1983, summer of 1986, and a brief visit during the summer of 1992 in eastern Turkey.

2. The use of honored guest in the title of this paper, however, refers to the overall treatment extended to me as a native anthropologist by the Kirghiz and others with whom I have worked in Afghanistan.

3. In the lecture version of the paper some of the details of Kirghiz feasts honoring the Khan were presented. Due to time constraints and space limitations, however, they are omitted here. It is hoped that those materials will be published separately at a later date.

4. The basic problem of finding and using acceptable labels for anthropologists doing research in their own culture and society as insiders, and the scale and scope of meanings attached to terms such as indigenous, native, and local that are currently in use, is not yet settled, but agreement on their importance is pervasive. For a discussion of some of the issues see Altorki and El-Solh (1988) and, especially, Messerschmidt (1981a:197, 1981b:13).

5. This is despite the fact that considerable research has been carried out, at least since the 1920s and especially since the 1960s, by native anthropologists in their own societies in the U.S. as well as in non-Western societies; for example, see Altorki and El-Solh (1988:3). The few exceptions are the published proceedings of a 1978 Burg Wartenstein symposium edited by Hussein Fahim (1982), Altorki and El-Solh (1988), Messerschmidt (1981a), Stephenson and Greer (1981), and Nakhleh (1979).

6. In this essay the term field is used, as in this instance, to mean both the place or community where ethnographic research is conducted during fieldwork, as well as membership in the scientific field or discipline of anthropology.

7. For a critical discussion of Ahmed and Asad's arguments on this topic and further analysis of this issue in Middle Eastern anthropological writings see Eickelman (1989:372–395). For a broader discussion of "national anthropologies," both Western and non-Western, see Gerholm and Hannerz (1982).

8. Stonequist states that the "Marginal Man" is "one whom fate has condemned to live in two societies and in two, not merely different, but antagonistic, cultures" (quoted in Freilich 1977:vii).

9. My elder brother completed the sixth grade the same year but was not among the seven chosen, and although he was later called upon by government officials to be sent to Kabul for further education, my father would not let him go. Since he was older and more capable of work around the house, he was kept home while I was "given to the government."

10. Dr. King had been interested in the anthropology of education and had studied native schools on reservations in Vancouver Island, British Columbia. He taught the class with the help of an Afghan translator, and was a remarkably dedicated, enthusiastic, and articulate teacher.

11. Some five hundred Kirghiz living in the Great Pamir Valley, an area further to the north and separated by high mountain passes from the Little Pamir where the Khan and the larger segment of the Kirghiz lived, were apparently unable to make their escape.

12. Such an expectation was logical in view of the fact that some meager assistance had been brought and distributed to them during the previous month by representatives of the Turkistani communities (Turkic-speaking Soviets and Chinese Central Asians) in the diaspora of Saudi Arabia and Turkey.

References Cited

Aguilar, John I.
1981   Insider Research: An Ethnography of a Debate. In *Anthropology at Home in North America: Methods and Issues in the Study of One's Own Society,* edited by D. A. Messerschmidt, pp. 15–28. Cambridge University Press, New York.

Ahmed, Akbar
1986   *Toward Islamic Anthropology: Definition, Dogma, and Directions.* New Era Publications, Ann Arbor.

Akhmedziyanov, A.
1978   The Bloody Paths of the Independent Khan. *FBIS-SOV,* September 1978 3(189):J1–J2.

Altorki, Soraya, and Camillia Fawzi El-Solh (editors)
1988   *Arab Women in the Field: Studying Your Own Society.* Syracuse University Press, Syracuse.

Asad, Talal
1986   *The Idea of an Anthropology of Islam.* Occasional Paper Series, Georgetown University Center for Contemporary Arab Studies, Washington.

Babcock, Barbara A.
1980   Reflexivity: Definitions and Discrimination. *Semiotica* 30(1–2):1–14.

Babur, Zahiruddin Muhammad
1921   *The Babur-nama in English (Memoirs of Babur).* Translated by Annette S. Beveridge. 2 vols. Luzac and Company, London.

Cesara, Manda
1982   *Reflections of a Woman Anthropologist: No Hiding Place.* Academic Press, New York.

Clifford, James
1988   *The Predicament of Culture: Twentieth-Century Ethnography, Literature, and Art.* Harvard University Press, Cambridge.
Clifford, James, and George E. Marcus (editors)
1986   *Writing Culture: The Poetics and Politics of Ethnography.* University of California Press, Berkeley and Los Angeles.
Crapanzano, Vincent
1977   The Writing of Ethnography. *Dialectical Anthropology* 2:69–73.
1980   *Tuhami: Portrait of a Moroccan.* University of Chicago Press, Chicago.
Eickeleman, Dale F.
1989   *The Middle East: An Anthropological Approach.* 2d edition. Prentice-Hall, Englewood Cliffs.
Fabian, Johannes
1983   *Time and the Other: How Anthropology Makes its Object.* Columbia University Press, New York.
Fahim, Hussein
1982   *Indigenous Anthropology in Non-Western Countries.* Carolina Academic Press, Durham, North Carolina.
Fahim, Hussein, and Katherine Helmer
1982   Themes and Counter-Themes: The Burg Wartenstein Symposium. In *Indigenous Anthropology in Non-Western Countries,* edited by H. Fahim. Carolina Academic Press, Durham, North Carolina.
Fahim, Hussein, K. Helmer, E. Colson, T. N. Madan, H. B. Kelman, and T. Asad
1980   Indigenous Anthropology in Non-Western Countries: A Further Elaboration. *Current Anthropology* 21:644–663.
Foster, George M., Thayar Scudder, Elizabeth Colson, and Robert Kemper (editors)
1979   *Long-Term Field Research in Social Anthropology.* Academic Press, New York.
Freilich, Morris (editor)
1977   *Marginal Natives at Work: Anthropologists in the Field.* Schenkman Publishing Co., New York.
Geertz, Clifford
1988   *Works and Lives: The Anthropologist as Author.* Stanford University Press, Stanford.
Gerholm, Tomas, and Ulf Hannerz
1982   Introduction: The Shaping of National Anthropologies. *Ethnos* 47(1–2):5–35.
Hymes, Dell (editor)
1972   *Reinventing Anthropology.* Random House, New York.
Keyes, Charles
1977   The Kirghiz. *Royal Anthropological Institute News (RAIN)* 18:14.
Madan, T. N.
1982   Anthropology as Mutual Interpretation of Cultures: Indian Perspectives.

In *Indigenous Anthropology in Non-Western Countries,* edited by Hussein Fahim, pp. 14–29. Carolina Academic Press, Durham, North Carolina.

Manganaro, Marc
1990 *Modernist Anthropology: From Fieldwork to Text.* Princeton University Press, Princeton.

Maquet, Jacques J.
1964 Objectivity in Anthropology. *Current Anthropology* 5:47–55.

Marcus, George E., and Michael M. J. Fischer (editors)
1986 *Anthropology as Cultural Critique: An Experimental Moment in the Human Sciences.* University of Chicago Press, Chicago.

Messerschmidt, Donald A.
1981a On Indigenous Anthropology: Some Observations. *Current Anthropology* 22(2):197–198.

Messerschmidt, Donald A. (editor)
1981b *Anthropologists at Home in North America: Methods and Issues in the Study of One's Own Society.* Cambridge University Press, Cambridge.

Naipaul, V. S.
1990 Our Universal Civilization. *The New York Times,* Monday, November 5, 1990.

Nakhleh, Khalil
1979 On Being a Native Anthropologist. In *The Politics of Anthropology,* edited by G. Huizer and B. Mannheim, pp. 343–352. Mouton, The Hague.

Nash, Dennison
1963 The Ethnologist as Stranger: An Essay in the Sociology of Knowledge. *Southwestern Journal of Anthropology* 19:149–167.

Nash, Dennison, and Ronald Wintrob
1972 The Emergence of Self-Consciousness in Ethnography. *Current Anthropology* 13(15):527–542.

Paul, Arthur
1953 Interview Techniques and Field Relationships. In *Anthropology Today,* edited by A. L. Kroeber, pp. 430–451. University of Chicago Press, Chicago.

Rosaldo, Renato
1989 *Culture and Truth.* Beacon Press, Boston.

Ruby, Jay
1980 Exposing Yourself: Reflexivity, Anthropology and Film. *Semiotica* 30(1–2):153–179.

Said, Edward W.
1978 *Orientalism.* Pantheon, New York.
1985 Orientalism Revisited. In *Europe and Its Others,* edited by F. Baker, pp. 1–14. University of Essex Press, Colchester.
1989 Representing the Colonized: Anthropology's Interlocutors. *Critical Inquiry* 14:205–225.

Sass, Louis A.
1986   Anthropology's Native Problems: Revisionism in the Field. *Harper's Magazine,* May, pp. 49–57.

Schuetz, Alfred
1944   The Stranger: An Essay in Social Psychology. *American Journal of Sociology* 49:499–507.

Shahrani, M. Nazif
1976   Letters: The Kirghiz. *Royal Anthropological Institute News (RAIN)* 16:10.
1979   *The Kirghiz and Wakhi of Afghanistan: Adaptation to Closed Frontiers.* University of Washington Press, Seattle and London.
1980   Kirghiz Refugees of the Afghan Pamirs: A Report on Their Situation and Needs. Submitted to UNHCR and other international aid donor agencies. Also published in *Cultural Survival Newsletter* 4(4), Fall 1980.
1981   The Kirghiz Odyssey. In *Odyssey: The Human Adventure,* edited by Jane E. Aaron, pp. 16–19. Public Broadcasting Associates, Boston.
1984a   Introduction: Marxist 'Revolution' and Islamic Resistance in Afghanistan. In *Revolutions and Rebellions in Afghanistan: Anthropological Perspectives,* edited by M. Nazif Shahrani and Robert L. Canfield, pp. 3–57. Institute of International Studies, University of California, Berkeley.
1984b   Causes and Context of Responses to the Saur Revolution in Badakhshan. In *Revolutions and Rebellions in Afghanistan: Anthropological Perspectives,* edited by M. Nazif Shahrani and R. L. Canfield, pp. 139–169. Institute of International Studies, University of California, Berkeley.
1984c   The Kirghiz of Afghanistan Reach Turkey. *Cultural Survival Quarterly* 8(1):31–34.
1985   Revolutionary Islam in the Armed Resistance in Afghanistan. Paper presented at the 84th annual meetings of the American Anthropological Association, Washington, D.C., December 3–8.
1986a   State Building and Social Fragmentation in Afghanistan: A Historical Perspective. In *The State, Religion and Ethnic Politics: Afghanistan, Iran, and Pakistan,* edited by Ali Banuazizi and Myron Weiner, pp. 23–74. Syracuse University Press, Syracuse.
1986b   The Kirghiz Khans: Styles and Substance of Traditional Local Leadership in Central Asia. *Central Asian Survey* 5(3–4):255–271.
1986c   The Social Bases of Islamic Movements in Afghanistan. Presented in a panel on Social Bases of Islamic Movements, at 20th annual meetings of the Middle East Studies Association, November 20–23, Boston.
1987a   Geopolitics and the Moral Dimensions of the Russian-Afghan War. *Afghan Refugee Information Network (ARIN) Newsletter* 25:2–8.
1987b   Islamic Eschatology and the Kirghiz Interpretation of Modern Politics. Presented at the 86th annual meetings of the American Anthropological Association, Chicago, November 18–22, 1987.

1988a   Social Transformations in an Afghan Kirghiz Pastoral Nomadic Community Resettled in Turkey. *The American Research Institute in Turkey (ARIT) Newsletter* 7:3–4.

1988b   Jihad Against Communism in Central Asia: From Holy Wars to Islamist Revolutionary Struggles. Presented at the workshop on Approaches to Islam in Central and Inner Asian Studies. Columbia University, New York, March 3–4.

1989   Project Market Place: Sociocultural Dimension. Submitted to the UN-HCR, Geneva.

1990a   Afghanistan: State and Society in Retrospect. In *The Cultural Basis of Afghan Nationalism,* edited by Ewan W. Anderson and Nancy H. Dupree, pp. 41–49. Pinter Publishers, New York.

1990b   Local Knowledge of Islam and Social Discourse in Afghanistan and Turkistan in the Modern Period. In *Turko-Persia in Historical Perspective,* edited by Robert L. Canfield, pp. 21–45. Cambridge University Press for the School of American Research, London and Santa Fe.

Simmel, George
1950   *The Sociology of George Simmel.* The Free Press, Glencoe, Illinois.

Singer, Andre
1976   Andre Singer Writes. *Royal Anthropological Institute News (RAIN)* 16:11.

Smith, Anthony
1983   *Theories of Nationalism.* 2d edition. Holmes and Meier, New York.

Stephenson, John B., and L. Sue Greer
1981   Ethnographers in Their Own Cultures: Two Appalachian Cases. *Human Organization* 40:123–130.

Tapper, Nancy
1976a   The Kirghiz of Afghanistan: Screened by Granada Television Last December. *Royal Anthropological Institute News (RAIN)* 13:6.

1976b   Nancy Tapper Writes. *Royal Anthropological Institute News (RAIN)* 16:11.

Werner, Oswald, and Mark Schoepfle
1986   *Systematic Fieldwork.* Sage Publications, Beverly Hills.

Whitehead, Tony Larry, and Mary Ellen Conaway (editors)
1986   *Self, Sex, and Gender in Cross-Cultural Fieldwork.* University of Illinois Press, Urbana.

Wolcott, Harry F.
1981   Home and Away: Personal Contrasts in Ethnographic Style. In *Anthropologists at Home in North America: Methods and Issues in the Study of One's Own Society,* edited by D. A. Messerschmidt, pp. 255–265. Cambridge University Press, Cambridge.

Interpreting Skulls: Reflections on Fieldwork in Malaysia

Robert L. Winzeler

Those of us familiar with the earlier articles in this volume are inevitably affected by them. Douglass (this volume) made this point regarding Simon Ottenberg, and his contribution in turn has influenced my own. Douglass notes that his fieldwork experiences seemed to parallel those of Ottenberg in a number of ways, and therefore he saw what he was doing as giving the same kaleidoscope a new twist. The metaphor is perhaps appropriate in my case as well, although my kaleidoscope is not quite the same. Perhaps I would do better to quote the Malay saying that "different ponds have different fish," or the Indonesian version, "different fields, different grasshoppers," which is all the more appropriate in my case since my grasshoppers are still hopping around and I had serious doubts that I would have them rounded up in time for this article.

I came to the University of Nevada in 1969 after a year and a half of fieldwork in Malaysia in 1966–67 for my Ph.D. at the University of Chicago. At that time there were two recent Chicago graduates at the University of Nevada—Bill Douglass and Peter Benedict—both of whom had done extensive fieldwork in foreign areas, Bill in Spain and Peter in Turkey. There was also, of course, Warren d'Azevedo, who had done extensive work in Africa as well as in the Great Basin, and Catherine Fowler, already working in the Great Basin. The next appointment was the late Kenneth

Knudson who did his research in the Pacific Islands. The evident commitment of the anthropology department to a comparative orientation was one of the things that drew me to the University of Nevada and has continued to make it a compatible place. Given the comparatively small size of the faculty, and its natural orientation to the American West, it has not always been easy to maintain a comparative as well as a local emphasis, but I think we have done fairly well in this respect, both in cultural anthropology and in archaeology. D'Azevedo's long-term fieldwork commitment to both Liberia and the Great Basin has always seemed like an ideal to me, and one I regret that I have not been able to approximate. This article relates more to the Liberian than the Great Basin side of d'Azevedo's fieldwork. Indeed, the ethnic situation in Liberia that I have read about in Warren's work reminds me of Sarawak, minus the headhunting.

My experience has been something of a departure from the usual pattern of long-term fieldwork, at least as usually conceived.[1] Douglass (this volume) notes that while pursuing a research career focusing on Basques he never returned to the Basque villages that he had originally studied. So much for growing old with your informants and seeing life change for them as it also changes for you. Instead of returning and restudying those villages, he has worked with immigrant Basque communities in various places in the world. In my case I have returned frequently to my original field site in Kelantan on the northwest coast of peninsular Malaysia for further research. But I have not attempted to restudy the specific communities in terms of change. Of course I know a good deal about the general changes in Malaysia and the more specific change that has occurred in the lives of friends and informants with whom I have remained in contact over the past twenty-three years. Such change has certainly been impressive. But this is to be expected. Stability in that sort of developing setting would be remarkable. Further, returning every several years has had the effect of dulling my own sense of change. Had I waited ten or twenty years I would have been able to marvel at all sorts of new developments, as well as how much older people had curiously become. Finally, I must confess that I liked Kelantan more in the 1960s than I did in the 1980s. I am speaking from a selfish perspective, and, of course, partly because I have changed. People there may or may not be better off—an argument could be made either way—but the culture now seems less interesting. All sorts of traditional practices, folk arts, and performances flourished in the 1960s. Now people tend to watch a lot of television. More than it was formerly, the local way of life seems to be a version of developing culture that one might well find in Africa or Latin America, as well as in Southeast Asia. Plastic culture and modern technology tend to look much the same everywhere, as do the lifestyles that go with them.

Of course differences and cultural continuities also can be stressed. People do other things than watch television. Certain traditional practices, beliefs, and modes of behavior continue to flourish. Instances of mass spirit possession now seem to be more common than in the past, though this may be only a consequence of their being widely reported in the local news media. And *latah*, the 'hyperstartle' complex, which was the focus of my research in 1985–86, certainly does not seem to have declined. *Latah* is perhaps the most famous of all the so-called culture-bound syndromes, although it is neither really culture-bound nor (in my view) a syndrome. It involves a severe reaction to startle, in some instances a loss of consciousness and a tendency to involuntarily imitate the words and actions of others or to follow orders. Since it first was noted by Europeans in the nineteenth century, it has been supposed that *latah* was disappearing as the Malays came under modern influence, that it would continue to appear only in backward and traditional areas, and that it would eventually die out entirely. Some modern writers who have read these old accounts in fact report that while *latah* was once common it has now died out. It has not. In some areas in Malaysia—that is, ones that I know—*latah* is at the present time (1990) extremely common. Since no real statistical information about the occurrence of the phenomenon is available for earlier periods, it is not really possible to know whether it is more or less common than it was at some point in the past. But in some ways at least it must be more common. It has now clearly spread from Malays to other groups in both Kelantan and Sarawak, among which it was not known to have previously occurred (Winzeler 1994).

As to my topic, I do not wish to repeat previous statements I have made about *latah*, and therefore will elaborate on my recent interests that I think pose some interesting methodological issues. The particular problem I wish to address in this paper concerns a recent phase of my own fieldwork. Moreover, it concerns fieldwork in general. The topic is headhunting in

Southeast Asia, more specifically the interpretations that anthropologists have offered about this practice over the years, partly on the basis of field-work. As I shall show, however, my particular interest in headhunting has more to do with modern ethnicity than with what actually occurred in the past. The place of concern is Sarawak, one of the two states that comprise Malaysian Borneo.

Sarawak and Headhunting

Douglass (this volume) notes that the social anthropology of European soci-eties developed late and has been concentrated especially on the margins. In some ways the situation is similar in Southeast Asia. We think of field-oriented social and cultural anthropology as a twentieth-century phenome-na. But in terms of its modern scale and range, especially outside North America and Africa, it is more a postwar development. In Southeast Asia, with a few exceptions perhaps, this has been true. Until the end of World War II, anthropological attention was limited to the tribal regions and much of what was done was ethnology—perhaps the equivalent of Euro-peanist folklore—rather than social anthropology. The scholars associated with such research were missionaries, colonial civil servants, and others, some of whom provided very detailed and valuable material. There also were "expeditions," but these too were focused on ethnology and explo-ration and were undertaken most often by natural scientists, for example, Wallace (1864). In Malaya, that is peninsular Malaysia, Raymond Firth (1946) and Rosemary Firth (1943, 1972) were the first social anthropolo-gists to do fieldwork. They did a pioneering study of Malay fishermen in 1939–40, one of the first anthropological studies of "peasants" (as they called them) anywhere. But their study, like Malinowski's in the Trobriands, was a quasi-accident. They had been planning to go to China but were di-verted by the second World War (Parkin 1988).

Sarawak is a very interesting place, a veritable anthropological paradise of—to use post-modern anthropology's favorite word—"otherness," where several famous anthropologists have worked. Social anthropological research there also has been mainly a postwar phenomenon. From the mid-nine-teenth century onward a great deal of ethnological research was done in

Sarawak but, as in Borneo in general, it was done by missionaries, government administrators, and natural scientists. Edmund Leach (1950) was commissioned by the Colonial Research Council in the late 1940s to do an ethnographic survey of the country and to organize social anthropological projects that would provide information regarding economic development. Studies were carried out under his direction by Derek Freeman (1955) among the Iban or Sea Dayak, by William Geddes (1954) among the Bukar Sadong (one of the Bidayuh or Land Dayak groups), and by Stephen Morris (1953) among the Melanau. Later, Rodney Needham (1976) undertook fieldwork also, especially among the Penan hunter-gatherers but also among the Kenyah.

The practice of headhunting is closely associated with Sarawak in Western thought. I begin with a few general and very unoriginal observations. As far as we know, headhunting was traditionally practiced by all of the indigenous peoples of Sarawak except the various hunter-gatherers, the Malays, and other coastal Muslims. Evidently there were, however, major differences in its extent and frequency among different groups, and in the reluctance with which they abandoned the practice when subjected to European influence or power. In the nineteenth and early twentieth century, the Sea Dayaks or Iban, as they came to be known later, were the largest and the most warlike of the Dayak groups.

The frequency of headhunting was linked to migration on the one hand, and to the arrival of Europeans on the other. For poorly understood reasons, the nineteenth century saw a great deal of Dayak migration from the interior of Borneo, that is, from south to north, into present-day Sarawak. The most extensive of these migrations involved the Iban, but other warlike groups were also involved, especially the Kenyah and Kayan (Rousseau 1990:331–339). As migrating groups who practiced shifting agriculture arrived in new areas, incentives and opportunities for warfare and headhunting increased. Since headhunting for all groups also was linked to internal cultural motives, it occurred in the absence of migration and territorial instability. Because of the latter, however, it may have reached a peak in Sarawak in the nineteenth century (see Metcalf 1982:129).

Headhunting played a major part in the events through which the Englishman James Brooke gained control of Sarawak and became the first White Rajah, the king of a unique state that lasted from 1841 to 1941, when the invasion of the Japanese brought its end, its eventual incorporation as a British colony, and then (in 1963) as a state in Malaysia. A major element in the mythical charter of the regime was that, when Brooke arrived in 1839, a civil war among Malay nobles was occurring, and Sea Dayak (that is Iban) headhunters and Malay pirates were terrorizing coastal villages and weaker tribal groups in the interior. He was implored to intervene and did so successfully. As a reward, he was made Raja by the Sultan of Brunei. Headhunting diminished as state control was established and expanded, though over a long period of time.

Brooke's version of events was questioned early on in England and there was eventually a full Parliamentary inquiry as to whether Brooke was justified in his actions. Headhunting was a main issue. Brooke's critics charged that he was an adventurer who had taken advantage of his situation by getting involved in processes that were best regarded as "routine intertribal warfare," which, as such, did not warrant outside intervention. Brooke's supporters claimed that the Sea Dayaks were not ordinary headhunters going about the usual business of intertribal raiding. They were leaving the rivers along which they lived and raiding coastal settlements and ships hundreds of miles away. Therefore they were "pirates," the scourge of eastern traders, and Brooke was a hero for going after them. The inquiry brought out facts in support of both positions. The Iban were raiding over very long distances, attacking peoples with whom they had not been at war, and were thus not ordinary headhunters. But it also was shown that they were not ordinary Southeast Asian pirates. The latter often cruised over thousands of miles for a year or more at a time and did so in order to gain slaves and goods. The Sea Dayaks, however, were raiding between the harvesting and planting seasons in the usual manner of tribal warfare and were primarily interested in heads and only secondarily in slaves and material property.

It was eventually decided that the Iban were engaged in piracy rather than simply in intertribal warfare. In any case, the suppression of headhunting in all forms and among all groups continued to be a principal justification of the European state in Sarawak. Indeed, since the Brooke regime was relatively uninterested in promoting trade and development (which, along with the elimination of piracy, oppression, and slavery, were the main reasons advanced for European control in Southeast Asia), the suppression of tribal warfare and aggressive migration assumed a particular importance in colonial ideology. It is now known that European policies aimed at suppressing warfare, migration, and headhunting in some ways made them worse. For whatever reasons, "traditional" warfare and headhunting continued in some regions of Sarawak into the fourth decade of this century when the last government punitive expedition against the Iban was undertaken (Pringle 1970:245). The end of traditional warfare did not bring an end to the ritual use of skulls or their religious significance. To varying degrees headhunting ceremonies continue to the present among those groups that have not converted to Christianity.

The point remains, however, that by the post World War II period in modern anthropological research, nearly all headhunting had ended everywhere; in many areas it had ceased by the end of the nineteenth century or before. *Nearly,* perhaps, needs to be emphasized. Evidently—the evidence, however, is not very detailed—many heads were taken, at least by the Iban, toward the close of the second World War. This presumably involved resistance activities against retreating Japanese forces instigated by behind-the-lines British operators (MacDonald 1956:101). More recently, in the middle 1960s during the border war in Borneo between Indonesia and Malaysian, Iban soldiers are reported in one recorded account to have taken the heads of slain enemy Indonesian soldiers (Dickens 1983:193–194). But aside from such relatively isolated incidents, headhunting as a part of regular or episodic tribal raiding and warfare ended well before modern anthropology arrived in the late 1940s.

The fact that active traditional headhunting ended earlier in the twentieth century or before, notwithstanding, is a matter that has been hard to avoid for anyone who has done ethnography or social anthropology in Sarawak. It seems to be something like kinship for anthropologists who study Australian aborigines or witchcraft for Africanists, that is, a topic that presents a major set of intellectual problems. Of the four British social anthropologists who carried out seminal studies around 1950, all but Stephen Morris have written extensively about headhunting or have offered ambitious interpretations of its meaning and nature (Freeman 1979; Geddes 1961:50–55; Needham 1976). And there have been many other accounts and interpretations (see Haddon 1901; McKinley 1976; Metcalf 1982:112–136; Vayda 1976). In the broader field of Southeast Asian studies, papers delivered and articles published about headhunting seem to be on the increase, especially regarding Indonesian societies. I tend to be skeptical of those efforts that deal with matters of emotion and meaning in relation to processes and events that took place well in the past on the basis of present-day informant accounts.

I should also note at this point that headhunting is not exactly a matter about which even a few years ago I would have ever expected to find myself having anything to say. Douglass (this volume) indicates that the research projects in which he has been involved seem to represent logical movement on a course he set early in his career. My own development, if that is the right word, seems more the opposite. I have continued to become interested in new things, which have required new modes of research. I suppose, however, there have been certain continuities. In the early 1970s, as a result of my earlier fieldwork, I became interested in matters of ethnicity, minorities, and social change. I have continued to be interested in these, which is one of the reasons I have been especially fascinated with western Sarawak. Along with a volume on shamans and other religious specialists in Borneo (Winzeler 1993), I am currently editing a collection of papers on ethnicity and ethnogenesis in Borneo and the Malay Peninsula. My own interest in headhunting mainly concerns problems of ethnicity and ethnohistory, especially among Bidayuh.

I have also long been interested in the matter of how anthropologists and others use historical evidence. I have recently completed a study of the ways that Europeans have interpreted various aspects of Malay religion, culture, and character over time. The field study that I did of *latah* in 1984 to 1987 actually grew out of my reading of how the topic had been treated over time and of how the historical sources were being used by modern scholars to infer change. Again, the European literature on headhunting is especially interesting and problematic in this regard. A considerable amount has been written, but the more you read the more ambiguous and uncertain various matters become. Much remains to be sorted out.

This is part of the reason I became interested in the topic of fieldwork and interpretations of headhunting, though I went to Borneo initially in relation to my project on *latah*. The research project was supposed to be carried out both in Kelantan (in northeastern peninsular Malaysia) and in Sarawak. Since I was already familiar with the Malay, Thai, and Chinese villages in Kelantan in which I needed to collect survey information, I was able to complete that part of the project sooner than I had expected and so was able to get to Sarawak earlier and stay longer than I had anticipated. The plan was to study the distribution of *latah* among the various tribal and ethnic groups who make up the population. This turned out be a very productive line of research. Since I speak Malay, the national language, which many people there now know, and which in any case is close to several of the Bornean languages, and since my research had been approved by the government, I was able to move wherever I wanted. I bought a boat and outboard motor and traveled extensively up and down rivers surveying villages to see if they had *latah*. With local assistants I had no real difficulties and was consequently able to cover a large amount of territory, to learn something about many different groups, and to acquire some sense of the different patterns of change occurring in different areas. I also was able to spend longer periods in particular places, to which I have subsequently returned in later trips and to which I will continue to go.

During the course of these activities I came upon, by accident, several interesting things relating to headhunting. At one point I was taken for a headhunter myself. This happened on the lower Oya River near the coast while I was working on a survey among the Melanau. My Melanau assistant and I went up to the house of a villager living near the river to make inquiries but we did not get anywhere. Quite uncharacteristically we were not invited in. The man would not even open the door very far and made it clear that he did not want to talk to us. As soon as we left I asked my Melanau assistant what was wrong. He said that the man had been afraid of me and had thought I was a *penyamun* or headhunter. I thought my assistant was joking. The situation struck me as ironic and funny, for there I was, a harmless, civilized white man. He explained that there had been rumors lately about headhunters being around trying to kidnap children, and I was a stranger. This was my introduction to *penyamun* rumors and I was the *penyamun!* I thus learned that if headhunting had ceased, rumors about it had not. Those of you who know something about urban folklore from the books of Alan Dundes (Dundes and Pagter 1975, 1991) or Jan Brunvand (1981), or have heard about the vanishing hitchhiker and the like, will know that many interesting notions circulate as oral tradition in our own society. In Borneo there are various versions of *penyamun* rumor—a new one was reported in the newspapers there in 1989.[2] Many such rumors concern the Iban, who have continued to migrate to new areas and of whom other groups tend to remain apprehensive. Among the Melanau and related central Bornean groups, *penyamun* rumors tend to harken back to traditional practices of human sacrifice and to focus on the off-shore oil and gas rigs, which sit out in the ocean. The oil rigs, the rumor goes, require human heads or sacrifices, and since oil rigs are run by Europeans it follows that they may be *penyamun* (see Metcalf 1982:129).

Another accidental experience that drew my attention to headhunting occurred in rural Lundu in far western Sarawak where I had earlier done surveys, and where subsequently I often went to stay in a Selako Dayak village with a particular family that had taken me in. On one occasion the topic of headhunting came up and my host told me that a few families around there still kept skulls; one who did lived just down the road. This was a real revelation, something I had not expected to hear. The Selako (at least those living in Sarawak) had given up headhunting in the distant past. They live in single family dwellings rather than long houses and supposedly had never had skull houses. I had never read anything in the meager literature on the Selako about their skull cult. The next day we walked to the house and sure enough there were two skulls, both sitting on an altarlike shelf up near the ceiling in the main room, surrounded by dried betel leaves and the remnants of other offerings that have to be given to skulls periodically to keep them happy. The old woman who owned them told me about where they had come from, how long they had been in her family, what taboos had to be observed in the house because of them, how they would warn her of robbers or headhunters by clacking their teeth or throwing themselves down and rolling on the floor. I subsequently visited other houses in the area that also had skulls.

Intrigued with such experiences, I have attempted over the last several years to read the literature on Bornean headhunting and Sarawak ethnology and history. It is useful to say something about this literature at this point. To begin with, in contrast to cannibalism, for example, there is no doubt that headhunting did take place. Europeans have frequently witnessed head taking and they also have provided eye-witness accounts of the ritual treatment of new heads, though I am not aware of any first-hand account that begins with a beheading and follows all of the subsequent ritual activities. Skulls may be readily seen today in long houses in Sarawak and certain rituals connected with headhunting and the head cult are still performed.

At the same time much is not known or is a matter of dispute. For example, Derek Freeman (1979:234), who lived with the Iban (on the Baleh River in what was then the Third Division) for two years from 1949 to 1951, has written that headhunting at that time was still a matter of passionate concern. But Eric Jensen (1974:6), another social anthropologist who lived with the Iban for an equally long period in the 1950s, has written that since headhunting was successfully suppressed in the 1920s it has not played an active role in Iban life. Such claims are not quite as contradictory as they might seem, for Jensen lived with the Iban in the Second Division where headhunting was eliminated much earlier than it was in the upper part of the Third Division where Freeman worked. Still, as a general statement I do not know who is more correct.

To take another example, Vinson Sutlive (1978:31), who had lived in Sarawak as a missionary before becoming an anthropologist, asserts that Iban were more prone to take captives than heads. Freeman (1981:62) challenges this in a footnote in which he claims it is not true of the Ulu Ai Iban of the Baleh. He offers as supporting evidence a survey he did of the number of skulls in 1949–50 kept in long houses on the Baleh. The survey showed an average of one skull for about every eight persons, from which he infers a total of about 1,260 skulls for all of the Baleh. European accounts of the region, he goes on, suggest relatively few captives. Such evidence is not wholly convincing since Freeman makes no effort to determine the time period in which such a number of skulls had been accumulated. Further, since as he notes, the Brooke government tried to have captives returned; Iban who had them were likely to have kept it secret. Again, this question of captives versus skulls is one that perhaps cannot be resolved.

Among other groups, matters are also vague. For the Berawan, a central Bornean stratified chiefdom, Peter Metcalf (1982:113–136) has given perhaps the most detailed and interesting account of headhunting for a specific group in the recent period. His concern is limited mainly to headhunting in relation to mourning rituals and beliefs, however, and even there he is not able to describe everything. The Berawan were willing to perform the major headhunting festival for him, which they had last performed thirty years earlier when Japanese heads had been taken. But they had expected him to supply the heads, presumably in the manner that government officials had previously done from a supply of old skulls kept at the local fort to be loaned out for ritual use as a substitute for freshly taken heads (Metcalf 1982:114). Since he did not have the skulls, the festival was not held. In addition, Metcalf was not even able to obtain a verbal description of one of the central rituals, the dance performed by the women to incorporate the new head into the long house. This dance involved what the Berawan had subsequently come to regard as acts of unspeakable obscenity (Metcalf 1982:132).

If we attempt to understand the ideas that underlay the practice of headhunting, matters become more complicated. Recently there have been a number of attempts to do this on the basis of older evidence or of accounts given by informants. For Southeast Asia in general it has often been supposed that the part of the motive for headhunting was to capture the "soulstuff" stored in the head of an enemy. This apparently does not work for Borneo. Significantly, Rodney Needham (1976:76–78) and Derek Freeman (1979:235–236), who do not seem to agree on much else, both reject the soul-stuff argument. In his earlier account of Iban headhunting, migration, and ecology, Freeman (1970:130–151) linked Iban headhunting to aggressiveness and a desire for new and fertile lands. Twenty years later (after turning to psychoanalysis [see Appell and Madan 1988:12–14]) he wrote that he had determined what had previously eluded him and what the Iban had been unable to explain concerning the central Iban myth of headhunting. This was that the head was a phallic object and that the whole complex was a fertility cult (Freeman 1979:236–238).

Since the nineteenth century, when Europeans began to note or explain the motives for headhunting in Borneo, various reasons have been offered. These include vengeance, the desire to achieve status and demonstrate bravery, the need to take heads in order to impress women and obtain wives, to promote the growth of rice and the general fertility and well-being of the community, and to complete the ritual necessary to end a period of mourning. Of these motives, the first two are likely to be associated with tribal warfare in any society while the remainder could all be linked to underlying notions of sexual energy and fertility. The latter notions are also suggested by the extensive involvement of women in the cult of skulls. The willingness of some groups to use existing skulls from other villages as a substitute for ones from freshly taken enemy meant that headhunting could be divorced from warfare and vengeance. It is not clear, however, that all headhunting groups were willing to use old skulls rather than new ones. Both the central Bornean groups and some of the Bidayuh groups did so. The Iban have not been reported to exchange old skulls insofar as I am aware.

While there are certain apparent commonalities associated with headhunting in Borneo, and perhaps with other areas in Southeast Asia, there also appears to be extensive variation. Observers who have obtained information about beliefs and motives have tended to offer general explanations. There is also reason to be skeptical about what can be learned about motives and beliefs in the past from informants in much later periods or from witnessing later rituals related to headhunting and the head cults. This, however, has been a popular mode of interpretation in recent years.

Headhunting and Post-Modernist Doubt

Headhunting continues to be a matter of interesting argument, but is it still justified as a topic of anthropological research and discussion? This is a matter of ambiguity. Among the criticisms that have been made of cultural anthropology in recent years is that it focuses on the exotic. Anthropologists, it has been said, emphasize otherness, relativism, uniqueness, and cultural particularity over human universals, commonalities, and ordinariness (Keesing 1989:459–460). We offer glimpses of the bizarre through the lens of scholarly respectability. We are the science of the strange. Most people in most societies do most things in similar ways, but we dwell upon—and perhaps overemphasize—the differences. If bad news sells newspapers, otherness gets anthropology books published and sold, and anthropologists funded, hired, tenured, promoted, and, in some cases, made famous.

Scholarly discussions of headhunting and the head cults of Southeast Asia obviously fit the scope of such criticism. Along with cannibalism, human sacrifice, and culturally sanctioned sexual promiscuity, it is among the best known bits of ethnographic exotica in anthropology. As much as anything else it symbolizes savagery. Further, emphasizing savage otherness has not been a harmless pursuit from the perspective of the native peoples involved.

This idea, it has often been said, served to justify imperial expansion, warfare, Christian evangelism, colonial control, and, in some instances, slavery and the expropriation of aboriginal lands and genocide. In Sarawak, headhunting played a major role in the developments that led to the establishment of a European controlled state in 1841, and in the subsequent justification for its existence and continued expansion (Keppel 1853). Anyone who writes about it should keep this in mind.

Headhunting has thus assumed a particular importance in the history of Sarawak as it has been written by European participants and later historians and anthropologists. Perhaps both because of this and their own oral traditions, it continues to be an important part of the view that the Iban and the other Dayak groups have of themselves and their past. Such notions are, moreover, bound up with present-day ethnicity. The processes of intertribal warfare and headhunting, which were in some ways intensified by European involvement, were associated with patterns of ethnic migration, dislocation, assimilation, and extinction, which profoundly altered the ethnic composition of northern Borneo. As more powerful groups moved from the interior toward the coast, less powerful ones were absorbed or driven out of their way. In the late nineteenth and twentieth centuries, the Iban came to be by far the largest and most powerful of the Dayak groups. As a result of warfare and migration, the Iban came to control a large area of Sarawak, often at the expense of other groups. In the more recent period, Iban migration into new regions has continued. This has been peaceful but it also has been a source of anxiety to the peoples inhabiting the areas into which they have moved. Present-day rumors about headhunters would seem to reflect such anxieties.

Local Views

Current attitudes about headhunting are thus bound up with patterns of ethnicity, that is, ethnic identity and ethnic interaction. Such attitudes tend to be ambivalent and to vary among various Dayak groups and subgroups of each in relation to patterns of acculturation. In 1988 I attended several meetings in Sarawak that were particularly interesting in this regard. Politics and culture in Sarawak, as in Malaysia generally, tend to be organized along ethnic lines. It was thus decided to celebrate the twenty-fifth anniversary of the incorporation of Sarawak into Malaysia in 1963 by holding a series of conferences and workshops on cultural diversity and integration. Malays, Chinese, Bidayuh, Iban, Melanau, and Orang Ulu ("up-river") peoples were each to have a workshop of several days to be held in a town in their own ethnic region so that local people—as well as state elites and outsiders—could attend. A primary purpose of each workshop was to provide an opportunity for the representatives of each ethnic sector to discuss its culture, traditions, and history, to determine what was worth keeping and what was not, and what could be contributed to a "national culture." All of this made for very interesting discussion in the several (Bidayuh, Iban, and Orang Ulu) workshops I attended. There were also feasts, dances, and ceremonial openings and closings by state and local dignitaries at each gathering.

The discussions at the different ethnic workshops focused on different concerns. Headhunting was a matter of much interest at the Iban gathering. Although it was not discussed in any of the formal papers that had been prepared by outside scholars or local Iban participants, it was soon brought up in the discussion by Iban commentators. The Iban, it was said, had been maligned by outside scholars who had written about them as pirates and headhunters. Speaker after speaker got up to second these remarks. The speakers were not really denying that the Iban had been headhunters. Several, including prominent political leaders, said that skulls still hung in their long houses. The Iban, it was made clear, are proud of their culture and their history, in which warfare and headhunting had a prominent place. The Iban heroes in the history of the Kapit region, where the meeting was held, had been famous warriors who had fought against the Brooke regime and led migrations into new rivers and taken many heads. Some had become allies of the Brooke government and been made district and paramount chiefs—offices created by the government. Several of the descendants of such men who themselves had in some cases become rich and influential in modern political affairs, were present at the meeting and spoke about their lives and the changes that had occurred.

The Iban concern at the meeting was that their reputation and history had been distorted and bloodied up too much by outside writers. This reputation had been formed in the mid-nineteenth century in relation to the founding of Sarawak by James Brooke, his efforts to eradicate piracy on the coast, in the parliamentary inquiry into his actions, and in the books that were written about these events. Too little, the speakers thought, had been written about the Iban in these accounts except in regard to coastal raiding, warfare, and headhunting. They were portrayed as mysterious, blood-thirsty marauders. In fact, as the Iban of the Skrang and Saribas rivers were subdued and as the British got to know them in their homes, they generally came to admire them. Accounts became less one-sided, but perhaps since Iban resistance, headhunting, and "illegal" migration continued in the up-river areas, the existing reputation continued. Postwar treatments of Iban by anthropologists and historians have been generally sympathetic. The most thorough history of the Iban during Brooke rule, by Robert Pringle, blames the Brooke government's practices—especially those relating to punitive expeditions, which made use of Iban from lower river areas to subdue those in the upper rivers—for the persistence of headhunting and intertribal war (Pringle 1970:244–245). The work of later foreign scholars, however, is perhaps inevitably linked to those of earlier periods.

The present-day Bidayuh also were interested in the matter of headhunting in their history. But there were no objections at their workshop about foreign scholars distorting their culture by overemphasizing headhunting and warfare. Little was said about headhunting at their meeting where the main emphasis was on economic development and the ethnic integration of the linguistically separate Bidayuh groups. At one evening performance of dances put on by the various Bidayuh cultural groups, however, a skull dance was performed. The girls who performed the dance held monkey skulls suspended on strings as substitutes for human skulls. The narrator who introduced the dance informed the audience that the Bidayuh also had been headhunters, "like the Iban." At the welcoming ceremony the men of the dance groups had worn war gear and carried headhunting swords. And a photograph of a Bidayuh skull house was featured on the front of the program for their meeting, as it was also on a program prepared for a local version of the anniversary celebration held in Bau district. While questions have been raised about whether "skull house" or "head house" are the proper translation of *baruk* and the other terms by which these ceremonial structures are known in the various Bidayuh languages, this is the term that was used to refer to them in the program.

These various symbolic expressions suggest that the concerns of the Bidayuh about headhunting and their past are somewhat the opposite of those of the Iban. The Bidayuh would like to be taken more seriously as former headhunters. They would like to have their history cast in more heroic terms. I am speaking here especially of modern Bidayuh political and ethnic leaders with western educations, but I think it is also true of more traditional villagers as well. Why should this be so?

The history of the Bidayuh produced over the past century and a half by European observers has been slanted in the opposite direction from that concerning the Iban. Both groups played roles in the mythical charter of the Brooke regime. But while the Iban were cast in the role of aggressor, the Land Dayaks were cast as victims who were oppressed by coastal Malays and raided by Iban until the arrival of Brooke saved them (see, for example, Wallace 1869:71 and MacDonald 1956:51–52). In reality, some of the Bidayuh groups seem to have been quite heavily involved in headhunting and warfare, though they all gave it up more readily than did the more numerous and powerful Iban.

Present-day Bidayuh interests in their history, including their traditions of headhunting, are in part "symbolic." And what they symbolize is the present-day ethnic situation of Sarawak in which the Bidayuh see themselves as occupying a low position in the local hierarchy of prestige, power, and wealth. The Bidayuh are aware of some of the objective, material bases of their position as an ethnic population in one corner of Malaysia. Agricultural lands in the areas they occupy have frequently been depleted, and there are few areas of mature rain forest suitable for logging, a major source of income in some other regions. Bidayuh leaders emphasize modern developmental solutions to their problems, but symbolic and ideological concerns also are stressed.

These concerns focus especially upon the problem of ethnic unity. The modern Bidayuh leadership is convinced that they lack political power and ethnic prestige because they have been fragmented into local areas with separate dialects. They would like to have a common Bidayuh language instead of the half-dozen distinct ones they now speak. Their concern for unity also is linked to an interest in their origins. They would like to believe that they had a recent common origin and that they diverged only lately as a result of intense warfare and raiding during the nineteenth century. The last time I was in Sarawak, my Bidayuh friends were excited about what they hoped was the site of their ancestral homeland. This was a mountain top where the Bidayuh had supposedly lived until it was destroyed by an Iban raid in the early part of the nineteenth century.

The Bidayuh also made it clear that they are quite willing to be studied. They are interested in knowing about their past, including the part relating to headhunting. Unlike the Iban, they as yet have little interest in deconstructing what has been written about them. Perhaps they should and probably they eventually will. At the present time, however, they are interested in improving their ethnic position and in understanding their past, about which very little is now known.

Headhunting does present some very interesting problems in relation to the Bidayuh. I doubt that much can be recovered about matters of meaning and emotion in relation to headhunting activities, which took place long ago. On the other hand, there are various things that can be studied that should be of long-term value. The rituals that surround the head cult in the different Bidayuh groups have never been well described. In most cases they have never been described at all. Some of them are still being performed. The skull houses, which are (or were) found among most of the Bidayuh groups, are very significant for several reasons. In Sarawak they occur only among the Bidayuh, and they are usually round rather than square or rectangular in shape. They are thus quite unlike almost any other indigenous residential or ceremonial structure in Borneo or elsewhere in Southeast Asia. Finally, Bidayuh villages present a very interesting problem in terms of ethnic history and linguistic diversity. In the past, these villages were located mainly on the slopes and tops of mountains from which they moved into lowland areas only after cessation of warfare. The Bidayuh themselves note that the people who occupied the different mountains spoke different dialects of the various Bidayuh languages. It has been argued by one colonial scholar that the Bidayuh *had* previously lived in lowland areas until Iban raiding drove them up into the mountains (MacDonald 1956:51). It is equally possible that this is incorrect, that most of the Bidayuh groups had been living on hill tops before the Iban arrived, because they were actively engaged in headhunting among themselves.

These are questions in which the Bidayuh themselves are very interested and in regard to which they would welcome outside scholars. They are also a matter of some urgency for if the modern Bidayuh are trying to understand their past, they also are trying to get out of much of it as quickly as possible. The skull house, which has recently become an important symbol of Bidayuh ethnic pride, is almost extinct. Based upon his study of the Bukar Sadong Bidayuh circa 1950, Geddes reported that nearly every long house had a skull house, and some had several; there were thus perhaps hundreds throughout the Bidayuh region. Now there are only a handful, some of them in danger of collapsing in disrepair.

As a result of my field experiences in Borneo, I have thus become interested in material culture in a way that I never was before. The documentation of traditional structures there—not only the skull houses, which I have talked about, but all sorts of other fine things—deserve more attention than they have so far received, especially from anthropologists. I hope to be able to document some of this.

Endnotes

1. My earliest research in Malaysia was supported by the National Science Foundation. Subsequent studies were funded by the National Institute of Mental Health and the Research Advisory Board of the University of Nevada, Reno. My research in the mid-1980s was supported by the National Science Foundation and the Fulbright Program.
2. "Police Deny 'Penyamun' Rumors." *Sarawak Tribune,* July 16, 1989.

References Cited

Appell, G. N., and T. N. Madan
1988   Derek Freeman: Notes Toward an Intellectual Biography. In *Choice and Morality in Anthropological Perspective: Essays in Honor of Derek Freeman,* edited by G. N. Appell and T. N. Madan, pp. 3–25. State University of New York Press, Albany.

Brunvand, Jan
1981   *The Vanishing Hitchhiker: American Urban Legends and Their Meaning.* Norton, New York.

Dickens, Peter
1983   *SAS The Jungle Frontier: 22 Special Air Service Regiment in the Borneo Campaign, 1963–1966.* Arms and Armour Press, London.

Dundes, Alan, and Carl R. Pagter (compilers)

1975   *Urban Folklore from the Paperwork Empire.* American Folklore Society, Austin, Texas.

1991   *Never Try to Teach a Pig to Sing: Still More Urban Folklore from the Paperwork Empire.* Wayne State University Press, Detroit, Michigan.

Firth, Raymond

1946   *Malay Fishermen: Their Peasant Economy.* London School of Economics Monographs on Social Anthropology. Athlone Press, London (republished 1966).

Firth, Rosemary

1943   *Housekeeping among Malay Peasants.* London School of Economics Monographs on Social Anthropology. Athlone Press, London (republished 1966).

1972   From Wife to Anthropologist. In *Crossing Cultural Boundaries,* edited by S. T. Kimball and J. B. Watson, p. 10–32. Chandler Publishing Co., San Francisco.

Freeman, Derek

1970   *Report on the Iban.* Athlone Press, London (originally published in 1955).

1979   Severed Heads that Germinate. In *Fantasy and Symbol: Studies in Anthropological Interpretation,* edited by R. H. Hook, pp. 233–246. Academic Press, New York.

1981   *Some Reflections on the Nature of Iban Society.* Occasional Paper of the Department of Anthropology, Research School of Pacific Studies. Australian National University, Canberra.

Geddes, W. R.

1954   *The Land Dayaks of Sarawak: A Report on a Social Economic Survey of the Land Dayaks of Sarawak Presented to the Colonial Social Science Research Council.* Her Majesty's Stationery Office, London.

1961   *Nine Dayak Nights.* Oxford University Press, Oxford.

Haddon, Alfred C.

1901   *Headhunters: Black, White and Brown.* Methuen, London.

Jensen, E.

1974   *The Iban and Their Religion.* Clarendon Press, Oxford.

Keesing, R.

1989   The Anthropologist as Orientalist: Exotic Readings of Cultural Texts. *Current Anthropology* 30(4):459–469.

Keppel, Henry

1853   *A Visit to the Indian Archipelago, in H. M. Ship Meander.* Richard Bentley, London.

Leach, Edmund

1950   *Social Science Research in Sarawak.* His Majesty's Stationary Office, London.

MacDonald, Malcolm

1956   *Borneo People.* Jonathan Cape, London.

McKinley, Robert

1976   Human and Proud of It! A Structural Treatment of Headhunting Rites and the Social Definition of Enemies. In *Studies in Borneo Societies: Social Process and Anthropological Explanation,* edited by G. N. Appell, pp. 92–126. Special Report no. 12, Center for Southeast Asian Studies, Northern Illinois University, DeKalb.

Metcalf, Peter

1982   *A Borneo Journey in Death: Berawan Eschatology from its Rituals.* University of Pennsylvania Press, Philadelphia.

Morris, H. S.

1953   *Report on a Melanau Sago Producing Community in Sarawak.* Her Majesty's Stationery Office, London.

Needham, Rodney

1976   Skulls and Causality. *Man* 11(2):71–88.

Parkin, David

1988   An Interview with Raymond Firth. *Current Anthropology* 29(2):327–340.

Pringle, Robert

1970   *Rajahs and Rebels: The Ibans of Sarawak under Brooke Rule, 1841–1941.* Cornell University Press, Ithaca.

Rousseau, Jérôme

1990   *Central Borneo: Ethnic Identity and Social Life in a Stratified Society.* Clarendon Press, Oxford.

Sutlive, Vinson

1978   *The Iban of Sarawak.* AHM Publishing Corp, Arlington Heights, Virginia.

Vayda, Andrew P.

1976   *War In Ecological Perspective: Persistence, Change, and Adaptive Processes in Three Oceanian Societies.* Plenum Press, New York.

Wallace, A. R.

1864   On the Varieties of Man in the Malay Archipelago. *Transactions of the Ethnological Society of London* 3:197–215.

1869   *The Malay Archipelago: The Land of the Orang-Utan and the Bird of Paradise* (reprinted Dover Publications, New York, 1962).

Winzeler, Robert L.

1993   The Seen and the Unseen: Shamanism, Mediumship, and Possession in Borneo. *Borneo Research Council Monograph Series,* vol. 2. The Borneo Research Council, Williamsburg.

1994   *Latah in Southeast Asia: The History and Ethnography of a Culture-Bound Syndrome.* Cambridge University Press, New York.

Changes over Time in an African Culture and in an Anthropologist

Simon Ottenberg

Long-term research in anthropology is a particular, specialized form of research, not well understood, and infrequently written about, yet it is probably more common than is often recognized (Foster et al. 1979). There is no universally accepted meaning for the term. This form of research may be defined as the lifetime experience of an anthropologist carried out with different peoples; as one who studies different problems in different cultures; or as one who analyzes a single major problem using different peoples. These concepts of long-term research tend to focus on the scholar. More commonly the term may define work performed over a length of time with one cultural group or in one area, which places equal focus on the field site and the anthropologist. I have done fieldwork in more than one area, but I will focus on my anthropological work among the Igbo (formerly Ibo) of southeastern Nigeria. I spent fifteen months in 1952–53 in a group of villages called Afikpo, another like period in 1959–60 at Afikpo and nearby Abakaliki Town, and brief visits to Afikpo in the summer of 1967, the winter of 1988, and in March and October 1992. What is curious about my Igbo project is that the field research aspect has not been that extensive, but the writing (S. Ottenberg 1990a) has been. Thus, long-term research has a somewhat different meaning for me than for others who have spent more time in the field. An earlier graduate student summer project in

1950 in an African American community south of Savannah, Georgia, of Gullah cultural background (S. Ottenberg 1959a), provided me with needed field experience, and I carried out two years of research in 1978–80 among the Limba of Bafodea chiefdom in northern Sierra Leone.[1] In the past five years I have also conducted research on the contemporary arts of the Coast Salish Indians of Washington and British Columbia (S. Ottenberg n.d.a), and I am two years into a project on contemporary art of eastern Nigeria.

My Igbo research may be discussed along five intertwined processual lines. These are (1) changes in the society studied over time, generally as a consequence of external factors, as well as some internal ones, (2) changes in ideologies and practices in the Western world, from colonialism to various forms of neocolonialism, to the recent moves toward democratization in many parts of the world, (3) changes in concepts and approaches in anthropology over time—this has particularly characterized fashion-ridden American anthropology, (4) changes in the life experiences of the long-term research anthropologist as a scholar and person, and (5) changes in the lifeways of those individuals that the anthropologist works with in the field. Of these five complexly interrelated processes, the driving force is probably changes in the Western world, which have had evident influences on the course of anthropology and on the societies that the anthropologist studies, thus also influencing the long-term researcher as scholar and person and the lives of the people he works with in the field. But there are other cross-linkages: the interrelationships arising out of changing anthropological approaches and the life experience of those one works with in the field. These cross-cutting levels of interlinkages give long-term field research its vitality.

There is a uniqueness to each anthropological field experience and to each long-term project. But there are also commonalities, despite the individualism of much research and writing in our field, the solo nature of most research, the particular personalities of the anthropologists and those they study, and the vast differences in the cultures studied and their extent and nature of exposure to the West. Every field experience differs in detail, yet many follow a similar process of development. This makes for interesting talk among anthropologists when they gather—those tales of field research we so delight in—and creates a common frame for much anthropological understanding.

As graduate students we do not usually plan, before our first field trip, to devote our research life or a good part of it, to the study of one people. Certainly, I did not. Frequently, toward the end of his or her first research trip, the budding scholar considers returning, perhaps to complete some unfinished projects, to probe in new directions, or because he or she has fallen in love with the people and the country. So there is a return some years later, as time and funds permit, often after first producing a dissertation and securing a teaching position. Or perhaps long-term research only begins after earlier work elsewhere, as Elizabeth Colson has done, first working with the Makah Indians of Washington State (1953), and then the Tonga of Zambia (1960, 1962, 1971, 1980).

Other paths toward long-term research occur. A number of American anthropologists spent two years in the Peace Corps and then, after training, returned to their work area for anthropological research; similar experiences have occurred with missionary children. Pre-anthropological overseas experience thus turns into an aspect of long-range research, earlier knowledge becoming incorporated into later work. I also know one anthropologist who has been fascinated by an American Indian group ever since childhood, and has devoted much of her life to studying them. In any case, long-term research is an unfolding process of increasing association, sometimes including a desire to help people through applied research, as in the work of Elizabeth Colson, Thayer Scudder, and David Maybury-Lewis, working on assistance and development projects. Yet there may be obstacles; political problems in some countries have made long-term research difficult and sometimes it had to be terminated, as in Iran and in Ethiopia. I could not return to Igbo country for some years because of the Nigerian civil war and its aftermath, though I continued writing.

As the anthropologist returns to the field, he or she seeks relationships with new persons, sometimes of different ages and gender, as well as with new groups, while often retaining older ties. My wife, Phoebe Ottenberg, an anthropologist, and I each had a new field assistant during our second research period, which gave us new perspectives into Afikpo culture. During the second research visit the scholar may be adopted into groups denied to him or her during the first research period. Concepts about the culture under study alter. Individuals met during the first visit have grown and matured and changed in status and power, leading to the researcher's better understanding of the processes of culture through time. The anthropologist develops a clearer view of the impact of neighboring cultures and of the influence of our Western, materialistic, role-specialized, politically hierarchical, capitalist society. A two-dimensional view of culture, the result of a single field trip, becomes, on return visits, culture with a more dynamic, temporal dimension. New ideas arise in which the deeply continuing cultural elements can be matched against significant changes. At Afikpo, from my later brief visits, it was clear that there had been impressive material changes since my initial fieldwork, but people related to each other as they had in the past, with two exceptions. First, there was considerably greater political hierarchy, associated with differences of wealth and of being part of an independent nation; second, women had greater independence in their relationships with men. These were gradual processes of change, beginning as early as my first fieldwork in the 1950s.

Returning to the field raises problems. The processual time-depth approach of the long-term researcher greatly complicates the write-up of field materials. What is an Afikpo funeral? Is it that which I reconstructed for the 1930–40s period? Is it that which I first encountered in 1952? Is it that which I recorded in 1959–60 during my second field season, or that of later times? Clearly it is all of these, but how should it be written up? Masses of data are collected over time, so much so that organizing them becomes a management problem. But this makes for a richer anthropology (S. Ottenberg 1990a).

Long-term research allows the anthropologist to focus on one major topic after another in detail, while a single research trip allows time for a narrower focus, perhaps on a single subject, such as religion, initiation, or to write a general ethnography, as was an older practice in anthropology. In long-term research, many topics may be covered. Whatever the conceptual scheme one goes to the field with, specific issues have to be met first. At Afikpo there were two initial problems to solve. One was the complex kinship system, which I was initially untrained to cope with; the other was the very diffuse system of leadership through elders, which took a long time for me to comprehend, for there were few formal political roles. I felt that it was necessary first to solve these puzzles, and they became the framework of my dissertation and subsequent publications (S. Ottenberg 1968b, 1971b). Then, using politics and kinship as a basis, I went on to study art and boys growing up from birth through adulthood (S. Ottenberg 1975, 1989a, 1989b). From today's vantage point it looks as if I had wisely planned this sequence, but rather it just occurred, as has been the case with other scholars. Other anthropologists have developed different sequences of long-term research, resulting from the culture and their research interests, sometimes returning to the same topic for a new look. A culture is like a jigsaw puzzle with many pieces of different shapes and sizes. It takes time and patience to put it together. But long-term research makes it clear that the pieces change in shape, size, design, and connectedness, and one is constantly trying to put them together again as they alter. Some scholars, James Fernandez (1982) for one, have written one substantial, detailed work on a people that synthesizes years of research. I have never been able to put together Afikpo culture in that manner; I lack that skill. I still cannot perceive its culture as a whole.

If long-term research allows the anthropologist greater movement outward both in subject matter and contacts, it also provides a sense of how various the culture and its social groups are from that first experienced. The anthropologist becomes a comparative scholar of the elements of a single culture. So during my second research trip in 1959–60 I explored other villages and their cultures at Afikpo and derived a better sense of cultural periphery, center, and variation. I also spent some months studying the Igbo town of Abakaliki, some 30 miles north of Afikpo, where some Afikpo had settled. This provided me with a sense of what was occurring in the growing urbanism in Nigeria and what life was like for those Afikpo who lived away from home (S. Ottenberg 1962, 1966).

An advantage of long-term research is the increasing knowledge one gains of the local language. You really do not understand a culture well unless you know the tongue. This is not just a gateway to understanding culture, it *is* culture. Building knowledge of the meanings of words, phrases, and sayings over time, one obtains a deepening sense of the complexity and variability of cultural concepts, nuances, and interpretations made by different individuals. At Afikpo I was interested in how, when the village elders met together, they talked through decisions and settled disputes. This required a good knowledge of how the language was employed. Metaphor, proverb, analogy, and historical references abounded: a people whose technology was simple compared to ours had such a complex language and such skill at speaking. At first it was maddening, as I listened to the elders; little was understood except the literal meaning of words. Gradually, through time, I improved, without ever becoming expert. Their speech was fascinating; I was struck with the richness of their metaphors, each with multiple meanings to be worked out. I began to think that English was relatively sterile of metaphor and metonym, only the language of our poets being rich in these. But now I realize how bountiful ours is as well, how many of our tropes are so commonplace that we are not aware of them. It is in learning a new language that we become particularly conscious of such features. "She pigeon-holed that idea," "He's in the dog house," "He has lost his marbles," "She is not playing with a full deck," "It's raining cats and dogs," and so on. Understanding the rich meanings of linguistic elements only comes with time and lengthy research.

So from first having concentrated on the great differences between the Afikpo and English, between a supposedly scientific, literate and a nonliterate language, I now appreciate the similarities in metaphoric usage, and see both languages as part of a universal community of speech. This helps me to place Afikpo in the general world, and my Afikpo research also has made me more aware of the richness and variety of our everyday English. This is one example of how the interaction between my long-range experiences in African culture and living in the West has enriched my comprehension of African culture and at the same time my comprehension of American culture. Interestingly, the longer I researched and wrote on Afikpo the more I sensed its similarity to other cultures. My earlier work largely focused on the differences.

As greater familiarity occurs between the long-term researcher and the people he or she studies, expectations of help are likely to increase—aid to send persons to school and to university, help in carrying out traditional rites, in well building, in constructing a new school or a road. Not all of the requests can be met (S. Ottenberg 1987). Even with the building of friendships and relationships over the years, which the anthropologist hopes is on the basis of equality, the fact remains that there are generally huge disparities of wealth and access to resources between the scholar and those he studies. Even if the anthropologist tends to deny this from time to time in the joy of participating in activities of the community, it is always there. We come from wealthy, industrial societies; the people that we usually study are from poorer, nonindustrial, or slowly industrializing ones. They are often more sensitive to these differences than we; consequently, the frequent requests for help may bother us if we do not understand this. It is easier to take—of knowledge of the culture, of its material objects—if only one trip is made. But one is expected to give on return trips (as should really occur the first time). Over time, the relationship increasingly turns to giving, not only copies of one's writing, but financial and other forms of assistance. Those studied try to equalize the relationship if the anthropologist does not give. And why should we not share? A major part of my professional success I owe to Igbo cooperation in my research, to my appropriation of their culture. I do not consider my research an exploitation of them in a political and economic sense, but it has raised issues of return value. Long-term research is not only long in time but binding in ties over long distances. One becomes a member of two cultures, working ideas and relationships back and forth between them again and again, focusing now on the values and items of one culture, and then on those of the other culture, a continual mental dialogue, associated with research, writing, and speaking.

Another striking factor that affects the anthropologist in long-term research more than in one-time study is that friends and pseudo-relatives and their spouses and children met during fieldwork die more frequently than friends and relatives back home, for the death rate is often significantly higher among those cultures. Of course, the longer one is in the field the more this is likely to occur. This always has disturbed me. I wish to help, but to plan a medical campaign to radically change the illness and death figures would make my own anthropological goals impossible and require special training that I lack. There is the loss of valuable friends, field assistants, and those who explore the culture with the anthropologist. One's work is affected, as is the sense of order. The frequent opportunities to attend funerals and related rites may be helpful to fieldwork but it also is saddening and sobering. The longer I remained in the field the more I had to come to grips with the realities of life and death. One can intellectually compartmentalize another culture, but not these realities. The anthropologist may be more acutely aware of the health differences between cultures, having experienced the lower illness and mortality figures of the West. He or she can supply some medicine and take people to clinics and hospitals, but the researcher is largely helpless in this regard. In long-term research one makes greater and greater adjustments to this. The somewhat make-believe jigsaw puzzle of the culture that the anthropologist plays with develops a deep reality. Social actors become real persons through loss: the double loss of personal ties and of potential insights and knowledge into the culture.

Culture change in the people that anthropologists study is often related to major external pressures. I first conducted research at Afikpo in 1952–53 during the colonial period. Nigeria was British. There were few secondary schools and no university graduates, and my wife and I felt ourselves to be spokespersons to the world for the Afikpo. I saw one of my missions as explaining Afikpo culture and its customs to others. Aware of the extent of racism and ignorance about Africa that existed in the United States and Europe, I believed that I could help overcome this through my writing and speech-making. I failed by not being a skilled popular writer, such as Margaret Mead, with a message Americans were particularly anxious to hear, and by being preoccupied with my own career; I wrote for the converted—my colleagues and students. Yet, for a time, my wife and I were the authorities on Afikpo in the Western world. We largely controlled knowledge of their culture outside Nigeria, except for some information known to a few Nigerian government officers.

On that first field trip we were the only whites at Afikpo who were not colonial officials or missionaries. We were clearly associated with power, whether we, as American graduate students at that time, wished it or not. We had some mannerisms, rare today, that reflected this, such as, after returning home to the U.S. referring to the Afikpo as "my people," or "our tribe," as if we owned them! Such statements of unequal relationships were common among scholars at the time. What my wife and I did was to gain knowledge of their culture in a colonial setting, without fully understanding the influence of the colonial culture on Africans or on us. Several days after we returned to Africa in 1959–60, I visited Dr. Hinds at the Catholic mission hospital at Afikpo. I said rather naively: "Gee, you and my wife and I are the only ones left from the old days," meaning all the other whites had left or been replaced from the time of our first trip. He replied: "Well, there are the Africans." This gentle put-down reminded me that I still carried certain ideas of differentiation, that even in field research I associated unconsciously with other whites.

Today, Nigeria is an independent country. There are a surprising number of Afikpo who have been to a university, and many to secondary school. They have begun to write about their own culture and history (*Adu Ehugbo* 1985; Oko 1987) and have for some years been reading and evaluating my work. They are gradually becoming their own spokespersons (S. Ottenberg 1987, 1989a). I see my present anthropological role as a more modest contribution than in the past, of providing complementary work and encouraging the Afikpo's endeavors to understand their own society. If I failed to have an impact on America with my writing, I unexpectedly did on Afikpo, who are proud of my work, though sometimes critical of its errors and biases. Their sense of ethnic identity as a subgroup of the Igbo has been raised by my publications vis-à-vis neighboring subgroups that have not been researched, and they are overproudful of the differences. This disturbs me, as there is vanity in it, though it pleases me that attention has been paid to my research outside of the anthropological world. Long-term research involves a continually changing dialogue between the anthropologist and the people he studies as well as between himself and other anthropologists. These two types of discourse feed into one another, refreshing the researcher, bringing together two disparate worlds.

The equalizing of relationships that I have just described is related to changes in the political and economic climate of the research area, to alterations in the Western world, and to changes in the concerns and ideology of the anthropological profession. Let us look at these.

When we first went to Afikpo in 1952 and 1953 there was a British colonial district officer and an assistant district officer, a visiting medical officer who appeared from time to time, and an engineer working on a new government secondary school who was temporarily stationed there. The white population was completed by the Irish Catholic mission and hospital, several American sisters operating a Catholic mission school, and a Scottish Presbyterian minister and his wife. No Africans were in senior colonial government positions. There were two distinct worlds, an African and a European, which met around specific issues at set places—in the district officer's office, in the schools, and in church. But each group lived separately, the whites on the hills, the Africans in lower regions; they rarely socialized with one another. Africans and Europeans all knew that Afikpo had been conquered shortly after the turn of the century.

Into this situation my anthropological wife and I appeared on the scene.

There was no way we could be totally disassociated from the white world in African eyes, nor in the whites' view, nor even in terms of our own interests and curiosity. We looked like the other whites, dressed and ate much like them, had a vehicle like theirs at a time when no Africans in the area had a car. We spoke English much as other whites did. Some Afikpo elders, to whom I tried to explain that we were not British, thought that there was a group of villages a long way off called "Inglani," where the British lived, and near them other villages called "Amerikani," where we resided.

I never realized until years later what authority this gave us in African eyes, what anxieties this must have raised in them, how they must have tried to figure out our mission. Every other white they had met was trying to change their ways, to bring them a new religion and language and to deny them theirs, to change their health practices, their bathing habits, and their dress. But we were trying to learn their language, to understand their religion, to study their family life, and were the only whites they had ever met who were not attempting to change or pass judgment on them. What was our mission from their point of view? Clearly, from our investigations we would issue reports for someone and some changes would result. Evidently we would "write book" on them and become wealthy. During our first visit to Afikpo we saw ourselves as poor graduate students with just barely enough funds; to them we were wealthy whites related to a people who had conquered them by military force in 1902.

Although we entered into their lives, socialized with them, were adopted into their organizations, and joined in their activities, and they were generally very open and not afraid to engage us, this did little to erase the overall barrier. We were the gatherers of information, they the givers, we were in a colonial situation, which they recognized better than we. We were associated with power and influence. For all of our cultural relativism, our belief in the inherent value of their culture and the intrinsic interest in it, for all the friends we made there, there was a barrier of authority that went beyond cultural differences.

There were also anthropological values that shaped our work on this first trip that reflected the interests of our main professor, Melville J. Herskovits (1946). Herskovits never carried out long-term research with a single group, though he studied many peoples, but he did study a single problem much of his life: the influence of African culture on African Americans throughout our continent. There was also William R. Bascom, who worked for years with the Yoruba, though he was not particularly an advocate of long-term research. The anthropological ideologies of these two scholars included the belief that every culture had merit as great as any other, a simplified statement of what they called cultural relativism (Herskovits 1972). They believed that one should study a group that had not been studied before, rather than one that had been studied at an earlier time. One should get the "facts," as scientists, focus on religion as a key to understanding a culture, be suspicious of colonialism, but have no real critique of it, express a hostility to British social anthropology, with its emphasis on social relationships and social structure, and study a single culture or "tribe" (S. Ottenberg n.d.b). Each of us was to gain a culture, almost literally to own it, in the absence of other literate interpreters. We were the latest type of explorers. After the first explorers of Africa came the traders, the military, the colonial officials, and the missionaries, and then the twentieth-century anthropologists from the West, to investigate and gain control of cultural knowledge, bringing it back to Europe and America to chew over and interpret, and occasionally for government use. More recently have come the economists, the political scientists, the agricultural and management experts, those who direct public and private aid programs, and the bankers. Tragically, the anthropologist has sunk nearly into oblivion today in the face of these others. Anthropology's always small voice has become smaller. Long-term research in Nigeria has allowed me to perceive these changes.

But there was another kind of exploration going on during our first field trip: the movement of Nigerians out of their own localities, and the development of their own national political and economic agendas, moving toward independence. In 1959–60, when Phoebe and I returned to Afikpo, Nigerian independence occurred. At Afikpo, a system of elected local government on the British model had been introduced, the administrative officers were largely African, the missions were beginning to be Africanized, universal primary school education had been introduced in southeastern Nigeria, and some Afikpo had been to, or were beginning to go to, university. There were somewhat better roads, a little piped water, and a number of Afikpo had moved to urban centers for work and schooling, though still retaining ties with home. And Afikpo had a better concept of what Americans were, and even of anthropologists. In contrast to our first field trip, there was a more equal air about our relationships with them. We were not such unusual persons, we were not as unique or important. Many Afikpo were pleased to see us interested enough to return, to make a second trip for which we did not ask their permission; we just appeared. Things were on the move, especially national politics and independence, and our relationships with them altered. While I had a teaching job at the University of Washington and we were financially better off, some Afikpo were now more prosperous, more linked to the growing Nigerian economy.

In America, British social anthropology was becoming better known, emphasizing the study of social relationships and social structure as the core around which belief, religion, ritual, and virtually everything else was to be understood. I was influenced by it, partially as a result of a temporary teaching position at the University of Chicago from January to June 1954, and through personal contact with Meyer Fortes of Cambridge University. This shaped my research and writing at the time, as I put aside some of the concepts of my anthropological teachers from my graduate student days.

By then it was clear to me that *all* people that anthropologists study were undergoing tremendous change. Much of the pressure for change came from outside those local communities that anthropologists were able to get to know—pressures issuing from the region, the nation, from other members of the same ethnic group, from other cultural groups in the country, and from the world at large, especially Western Europe and America. Long-term researchers simply cannot ignore these issues and still do an adequate job. So in my second major trip to Afikpo I focused on changes in local leadership as independence approached, and expanded my concerns to the Igbo town of Abakaliki, north of Afikpo, a community formed in 1906 around a British administrative settlement. In the 1950s the British introduced to southern Nigeria a local government system modeled on theirs, and one of my self-set anthropological tasks was to analyze its workings. In the process I discovered the British model to be quite unworkable in the African cultural setting, where history, different styles of leadership, and differing ethical standards existed. Here, and at Afikpo, where I also studied the new local government, I was unable to keep my much self-prized ethical neutrality as a researcher, for at both places a fair number of the Igbo local government councilors were involved in obvious self-aggrandizement and in disruptive subethnic conflicts among different Igbo groups. I was appalled; I had not expected this. It did not fit my ideology of political development. Traditional controls had broken down and little replaced them. I lost my anthropological cool and discovered that, after all, I was a human being with deep-set values, yet trying to be an objective social scientist. True, I wrote an article on widespread corruption in the new local governments in southern Nigeria (S. Ottenberg 1967), although at that time I did not use the word, then unfashionable, but now so common in Nigeria. And I wrote several papers incorporating the history of local government in Abakaliki (S. Ottenberg 1962, 1966, 1976). But I could not write a projected book-length study on that town, though I feel that I could today as history.

My easy ability to emotionally handle traditional religious beliefs, which I myself did not believe (the power of ancestral spirits, of the spirits of the ground and fertility, of divination, of the yam spirit), and the acceptance of practices that I could not accept in my own society (polygyny, clitoridectomy, patriarchialism), did not hold for corruption and subethnic divisiveness in contemporary government. Naively, I expected those who emulated my type of society to behave as it was ideally presented, not as it actually existed. Paradoxically, cultural relativism worked best for me the greater the difference in sociocultural forms from my own. Exotica permitted more generous understanding and acceptance. In addition, I still wanted to present a favorable and positive image of Africans to the world. This newer, somewhat nasty ethnographic stuff contradicted that aim at a time when much of the Western world, including its scholars, were talking and writing in very positive tones on the likelihood of the success of governments and economies in the newly emerging independent African states.

So I turned away from governmental topics and set to writing on Afikpo religion and art, seemingly less conflicting among the Afikpo and with my personal values. I have had some success without using a social anthropology framework, but rather returning to some of the concepts of my teachers, Herskovits and Bascom, including psychologically oriented ideas (S. Ottenberg 1975, 1982, 1989a), again a conceptual change for me. But I regret that I did not continue my political work. It would have presaged what was to occur on a much larger scale in national life and politics in the country a few years after Nigeria's independence in 1960. Personal emotional involvement is an important factor in long-term research, more so than in one-time work, because the anthropologist has made a greater commitment to a people and a culture.

I was in Abakaliki Town for Nigerian Independence Day in 1960. I saw the British flag lowered, the Nigerian one raised. I was one of the judges at the ethnic dance festival and the Miss Independence of Abakaliki Township contest. I had the pleasure of dancing with the winning contestant! I also was able to observe Afikpo celebrating independence. The Igbo world and the Western world were mixing in unexpected patterns to me. There was an air of great hope, of expectation. Africans would control their own destiny. Nigeria had gained its independence, as the United States had, and everything would go well. These feelings were shared by other scholars of Nigeria and other regions of Africa, which also were becoming independent.

As independence in Nigeria continued, there were coups, and a bitter civil war ensued in which Afikpo and Abakaliki were minor battlegrounds but suffered greatly. There were problems of leadership and corruption increased at the national level. During much of the post-independence time I was at home teaching and writing on Afikpo, and worked a year at the University of Ghana, where I finished the draft of a book on Afikpo masquerades (S. Ottenberg 1975). Away from the field, I was writing as if somehow the information about a traditional African culture would counterbalance the evident problems of Nigeria as a developing country, and would somehow set the record straight for the world. My writing did nothing of the kind, although it has been useful to some anthropologists and students, and to Afikpo in several court cases over land issues.

The oil boom came to Nigeria in the 1970s and Afikpo, although not in the oil area, prospered from it, as did the whole country. To many Nigerians and even to myself, government problems and inefficiencies did not seem to matter so much; everyone seemed to be doing well. I kept on writing about Afikpo, beginning to feel that some of my material was truly history. But since the slump in oil prices in the 1980s, Nigeria has suffered greatly from overcommitments to development that it cannot fulfill, resulting in a dramatic rise in prices and reduced growth and unemployment.

When I returned to Afikpo in 1988 for a brief trip after many years away and again twice in 1992, many individuals complained about the quality of life. Looking at Afikpo now more as an historian, I was amazed at the changes that had occurred since my earliest research there (S. Ottenberg 1987, 1989a). The roads were much improved, there was better housing, electricity, piped water, a greatly enlarged market, many more schools, numerous taxis, even two-seater motorcycle taxis, outboard motors on traditional canoes, radios, cassette players, VCRs and Afikpo taping their own rituals, hotels and two-story homes, and there was more money around. Educated Afikpo had decided to change their name to Ehugbo, close to the traditional pronunciation of their name, rather than the term Afikpo, derived from other Igbo groups and employed by the British. I met a number of Afikpo who had been to a university or were attending one, and there was a group of retired civil servants and teachers, among the first to be Western educated at Afikpo.

I had to balance my own interest and enthusiasm at these changes against the depressive consequences of the post-oil boom era as Afikpo felt it, to see their point of view on disappointed rising expectations. I tried to pass on to them my long-range vision that they were better off in health, education, prosperity, and in cultural variation and activity than when I first visited them in the early 1950s. Both views will be a necessary aspect of anything that I write of the Afikpo in the future. But I wonder if mine is not another case of being surprised by changes, a Westernized view of Afikpo, similar to the previously mentioned short discourse with Dr. Hinds. I may have unconsciously set my first experience at Afikpo in the early 1950s as a baseline for all future interpretation, without necessarily meaning to do so, because of its emotional and scholarly impact on me (S. Ottenberg 1990a). This may be a danger of long-term research, an intellectual nostalgia for the past.

Another aspect of change that a long-term researcher may become involved in, and that I only did to a limited extent, is to analyze the changing influence a cultural group has on the world outside their own home area. During my first fieldwork at Afikpo, I was aware of cultural similarities between Afikpo and certain groups around it, but never asked these other groups how they might have been influenced by the Afikpo. I looked largely at African influences that came to Afikpo from the outside—from other Igbo to the northwest, west and south, and from Ibibio and Cross River peoples. I largely saw Afikpo as a cultural sponge, absorbing peoples and cultures from surrounding areas to develop a complex and varied social structure and a rich variety of rituals. Was this a true picture? I doubt it, and I would prefer a more interactive, give-and-take model today, in which these incoming factors were viewed in the context of Afikpo's influence on others.

In terms of incoming influences, I initially did a good deal of research on the political and legal system established, guided, and controlled by the British for the Afikpo, the native authority structure, and I tried to show how the Afikpo reacted to this and manipulated it to their own personal advantage (S. Ottenberg 1971b). And I had some sense of how the colonial officers used and manipulated matters for their own purposes (S. Ottenberg 1956). But I did not sufficiently focus on the British administrative structure, its aims, methods, and goals, in relation to the colonial situation, being more concerned with what I considered traditional affairs at Afikpo.

Perhaps we are wiser today about the nature of external influences on the people we study, more aware of them, since anthropology is going through a period of self-reflection and introspection concerning its research and writing. But it seems to me rather easy to see the political and economic influences of our Western society upon the people that we have studied in past periods. It is immensely more difficult to perceive this today, since by nature they are likely to remain invisible until tomorrow. Are not current trends in anthropology, be they post-structuralism, hermeneutics, interpretative anthropology, or whatever, as much a reflection of current Western political and economic life and of the relationships of the West with the "other," as social anthropology, colonial anthropology, and cultural relativism were when I did most of my Afikpo research? Will not anthropologists of the future be as critical of the work of anthropologists of today for much the same reasons as those of today are critical of the scholarship of the time of my major research at Afikpo, the post-World War II colonial period? We may have greater awareness today of our own Western influences upon our scholarship, but I see no ready solution. It requires the anthropologist to have as thorough a knowledge of the underlying workings and assumptions of his own society and culture as that of the "other" that he studies, surely a monumental task. I do believe, however, that long-term research can provide the time and the insight on change to develop a sound awareness of the nature of Western influences on our scholarship and orientations to those we research. It should not leave us totally blind; we can do better than some missionaries, who for all their years in the field, know little of the culture of those they work with because of their own blind acceptance of external Western values.

The absorptive view of neighboring African external influences on the group that I studied during the first Igbo research period was reinforced on the second field trip by my concern with external governmental and other political influences on Afikpo and Abakalili Town. True, it was a time of great change from the outside in which these two groups responded rather than led. Yet by then a good number of Afikpo had moved to urban centers elsewhere in southern Nigeria but maintained strong contacts with home. The Afikpo Town Welfare Association had been initiated largely in some of these urban centers and was attempting to offer various kinds of support for individuals living away from home, as well as to influence home events (S. Ottenberg 1955, 1968a). In my brief 1988 trip, I became aware of Igbo artists established outside of Afikpo (Ota et al. 1974, Ota n.d.; S. Ottenberg 1989a), that an Afikpo dance group had appeared on Nigerian television, that Afikpo were teaching and working in many parts of Nigeria. Explaining the influence of these factors on Afikpo could have been an important element in understanding that group of villages and is the kind of work that should be possible with long-term research.

There is another element in this changing dialogue between myself and the Afikpo over the years. I was aging, maturing, changing as a person and so were my friends, my helpers in the field, those I had worked with who were still alive. My maturation brought changes in interpretation. In 1952–53 I was convinced that the traditional elders, as a gerontocratic group, made decisions in a democratic, consensual way for their communities. It, of course, pleased me, to perceive the Afikpo as being so democratic. By the end of the 1959–60 field research I realized that there were powerful elders who dominated the groups' decision-making and had the economic resources to do so. Matters were not so democratic. What had changed? Partly it was more sensitive field research, a deeper probing the second time, and partly my greater maturity and experience allowed me to see Afikpo politics more clearly. As a teacher I had had more experience in handling authority than as a graduate student.

In 1988, when I briefly returned to Afikpo, I was ritually made a junior elder; Afikpo elders presented me with a knit wool cap and a cane, two symbols of seniority at Afikpo, in recognition of my years. How many hours had I spent on earlier trips talking to elders, who embodied the wisdom and cultural knowledge of Afikpo, and now I was one of them, my relationship to Afikpo people altered by time! And for some young Afikpo I had become a repository of the past, as I had viewed elders in my earlier days there. True, some of the elders I sat with drinking palm wine and listening to speech-making were young when I was young, but the point was that I now had the authority of age, which I lacked before, not the authority of colonialism nor of the white man, and not so much the authority of a professor, as on my second trip. So there were major alterations in my relationship with them, supported by my writings on the Afikpo, which in 1988 they saw as largely representative of older customs, though some of these customs still occurred in various forms. Personal growth and change on my part, and also in the Afikpo, are features of long-term research, along with changes in theories in our anthropological field, and in the Afikpo's social and political lives. There has been a dialogue of these continually altering elements that feed into my writing and thoughts about the Afikpo. Everything is flux, there is no clear baseline, all is process.

And to those fellow scholars, both African and American (whom I shall not name here), who have damned me as a colonialist anthropologist, since much of my Igbo research was conducted before Nigeria received its independence on October 1, 1960, I can respond that there are substantial numbers of Igbo, at Afikpo and elsewhere, who have appreciated my work. On March 19, 1992, I received an honorary Doctor of Letters (D. Litt) from the University of Nigeria, a federal Nigerian institution in the Igbo area. And on October 19 of the same year I was awarded, before a substantial crowd at Afikpo, the title of *Enya Mba Ehugo*, "Mirror of the People of Afikpo," by the Chief *(Eze)* in honor of my Afikpo publications. I understand that Elizabeth Colson, who has carried out extensive research over many years in Zambia, is shortly to receive an honorary degree from the University of Zambia for her work in that nation. Amidst the scholarly fashion of anticolonialist discourse, it is good to know that my work has been appreciated at Afikpo and in Igbo country, albeit the Afikpo also willingly show me where my work has not always been correct.

There is also a cyclical pattern of experience for the long-term researcher and for those he or she studies. The anthropologist's absence from the field, when home writing and teaching, allows the people he or she has studied to return to a certain normality of experience and to reflect upon the presence of the strangers amongst them. It may lead them to make decisions regarding how to relate to the scholar and his or her family upon their return, and to reflect on Western influences in their society. It allows them to rest from the special attention and needs created by the presence of the anthropologist and his or her family. For the anthropologist, living under foreign conditions has its social, financial, and health stresses, and returning home between field trips permits the researcher to recharge one's batteries, to reconstitute one's life, to reflect on one's fieldwork, to write, and to plan new research goals. This is a fundamental anthropological cycle. Few anthropologists can write at length in the field, or live there for more than two years at a stretch.

Temporal processes have intruded into my anthropological life in another way. Though I do not see myself as an historian, and I have never been trained as such, I have become an historian of Afikpo in two senses. The culture I have written about is now substantially changed; I have produced a record of past times, one which today is much valued by the Afikpo, even with its imperfections. This creating of history as a consequence of the passage of time, of course, is associated with all anthropological research, even one-time fieldwork. I am also an historian in another manner. In my field notes and some publications (S. Ottenberg 1955, 1956, 1959b, 1968a, 1971a, 1971b, 1987, 1989a), I have specifically recorded changes that have occurred at Afikpo. This has been largely the consequence of long-range research and reflects the dynamism of life at Afikpo that only this approach can bring. Like Margaret Mead, when she returned to Samoa after many years (1956), and Kenneth Read (1986) to New Guinea, when I returned to Afikpo in 1988 after a long absence, I was astonished by the changes that had occurred. I suffered from a kind of displacement of the imagined past, which I had myself created through my writings. This is a problem for the long-range researcher, to which I have already referred. One cannot let the baseline of the earliest research with a people become so fixed, so comfortable, as to inhibit understanding of later events, especially where substantial change is involved, and particularly where the anthropologist may not like, or find helpful to the people, all the changes that have occurred.

Long-range research involves a very strong commitment that one-time research lacks. Maintaining social relationships, even though many elements of life are changing for both the anthropologist and the people he or she studies, is exciting. And it is exciting to have a commitment to publish and to share one's writings, which becomes the basis of further understanding and relationships. This differs from one-time research, where the anthropologist sends his or her publications to the research area (and, sadly, there are some who never bother to do so) and has little or no feedback or further ties. Long-range work means devoting a good part of one's life (and one's family) to understanding a single people. Although anthropologists and missionaries rarely see eye-to-eye in goals, morals, and in attitudes toward non-Western religions and cultures, there is a kind of missionary quality to long-range research, a dedication to a goal over a lifetime, perhaps not planned as such in the beginning, but growing through time. This is a commitment to involve those one studies, who become drawn into and excited by the research, and who turn into anthropologists of their own culture.

Long-range research, more so than one-time research, fosters a kind of ethnic identification, occurring when the anthropologist becomes a cultural member of and an advocate of another culture. At the present time in our Western pluralistic, capitalist societies, identification with another ethnic group than one's own is common. I know people in Seattle who are not Croatians but who have for years danced or played instruments with a Croatian performance group. One of them, of Scandinavian American background, also plays with Southeast Asian performing groups! There are skilled non-Indian artists in the Seattle area, for example, Bill Holm, Duane Pasco, and Barry Herem, who produce Northwest Coast Indian objects and who have close relationships with Indians. Non-Irish people become experts in playing Irish music. The folklife festivals in Washington, D.C., Seattle, and elsewhere are living monuments to ethnic attachments in music, dance, and food. The interest in other cultures in Western society has increased in recent years because of the growing uniformity of our own culture, the increasing importance of ethnic pluralism rather than cultural assimilation, the increasing ability of persons to travel and communicate rapidly, and perhaps a certain boredom with the uniformity of our own culture.

Of course, anthropologists have experienced ethnic identification in their research from the beginning of fieldwork in the early part of this century, when ethnic pluralism was not the mode and assimilationist policies dominated much of our Western cultural ideologies. The "exotic" in culture (outside of Europe) was not as fashionable as today, nor as approachable, when I was a graduate student in the 1950s; we operated more in opposition than in agreement with Western ethnic interests, unlike today. Yet I believe that then, as now, a substantial number of us go into anthropology because we unconsciously seek an identification with another people, whatever the conscious interest in living abroad, in travel, and in exotic languages may be. For some, including myself, long-term research continues to draw upon and to reinforce this quality. I have for some time felt an association between my work in Africa and my mother's small French Swiss-Catholic village of birth and early life, which I first visited when I was six years old, and where I have continued to visit relatives, so that somehow my field research is an unconscious attempt to associate with that place and with her. I have gone there after being in Africa and felt that there were many similarities—in family disputes and the way that they are settled, in leadership style and outlook on the world. This apparent need of mine for ethnic identification may also be the consequence of a search for my father's German-Jewish tradition, which I was never close to as a child but have been curious about, as well as an attempt to resolve the unsettled contradictions of my mixed ancestry. I am suggesting that the anthropologist's ethnic identification, particularly true in long-term research, may go back to childhood roots; it is deep and directing. Long-range research continually refuels it: the reason that scholars return to the same people again and again may be related to this ethnic association. Thus, one's experiences in the West and with the people he or she studies are connected in a deep and fundamental manner.

This commitment to another culture may lead the anthropologist from "pure" into applied research, as it has Elizabeth Colson with the Tonga of Zambia (1971, 1980; Colson and Thayer 1988), or, as in my case, it may not. But the concern for the people remains: the dual identity of the long-term anthropological researcher with his or her own culture and the one he or she studies has feedback; I believe that I perceive and understand American culture better and can puzzle out complex elements in it because I have a contrasting culture with which to compare it. I see with clearer eyes the wealth we have, the material goods, the greed and self-indulgence, the neglect of the unsuccessful, our aggressiveness, and our commodification of everything, as well as our very rich cultural variety, pluralism, freedom from kinship restraints, and the considerable possibility of making choices in certain areas of life. I can compare these with conditions at Afikpo, and the larger Igbo group of which it is a part, which have their own styles and problems. African peoples recently have been accused of large-scale corruption, which I do not deny. But my long-term research allows me to put this in perspective and to contrast it with the equally impressive corruption in our country, albeit different in style, which we call influence or mismanagement.

Long-term research should allow the fieldworker to deal more fairly with gender issues than one-time study. A good number of the societies that we study have strong gender distinctions—true for the Igbo of forty years ago—resulting in the fieldworker largely relating to persons of his or her sex if research is one-time, unless very strong efforts are made to overcome this. My own work in Igbo country has been largely with males, partly as a consequence of the sex dichotomy, but largely because Phoebe Ottenberg focused her work on females. And of course, the bulk of the Afikpo work was done before the gender revolution and feminist movement. In 1960, we did write a joint article on the Afikpo market that looked at the roles of both male and female traders (S. Ottenberg and P. Ottenberg 1962). I have written on male attitudes toward and concepts of females in my work on masquerades (S. Ottenberg 1972, 1975), and Phoebe Ottenberg's writings (1958, 1959; Miller 1982) have discussed female roles and concepts at Afikpo.

But when I reflect on the many arguments that my wife and I had while in the field and while writing our dissertations and afterwards on the very different interpretations of Afikpo life and events that females and males had, each of us incorporated our own gender viewpoints into our writing but without trying to put both viewpoints together. I now see how we neglected to present this material jointly, which would have been rich indeed. Our divorce in 1965 led to a termination of joint anthropological efforts. The reason we did not work jointly was because we were so firmly committed, or at least I was, to same gender-as-self views. Nevertheless, I see long-term research as allowing the time and the development of the skills necessary for those of one sex to work more thoroughly with members of the other in situations of strong sex-role distinctions and status. In October 1992 I worked with my former wife's 1959–60 field assistant on pottery and on body makeup, both female matters. How easily it went working with her.

There are at least two disadvantages of long-term commitment to the study of a single group. The finely crafted knowledge that it brings, the connoisseurship of its culture, the ability to make rich interpretations drawing on a wide range of culture knowledge and experience, are all strengths, but after some time on my Afikpo work, I began to miss the comparative perspective. I came to see all anthropological problems from an Afikpo perspective, or at the widest an Igbo one, referring to the larger cultural group to which the Afikpo belong. This limitation could be satisfied partly from reading the works of other anthropologists, and through discussions with them, but it is no substitute for the perspective and experience of field research in a substantially different culture. Warren d'Azevedo has resolved this issue through long-term research among Native Americans in addition to his extensive Liberian work. It would be fascinating to have him write comparative comments on these two groups and his experiences with them. I began to feel in the mid-1970s that I needed the perspective gained from another research culture, so I spent two years studying a Limba chiefdom in northern Sierra Leone in 1978–80, one that differs sufficiently from Afikpo to be rewarding. To study a different culture in a different setting has given me additional insight on the Afikpo, and I have begun to make some comparative observations (1990b). I have, however, still continued to write on Afikpo and, as I have indicated, I have returned, as I also did to my Sierra Leone research area (S. Ottenberg 1987, 1989a). Neither people, curiously enough, had interest in my research in the other group, some one thousand miles or more apart. In each case individuals wanted to relate to me only in reference to their own culture and experience, and to my American culture. Whether they saw themselves as competitors for my attention and resources, I do not know, but I suspect this to be true for some individuals in both societies. And my recent work on Coast Salish art is being complemented by work on modern Nigerian art.

A second major problem in long-term research is that as one gets deeper into the culture, he or she may come into knowledge of very secret areas. This is less likely to occur in one-time research. The secrets may be ephemeral matters, sometimes very personal information, but they may be very central to the core of the culture, involving secret societies and initiations and secret political processes of judgment and decision-making. The anthropologist may even become a member of a secret organization.

What does the long-term anthropologist do about important secret material? As a scholar, one is aware of its centrality to the understanding of the culture as he writes for his own academic world. On the other hand, publication may destroy or influence the very nature of the secret elements of the culture, and jeopardize friends and field assistants who have helped him or her gain the knowledge. And publication may inhibit one's ability to carry out further research in the area. Anthropologists have adopted various solutions. One is to go ahead and publish and let the chips fall where they may. Another is never to publish this sort of information, perhaps even to destroy the notes on it. Still another is to publish it with a fictive name for the group he or she worked with (Herdt 1981), whose identity, however, is soon known to the anthropological community, though not the general public. Some scholars write it up and leave it to be published at some unknown future date, or place the notes in a controlled access archive. I have approached the matter by waiting until changes have made the secret elements irrelevant, nonsecret, or of minor importance. I believe that this is now so with regard to the village men's secret society, and, in a recent book (1989b), I describe the traditional forms of boys' initiations into that group. I hope that my decision has been a correct one, but I await the Afikpo's reaction to the work with some uncertainty.

Despite these problems in long-term research, the rewards are substantial in terms of scholarship and personal experience. Clearly, the work is bound to be influenced by, and responsive to, the rapidly changing conditions of the people one devotes years of research to, and those of the anthropologist—the scholarly field and the society in which one lives. One becomes a reporter and historian. The work is endless. I could go back to Afikpo and write an ethnography of what their culture is like and it would differ greatly from what I have written in earlier times. In one-time research the anthropologist does fieldwork, leaves, and writes of that time. In long-term research one is always writing of the new and its relationship to the old, seeing people one knows change, mature, die, matching one's life experience against theirs, watching as they begin to write of their own culture, evaluating the external influences from the West and from elsewhere. Long-term research allows one to correct errors and misconceptions of earlier work, encourages working with new field assistants and informants to gain differing views, and gives us a sense that there may not be one culture, but differing ones in the eyes of those we work with. For me it has been an exciting, endless, changing occupation, full of hard work, struggle, and delight.

Endnote

1. The field work in Georgia was supported by a grant from the Program of African Studies, Northwestern University; in Nigeria in 1952–53 by a Social Science Research Council fellowship, and in 1959–60 by a National Science Foundation grant. Research in Sierra Leone was made possible by a National Endowment for the Humanities fellowship and sabbatical leave from the University of Washington.

   Igbo is spelled Ibo in my older publications, as that was the correct form at that time. In the references cited, S. Ottenberg (1987) refers to events in 1988. It was actually published in 1989 in a journal running behind schedule.

References Cited

1985   *Adu Ehugbo: A Publication of Nzuko Umuada Ehugbo (Afikpo)*. 1(1) (all published).

Colson, Elizabeth

1953   *The Makah Indians: A Study of an Indian Tribe in Modern American Society*. University of Minnesota Press, Minneapolis.

1960   *Social Organization of the Gwembe Tonga*. Manchester University Press, Manchester.

1962   *The Plateau Tonga of Northern Rhodesia, Social and Religious Studies*. University of Manchester Press, Manchester.

1971   *The Social Consequences of Resettlement*. Manchester University Press, Manchester.

1980   *Secondary Education and the Formation of an Elite: The Impact of Education on Gwembe District, Zambia*. Academic Press, New York.

Colson, Elizabeth, and Scudder Thayer

1988   *For Prayer and Profit: The Ritual, Economic and Social Importance of Beer in Gwembe District, Zambia, 1950–1982.* Stanford University Press, Stanford.

Fernandez, James

1982   *Bwiti. An Ethnography of the Religious Imagination in Africa.* Princeton University Press, Princeton.

Foster, George M., Thayer Scudder, Elizabeth Colson, and Robert V. Kemper

1979   *Long-Term Research in Social Anthropology.* Academic Press, New York.

Herdt, Gilbert H.

1981   *Guardians of the Flutes: Idioms of Masculinity.* McGraw-Hill, New York.

Herskovits, Melville J.

1946   *Man and His Works.* Alfred Knopf, New York.

1972   *Cultural Relativism: Perspectives in Cultural Pluralism.* Random House, New York.

Mead, Margaret

1956   *New Lives for Old: Cultural Transformations—Manus, 1928–1953.* Morrow, New York.

Miller, Phoebe

1982   Sex Polarity Among the Afikpo Igbo. In *African Religious Groups and Beliefs: Papers in Honor of William R. Bascom,* edited by Simon Ottenberg, pp. 79–94. Folklore Institute, Berkeley and Archana Publications, Meelut, India.

Oko, James B.

1987   *The School Head as an Interested Dramatist. "New Mock Court Trial of Mr. Ratus" for Primary and Post-Primary School and "Ehugbo" Proverbs, Idioms, Folklore and Axioms.* Published by the author, Afikpo, Nigeria.

Ota, Ota-Okoche

n.d.   *Re-Creation. An Exhibition of Visual Thoghts.*[sic] Published by the author, Enugu, Nigeria.

Ota, Okocha, Jr., Emmanuel C. Ayangaor, and Wilhelm Seidensticker

1974   *Afikpo Masks.* Published by the authors, Zaria, Nigeria.

Ottenberg, Phoebe

1958   *Marriage Relationships in the Double Descent System of Afikpo Ibo of Southeastern Nigeria.* Ph.D. dissertation, Department of Anthropology, Northwestern University.

1959   The Changing Economic Position of Women among the Afikpo Ibo. In *Continuity and Change in African Cultures,* edited by W. R. Bascom and M. J. Herskovits, pp. 205–223. University of Chicago Press, Chicago.

Ottenberg, Simon

1955   Improvement Associations among the Afikpo Ibo. *Africa* 25:1–25.

1956   Comments on Local Government in Afikpo Division, Southeastern Nigeria. *Journal of African Administration* 8:3–10.

1959a   Leadership and Change in a Coastal Georgia Negro Community. *Phylon* 20(1):7–18.

1959b   Ibo Receptivity to Change. In *Continuity and Change in African Cultures,* edited by W. R. Bascom and M. J. Herskovits, pp. 130–143. University of Chicago Press, Chicago.

1962   The Development of Local Government in a Nigerian Township. *Anthropologica* 4(1):121–161.

1966   The Social and Administrative History of a Nigerian Township. *International Journal of Comparative Sociology* 1(1):174–196.

1967   Local Government and the Law in Southern Nigeria. *Journal of Asian and African Studies* 2(1–2):26–43.

1968a   The Development of Credit Associations in the Changing Economy of an African Society. *Africa* 38(3):237–252.

1968b   *Double Descent in an African Society: The Afikpo Village-Group.* American Ethnological Society, Monograph Series no. 47. University of Washington Press, Seattle.

1971a   A Moslem Igbo Village. *Cahiers D'etudes Africaines* 11(2):31–60.

1971b   *Leadership and Authority in an African Society: The Afikpo Village-Group.* American Ethnological Society, Monograph Series no. 52. University of Washington Press, Seattle.

1972   Humorous Masks and Serious Politics among the Afikpo Ibo. In *African Art and Leadership,* edited by Douglas Fraser and Herbert M. Cole, pp. 91–121. University of Wisconsin Press, Madison.

1975   *Masked Rituals of Afikpo: The Context of an African Art.* University of Washington Press, Seattle.

1976   Ethnicity in a Nigerian Town and its Environs. *Ethnicity* 3:275–303.

1982   Illusion, Communication and Psychology in West African Masquerades. *Ethos* 10(2):149–185.

1987   Return to the Field: Anthropological *Deja Vue. Cambridge Anthropology* 12(3):16–31. [published 1989]

1989a   We Are Becoming Art Minded: Afikpo Arts 1988. *African Arts* 22(4):58–67, 88.

1989b   *Boyhood Rituals in an African Society: An Interpretation.* University of Washington Press, Seattle.

1990a   Thirty Years of Fieldnotes: Changing Relationships to the Text. In *Fieldnotes: The Making of Anthropology,* edited by Roger Sanjek, pp. 139–160. Cornell University Press, Ithaca.

1990b   Mannerbunde, Geschlechtzugehorigkeit und ihr kunstlerischer Ausdruck in zwei westafrikanischen Gesellschaften. In *Manner Bande. Manner Bunde. Zur Rolle des Mannes im Kulturvergleich, Band 1,* edited by Gisela Volger and Karin v. Welck, pp. 283–288. Rautenstrauch-Joest-Museum, Cologne.

n.d.a   Possibilities and Constraints: Contemporary Artists and Art of the Coast Salish Indians. Unpublished manuscript.

n.d.b   The American Anthropological Background to Herskovits' Scholarship. Unpublished paper presented at the 31st annual meeting, African Studies Association, Chicago, October 28, 1988.

Ottenberg, Simon, and Phoebe Ottenberg

1962   Afikpo Markets: 1900–1960. In *Markets in Africa,* edited by Paul Bohannan and George Dalton, pp. 117–169. Northwestern University Press, Evanston.

Read, Kenneth E.

1986   *Return to the High Valley: Coming Full Circle.* University of California Press, Berkeley.

Time on Our Hands

James W. Fernandez

**For Warren d'Azevedo and the Merchant Seaman he once was
and always is!**

. . . the act of formal retrospection is the duty of qualified
men of wisdom who are expected to apply their accumulated
memories to the solution of problems confronting the
living present.

—W. L. d'Azevedo, *Uses of the Past in Gola Discourse*

Hands across the Destructive Power of Time

It is now thirty-seven years—seven hands and two fingers—ago that I first
met Warren d'Azevedo. I remember shaking his hand in the second floor
corridor of old Lacy Hall at Northwestern University in front of Melville
Herskovits's office—an Ibero-Celt closing ranks with an Ibero-Scandina-
vian. Thirty-seven years is a long time—a generation and a half by most
calculations. You have to hand it to Herskovits. He certainly had interesting
students. Joseph Greenberg, Melford Spiro, William Bascom, just to mention the first generation. And when he brought those students together in
his memorable acculturation seminars, whereby critiquing the past, we
tried to take the future of anthropology into our hands, the synergy could
often be positively scintillating. Without doubt the most insightful and
stimulating "provocateur" in those seminars in my years at Northwestern
was Warren d'Azevedo. Tough-mindedly analytic and yet imaginative and
with more worldly experience than others in the cohort, he was heads
above, hands beyond the rest of us. He seemed to have read everything and
he had been a merchant sailor, too—a Harry Bridges man. He had a head
full of ideas and he had calloused hands. (And he was a handsome man, too,
with the vigorous head of hair he still has.) That's a combination, baldly

speaking, rarely found in academia, and we respected it. And it has continued to be the case that throughout his career in the life of learning, that combination of imaginative intellection and groundedness, that particularly convincing combination of the manual and the mental, which is everywhere negotiated but rarely satisfactorily resolved in the human equation, has impressed us all. In all this Warren d'Azevedo was and is a person whose reach of mind is always instructive but a person less grasping in the sharing out of his understanding you could not imagine.

Behind all the particular topics of each week in the acculturation seminar, what we basically had in mind in those days was the *mano a mano* between British social and American cultural anthropology—the excessive synchrony and neglect of temporal process of the one and the time awareness of the other. The anthropology we learned from Herskovits was smack in the core of a very American tradition. After all, when you shook Herskovits's hand you shook the hand that had shaken the hand of Franz Boas, who had himself, if not shaped, surely shaken the hand of practically all the important American anthropologists of the late nineteenth and the first half of the twentieth century. Now I continue to teach Boasian anthropology at Chicago. I offer our students the opportunity to shake the hand, that shook the hand, that shook the hand of Franz Boas.

Manual Memories

When I think of how we are bound to the past—even the very distant past I suppose—through an iteration of handshakes I am put in mind of several field experiences in which corporeal time binding of this or a related kind took place. In Africa I worked with a highly interesting religious movement, *Bwiti,*[1] whose members always began their night-long rituals by reciting genealogy—the upwards of twenty names of their family and clan ancestors ascendant. One of the objects of Bwiti was to come back into worshipful contact with these ancestors. For the ancestor cult had been decimated during Christianization. During this recitation the individual grasped an imitation umbilical cord of twisted red and white yarn tied around his or her waist. The idea was that men and women are tied to all their ancestors ascendant by a string of umbilical cords symbolized in the cord upon which their hand was laid. This notion of umbilical time-binding was a powerful one in Bwiti and animated their attempts to come into communicative contact with all their ancestors ascendent, with whom they were already, in this symbolic sense, corporeally linked.

For years now we have been working in northern Spain not far from the millennial pilgrimage route to Santiago de Compostela. For more than a thousand years, hundreds of thousands of pilgrims—millions by now—from all parts of Europe have trod the Jacobean route, the route of the Milky Way as it is called.[2] When they finally arrive in Santiago in the far northwest of Spain, one of the first things they do is enter the cathedral. In the entrance to the famous "Portico de la Gloria," carved by Master Mateo in the twelfth century, they approach the central pillar, known as the Tree of Jesse. There they place their right hand in a concavity in the lower branches of this finely carved tree. This recess, worn quite deep now by the thousands and thousands of hands that have there been poised over nearly a millennium, is a powerful form of manual time binding with all those who went before. In August 1989, the Pope, during his visit to Santiago, after making a short pilgrimage of his own, leaving the Popemobile and walking for about a half a mile, entered the cathedral and placed his hand in this recess before proceeding to offer Mass. So are a millennium of Christian pilgrims, from Polish peasants (for they came from that far even in the Middle Ages) to Polish Popes, symbolically linked. I assert a linkage that I myself feel, for I have placed my own hand in this recess five or six times now over the years, and this year I bound myself to time through my hands both before and after the Pope.

Taskmasters and the Work of Anthropology among Cattle-Keepers and Miners

My playful manipulation here of the manual metaphor is not gratuitous . . . not my conceit alone. Practically any paleoanthropologist interested in human evolution will testify to how crucial our manual dexterity—first fashioned in our ancient arboreal existence—has been to our adaptation and survival. Indeed, and this is of great relevance to my argument, the hand is written into the brain (or the brain is constructed upon the hand) in such an extensive network of nerves as to make it evident, whatever the purely intellectual prejudices of the academies to which we belong, how much the manual has shaped and continues to shape our mental experience and understanding. The evolutionary implications in respect to the important place of the hand in the brain's growth in humans seem obvious enough.

It is also the case that in most languages, perhaps in all, many of our abstract understandings can be traced back etymologically to corporeal experiences of one kind or another, and primary here is manual experience. Practically any good dictionary will be a handy index of this fact carrying us back, in the examination of word roots, pretty quickly to the hand and its associated appendages. For the emotions it's quite impressive how many words for feelings are derived from "touching," pressing, pinching, squeezing, gripping, breaking, and hitting.[3] It's touching to think how this tough, power-gripping appendage of ours, which is yet so gentle and precise in its grip, can be useful in anchoring in proprioceptive experience the most difficult to grasp internal emotions. In recent years, of course, we academicians with our Platonic and cerebral biases have been well reminded of the degree to which what the mind knows—how it organizes its experiences—is learned from the body and from the body's activity in the world. And it is clear that not only our emotions but our abstract concepts as well have their roots in body metaphor[4] just as our categorization of things are as often as not due to task requirements. They are, as it is called, "taskonomies" more than taxonomies.[5] Ward Goodenough in an oft-repeated phrase once argued that the ethnographer's task is to give a description of "whatever it is one has to know or believe in order to operate in a manner acceptable to a society's members." It has been the tendency in the academy to focus on knowing and believing and their impact on doing. A more pragmatic view brings equal focus to bear upon our operations in the world, the activity, of this doing, of carrying out our tasks and the impact of this activity on what we know and believe.[6] At least we have come to understand the integrally reciprocal relation between the subjective and the objective, the internal and the external, between image and action, between, as I am calling it here, the manual and the mental.

But I have a more workerlike reason, in respect to our present ethnographic task in among cattle-keepers and miners, for making this manual-mental argument. It is the expression of things impressed upon me—or demonstrated to me or handed to me, to say it better—in long-term field experience in northern Spain among cattle-keepers and miners. They are people who, par excellence, make their living with their hands . . . people who know what they know as much in what their hands know how to do as in what their heads know how to say. Their identity is very much bound up in their mastery of the intricate tasks of their milieu: milking, making butter and cheese, aiding the birth of a calf, mowing and laying windrows, hay binding and hauling, chopping trunks and knocking up mine timbers, drilling and scuttling coal seams. It is to this task mastery and its accompanying operational experiences of confident or frustrated task completion that one has to turn one's hand in writing an ethnography adequate to their life in culture.

This being the case, what I would like to do now is take up and consider some aspects of our ethnographic experience in manual terms. I am going to want to provide here, all too briefly, something of a manual of long-term field experience, working, in the fullest primary, hands-on sense of that term, with cattle-keepers and miners.

Such a manual is a handful for a short paper because we have, indeed, been working a long time, since the mid-sixties, in these northern Spanish mountain-valley villages. We now carry in our arms and lead by the hands infants and toddlers who are the children of the children we once, a generation ago, carried in our arms and led by the hand. This long-term fieldwork, I should say, contrasts with my African work, which, though we spent well over two years in our first fieldwork among Fang in Western Equatorial Africa, was always fieldwork of a particular moment, even though of a two-year stretch, in the flow—here a backwater there a rapid or eddy—of the river of time of that culture. It had flowed a millennia or more before we entered it. And it flows on there now long after we have left. In these Asturian villages, on the other hand, we feel that we have been more a recurrent part over time of the flow of culture. But before I turn to this abbreviated manual of the flow of time among field and meadow workers, stall workers, and mine workers, let me develop a bit further the mental part of this manual-mental argument.

A Sense of Proportion: Physical Fantasies and the Human Measure of Things

In our Spanish research, then, by long-term engagement we more closely satisfy a fantasy I remember having with some frequency in Africa under my mosquito net cat-napping of an afternoon or waiting to fall asleep during fevered nights (malaria was a frequent companion my first two years in Africa). This occurred well along into my second year. It was a Gulliveresque fantasy—some kind of cabin or hut fever—of somehow escaping the proportionality of human existence. Of somehow being, on the one hand, much larger than the village and the villagers and towering above both in serene objective contemplation, or being, on the other hand, much smaller, minuscule, than the human dimension and scurrying into and ferreting out the most private domains of experience. I believe I felt somehow inhibited in my research and my understanding by being of the same human dimensions as my informants. And I used to remember fantasizing time differences . . . fantasizing that the coevality, the equal amounts of time, and oh-so-slow pace of things we, anthropologist and villager alike, shared were in fact experienced differently. I might experience their slow time much more rapidly, or occasionally, at effervescent moments in village life, their fast time more slowly. I imagined that we lived in different time scales. It was the fantasy of living by a different drummer—of living much longer and much slower. (It was probably a reaction both to the, for the most part, slow pace of village life as well as a desire to be done with the research.) Thus their slow, oh so slow paced, year I would live in an instant of my millennial time scale. It's like those models of life on earth that biologists or paleoanthropologists present to us, in which the million-year human career is just a recent blip on the vast progression of biological time.

For an ethnographer there are, to be sure, advantages and disadvantages to coevality, of more or less sharing the human time scale with our informants and of having to measure things by the arm's length, by a hand's breadth or a foot's stride. (I don't mean to suggest that there are not interesting differences between cultures as regards their construction of time and space.) The advantages are those of participation—of knowing what it is like to live within the human skin sub-specie Fang or Gola.

But participation within the human proportions in such matters also confines us to the human condition and limits our powers of observation. If only we were Colossi or Tom Thumbs, what then could we know . . . or find out. If man is the measure of all things as the ancients argued, it's a measure that confines us as much as it confirms us.

Of course, we humans feel our confinement in the skin of human proportion. Of course, the imaginative lore and literature that fantasizes changes in that proportionality is vast indeed. It is the Gulliveresque literature of Thimbelinas and Tom Thumbs, Paul Bunyons and Cyclops, of Methuselah and Rip Van Winkle. The Field Museum of Natural History in Chicago has a marvelous exhibit for adults in which a kitchen is created with tables and chairs and utensils proportionately as large as when we were small children. The surface of the table is six feet high, an adult can just peep over it. Plates are as big as shields, and it is all an adult body can do, like any toddler, to awkwardly clamber up on the big kitchen chairs. Oh, what early memories are evoked from this sudden change of proportionality!

And, of course, evolutionary biologists constantly discourse on proportionality of animal size, which is to say on gigantism and miniaturization. Size has made a great difference in evolution. Giants have big present advantages but not long-term survival value. By and large the evolutionary story shows us very small creatures inheriting the earth. The bacteria will likely be here long after we humans are gone and until the sun explodes. We can see the difference that proportionality in size makes when we are asked to contemplate the disproportional consequences if our domestic tabbies were as big as St. Bernards. If we tried to only feed them in the evening, they might eat us for breakfast. And suppose that the human primate had never been able to exceed in life span the twenty years of a horse or the fourteen years of a cat or dog. What then? Our long life span, so crucial to our construction and maintenance of culture, compared to most denizens of the animal world, does take some explaining evolutionwise.

If we as humans feel our confinement in the human proportions even more, I am suggesting, do we anthropologists feel it? There are various strategies that we have adopted to deal with the problem of our confined relation to time's passage in ourselves and in our informants. One-shot fieldwork is one strategy in which we pretend only to a slice of time. Intense archival involvement is another. The ethnographic present is yet another of these strategies by which we deal with the problem of converting change into simultaneity—the diachronic into the synchronic, the irreversible or the transitory into the perpetual. Johannes Fabian sees in these temporal strategies the observer's desire to distance ourselves from coevality with the "other" with whom we have worked in gathering our material . . . and who have, as co-workers, an important claim upon it and what is done with it.[7]

In the post-modern mood to which his argument makes an important contribution he sees in this "construction of our subject" a hegemonic discourse, which denies to the other his or her crucial role, his or her voice, in our common work. No doubt there is, here, the arrogance of translating the lively discussions and communicative interchanges of the field into privileged and distanced professional discourse imbued with the sense of essential difference.[8] There is, as Fabian argues, the hegemonic impulse in these strategies of temporal congelation or distanciation. Still they also represent in the anthropologist's realm, the human struggle against time's winged chariot carrying us and our informants too precipitously along toward oblivion. We think we can stay the inexorable march by distancing ourselves or by postulating an eternal present—that is, Godlike, by a fundamental change of proportion. And this, of course, brings to the surface the problem that is so directly keyed into the human life cycle . . . it's the fish in the water problem, or the "logical types" problem of Godel's famous proof that no logical system of explanation can prove or explain its own postulates. It's the problem of hauling ourselves up by our own bootstraps. We can also call it the ultimate redundancy problem of our involvement within a cultural system. Since we swim in the human life cycle ourselves can we ever really understand, without redundancy, the cycle in which we along with all our informants are swimming? Though I do not recall that such abstruse logical problems motivated in any direct way my daydreams of distancing by gigantism or miniaturization, at the same time, fully in the swim of participatory fieldwork, I must have been feeling a bit suffocated and anxious in some way to jump out of the pool, out of the system as it were, in which we were all, villagers and anthropologist alike, steeped, and too thoroughly saturated.[9] I must have felt my understanding encumbered. Perhaps by some change of proportion, I must have fantasized, I *can* jump out of the system and obtain increments of understanding.

Changes in Activity over the Long Haul

The focus of our interest is long-term field research and its fruits. It is the kind of research that Warren d'Azevedo has carried on so patiently and fruitfully over so many years with both Washo in Nevada and Gola in Liberia. Until this point I have been approaching this topic indirectly, not to say backhandedly if not underhandedly. But, of course, I have wanted, in all due respect for the dexterities of the miners and cattle-keepers with whom we have been working these twenty-five years, to give the manual its due—to avoid treating it backhandedly as is so often the case in the academy. I want to make it primary to what we know and feel in this world. I think it has that primacy for our informants.

If our interest, then, is manual and long term, we might begin by making an inventory of the hand-held objects of these rural lifeways that have changed in the last twenty-five years. And we can ask a very objective question. What differences do these changes make in the feelings and ideas, and most importantly, in the lifeworlds of villagers? Perhaps we might begin with the plow and the scythe, which as far as agropastoralists are concerned lie at the heart of their mode of production. In the culture history of Europe the plow, that is, the shift from the Roman scratch plow to the northern European moldboard plow, has had powerful explanatory value in accounting for Cultural Product—to use Leslie White's term—and capital accumulation. In our villages in the first years of our research the ancient Roman plow, or something very similar to it, still was being used, hauled laboriously across the small *minifundia* landscape by a team of cows. Most villagers could not afford to keep the single purpose oxen and plowed with their cows, which otherwise served, in *pluriempleo,* for milk and meat production. Nowadays a few enterprising villagers have bought tractors, either on installment or because they belong to wealthier families, and multitracked mould board plows, which can plow a *minifundia* tract in a half hour. It has freed up cows and whole families—for cow-drawn scratch plowing occupied men, women, and children, one to guide the plow the other to guide and prod the cows. But it also has added to preexisting wealth differentials in the village. We now have an entrepreneurial class of machine-age men tied into the beneficiaries of—along with their neighbors who sell grains and fertilizers and insecticides—a multinational agricultural economy. That is an important change, for it has made villagers dependent as never before on outside influences. As they have long had to market their produce they have long been subject to outside pricing mechanisms at the moment of selling. But they have now become more intricately involved with outside influences in the moments of production.

The scythe and the mastery of its manipulation is something I could wax eloquent on. For it is a kind of mastery in which less is more, easy-does-it is beautiful. The scythe, if kept carefully honed, and that's the secret of it, by its own momentum should do the work virtually by itself. For if you try to muscle it you can easily overmaster it and butcher your stubble. Now the scythe—that proud tool of the countryman—and the beautiful windrows it laid down are things of the past. Countrymen have bought *motosegadoras*—hand tractors with a long multiteeth blade, which they wrestle and struggle to master over their steep meadows bucking and binding, fouling the air with fumes and noise. These machines often seem more to master them than the reverse—to have, themselves, become the task masters. A man can mechanically mow in an hour that which took him manually most of a day. But the aesthetic is gone—the quiet flow and swish of the blade through the grass in a steady effort of manual mastery, by means of self-mastery. And here again the countryman in the act of production is tied, in so many ways, into a multinational economy and those entrepreneurs who sell and maintain the *motosegadoras*. And while these villages and their country life have never been completely independent of larger systems of marketing and administration—so that we cannot speak of traditional life with the "epistemology of entitivity"[10] as something once entirely whole and isolated—yet there was, a quarter-century ago, greater self-sufficiency and circularity in their round of life. There was a capacity to make their tools out of local materials and, once used up, to dispose of them in a seemly manner. For the modern tools that have come into their hands, when they can no longer be maintained, can only be abandoned to rust away in unsightly heaps in the countryside. I hope my assessment of this change doesn't seem too much an instance of the pastoralist nostalgia that affects and often afflicts the anthropologist. Most countrymen, while guided by the principle of least effort as any accountant, and grateful for the time and effort saved by the machine world, at the same time, preserve in their hands the older skills of plow and scythe and recognize the manual world of self-mastery they have lost. And if, as we argue, the works of the hand build themselves into the mind's ideas and feelings, the implications of these manual changes is loss of independence and increase of dependency. And it is a loss that is felt both as an emotional condition, a dependency, of modern life and as an increasing lack of confidence in what local knowledge and local ideas can themselves produce.

In both cases of the replacement of the scythe and the plow we have instances of the increase of scale in village affairs as agropastoral production becomes increasingly dependent upon the outside world for supply and repair. Long-term field research practically anywhere in the world, at least as it is undertaken in relation to the expanding imperium of industrial capitalism, has shown us such increases of scale. Indeed, long ago in the 1930s in African studies, Godfrey and Monica Wilson, in a little book with large implications, drew our attention to the expansion of scale as the main dynamic of social change in the modern world.[11]

But let me mention another hand-held object whose whole nature speaks to us of wider horizons: the telephone. When we went out to these villages in 1965 there were no telephones in the village and for upwards of twelve years there was only one telephone. Now there are more than thirty telephones in the village—a small telephone book. We can even do our ethnography comfortably ensconced in the United States on a multiparty hookup. Here quite clearly is the expansion of the scale of relations of which we speak. But accompanying that is a corresponding decrease in what we might call the synesthetics of human relations. For with the telephone there is the tendency to concentrate these relations in one sense modality alone: the oral/aural. For those of us who live in the age of telecommunications, where so much of our contact with significant others is telecommunicated or otherwise sensorily reduced, the telephone's short circuiting impact on the synesthesia which makes up our relation with others—that is to say the full sense of our relations to each other as can be found in touching, tasting, smelling[12]—will not be appreciated. But in our villages they are yet aware, I think, of the new kind of relationships they now hold in their hands: expanded powerfully in scale, reduced significantly in synesthetic amplitude. It's a change in the meaning of human relationships, which has occurred widely in the world but which we have seen taking place over our long-term (although in history short-term) work in these villages.

For miners, since they are part of an industrial milieu that is always interested in making its technology more competitive and productive—although Asturian mining has been in somewhat of a backwater through the decades—there has been the change, as far as the hand is concerned, from the pickaxe to the air-hammer with corresponding great increases of production. The pickaxe required more acrobatics on the seam scaffolding and was back-breaking labor. Older generations of miners tend to mock the younger generations for the relative ease of extraction, and the comparatively high wages, that air-hammering has brought.[13] The younger generations respond that the danger of air-hammering is perhaps greater in respect to the risks of seam slumps and the greater dust levels and exposure to silicosis that hammering generates. On the other hand major efforts have been made in the last quarter-century to both eradicate coal damp by better air circulation and to keep down dust levels, in this low-grade bituminous coal, by seam wetting. Though our tough miner's hands have seen other changes in tools and in tasks than in this shift from pickaxes to air-hammers, this change can stand for a quarter-century of change in the miner's manual relation to time, which is to say production—for miner's time is measured in terms of production by both managers and the miners themselves. Of course there are many men who work in the mine who are not tied into the unit of production or performance measure, the *atajo*. But for the *picadores,* who are the predominant occupation and role model of mining, time is units of production and that in turn is predominantly a matter of the tools put in their hands.

In speaking of tool and task change among our agropastoralists we indicated increased dependency on imported tools and loss of a kind of slow circular, everything-in-its-season, aesthetic of life. This was the result of complete mastery of the tool as well as self-sufficiency in tool production and tool disposal, which is, of course, a kind of mastery as well. The miners have never really had this slow circular aesthetic. For the time-is-production aesthetic forces the pace away from the "everything-has-its-season" view of the agropastoralist, as the perpetual dark of underground production itself cuts the miner off from the circling of the seasons one after another. So there is a straight line, linear world view built into mining that has ever more pronouncedly come upon cattle keeping in this quarter-century.

There are many other things that have come into villagers' hands over these twenty-five years that have significant impact upon their emotional economy and their ideas about the world. From the women's perspective, bottles have replaced breasts, a subject my wife, Renate Lellep, has written informatively about.[14] And in the same realm of mother-child relations, handy throw-away diapers are now in local stores, at least for miner's families who can afford them, with all the disposal and environmental problems that we have learned they present.

In this regard, in our twenty-five years we have seen great efforts made in our villages to modernize their sanitary facilities, to have bathrooms worthy of the modern world. And most all villagers have done impressively well in this respect replacing septic tanks—black wells, the *pozo negro*—with often quite elegant bathrooms attached to a new sewer system. In the old days, of course, in the very old days and even in our first years, cattle-keeping families simply descended to the stable and mixed their night soil with that of the cattle—matter out of place from any middle class point of view, perhaps, although the villagers don't fool themselves that we are in any way different from the animals in this respect. And as this exuviae was all regularly redistributed on the fields the disposal problem was solved advantageously and not unduly offensively for the cattle manure was the overpowering substance in the mix.

But now the effluents all go into the sewer system and then, after some brief settling out in a large holding tank, go directly into the river. Local sanitation and dignity has been achieved at the expense of alarming pollution of these once rich salmon- and trout-bearing rivers. The dignity of bathroom propriety and cloacal modernity has been bought at the expense of a wider pollution of discouraging proportions.

Once again what was once at hand, local problems most all of which could be solved handily, has been transferred out to the larger world for others to solve. Since others, however, aren't solving them, modernity has been bought, as it has been long recognized for the European Mediterranean generally, at the expense of balanced development.[15] But is it really any different anywhere? My impression of a very modern but ghetto-afflicted and polluted city of Chicago is that our Second City modernity has been bought very often at the expense of a balanced and equitable urban development.

Of course, the point is that had our stay in those villages been only of one or two years we wouldn't have been so struck over these many years by the paradox and maladjustments of modernization and development, the change of scale, that is taking place. For practically every year we return there is a new bathroom of great elegance to impress us and comfort us and, also, worry us with the larger implications of it all.

In this problem of cloacal disposal there is also the increasing influence of the miner's world view. For the miners have never been interested in or seen the possibility of circulating their detritus. The time-is-production mentality militates against it. Mine tailings are simply thrown out of the mine and piled up in giant black vegetationless moon heaps in the bottoms of the green valleys. The mentality is linear. The mine is exploited by the time-is-production standard as rapidly as the market allows. The infertile and unprofitable leavings are thrown out and distributed willy-nilly upon the landscape and the miner moves on linearly to the next production. So in the handling of their own exuviae are the agropastoralists more and more operating linearly rather than circularly. These remains are distributed or cast away as cheaply as possible without profit and to the detriment of other dispensations.

As our friends and villagers join more fully the modern world, then, they are inevitably implicated in, but almost powerless to solve, its paradoxes and profound problems of distributive justice . . . "distributive justice" understood in a rather elemental way. It is an injustice, which they recognized sometime with a touch of malicious humor in view of intervillage rivalries, to distribute one's cloacal effluents to villages downriver (luckily our villages are mostly at the high points of the river). It is an injustice, in the nature of things, simply to waste the recuperative possibility and fertilizing power of detritus. But the ground swell of modernization is hard to resist.

Surprising Returns of Events

I could go on and on about other things that have come into our villagers' hands these twenty-five years and have passed from there into their emotional economy and the ideas that make up their world view. One could talk about the changes brought by a water distribution system to every house and the purchase of family washing machines. One got cold hands drawing water at the fountain, and especially scrubbing clothes on marble slabs at the edge of the stream . . . very cold hands. But there was a conviviality in it that is increasingly absent in village life as women are more and more confined to their houses and more and more bound to their increasing supply of "electro-domestic" machines, which they know much less about than any cow and which they can operate but can not really manipulate.

But I hardly have space for such an inventory. And, although I have wanted to be true to this point of the villagers' manual dexterities and to their pride—now disappearing pride—in such handy know-how as I have wanted to be true to the manual-mental interaction of human evolution, I now want to turn to some ideational implications of all this. These are the matters more comfortably treated by we soft-handed and hard-headed academicians who are rather calloused to manual argument. Nevertheless these ideational matters have their importance.

We shouldn't imagine that because I have focused on the manual—praxis in the most basic sense—that nothing mental has been going on in these villages. We shouldn't imagine that there is nothing in the mind there, that is, that wasn't first in the hand. There is a rich stock of folklore, of course, which is the subject of another essay. And the Church has been present for a thousand years or more, inculcating through catechism a whole set of religious ideas reenforcing the organization of village life, reinforcing kinship ties, and giving men and women an opportunity to purify their souls and prepare themselves for the fatalities of the human career. This social religiosity, its acceptance by cattle-keepers, and its increasing rejection by miners, is also subject for another essay. Though in our twenty-five years we have seen changes in religious practices that amount to secularization, this glacial shift so characteristic of the modern world has been surprised by a revitalized religiosity in some quarters, including among some miners who have been mainly the great secularizers, due to the coming of an enthusiastic young priest.

Let me speak rather to the ideas that have come to the miners through the international socialist movement. This movement, represented in a spectrum of parties, has been present among miners in this province for at least a hundred years. These ideas, as we know, embody notions of class relations, the mode of production, and the unjust accumulation of the rural gentry and mine owners, and ideas about the course of history. This movement was strong in Asturias during the 1920s and '30s of the Spanish Republic. It was drastically suppressed in the victory of the nationalists and went underground during the Franco regime, hardly mentionable in our first years of fieldwork. With the death of Franco, socialism and Communism revived almost overnight, such are the deep and enduring powers of cultural ideals, and have become widely influential in the villages, in the towns, and in the cities of the province. Where agropastoralism is strong more conservative parties prevail, of course, and in the villages we know best, where there are various mixes of cattle keeping and mining, conservative and populist forces share representation. But mainly Asturias has become a social province sending the famous Civil War leader, La Pasionaria, again and again to the national assembly (until her death in 1989) as it did during the Republic.

But it is the socialist ideas of the course of history that have undergone change. After the disappearance of the Franco regime there was strong animus for the realization of socialist version of history: a centrally planned economy in which the distributive injustices of the market system would be eliminated. Under the situation of the transition with a liberal monarchy supported by a still menacing army, nothing truly radical and revolutionary could be attempted, even if it would, and Spain and Asturias settled, as we know, for a very liberal socialism and an essentially Western Euro-American market system. In market terms it is a prospering country attracting high rates of foreign investment at the present time although there is still deep and often bitter debate about the distribution of surplus value in the economy.[16]

During the early years of fieldwork we could hardly have imagined a socialist Spain. In the early years of the post-Franco era, and the surging strength of socialism in Asturias, we could not easily have imagined the very centrist socialism that has emerged. History is, thus, full of surprises and retrospect should be wary of pretending to a wisdom that prospect never had.

Let me give one more example, also, by reference to labor, in the terms of our theme. We have pointed to the circularity and the husbandry of resources built into cattle-keeping and agropastoralism as a lifeway; its careful concern to redistribute its resources at every stage of their production and consumption. That is not just the same thing as the equitable redistribution of the surplus value produced in an economy, but there is a relationship. We also have spoken of the linearity of the miner's lifeway—the productive frenzy and the carelessness about redistribution so that the benefits tend to accumulate in one place and the worthless by-products accumulate in another. That, also, is not just the same thing as distributive injustice in an economy through excessive accumulation, although there's a relationship.

But history is full of surprises, to repeat, and one of these surprises is the untoward turn of events of the last five years in our province (and the northern provinces of Spain generally), and the consequent reappearance of cultural ideals more characteristic of the husbandry and redistributive circularity of agropastoralism than of mining. Two things have occurred: it suddenly has become clear that the bituminous coal of Asturias is running out or at least the coal, given its low-grade quality, that can be profitably extracted is running out. It also has become clear that the milk and meat produced by the cattle-keepers, for reason of price and quality, is not able to compete profitably with these products in the Common Market (Spain's full entry into the Common Market was in 1992). It is becoming clear that miners and cattle-keepers may have to turn their hands to something else. But what? There is much talk of reconversion, of retooling. But how?

And here is where an older cultural ideal is reasserting itself: the agropastoral ideal of redistributive husbandry and ecological circularity. "If we could raise cattle and produce milk more naturally and with less waste," it is argued, "on our own rich grass, without such dependence on fertilizer and feeds from the outside!" "If we could return again to that relative independence of former times, then our meat and our milk might be profitable again!" And as for the disappearance of coal mining: "Why it will enable Asturians to return to a more natural and healthy relation to the land!" "Everyone recognized that coal mining was polluting and contaminating."

Of course there are the ideas of the international ecology movement in this; ideas combined with the independent impulse of provincial nationalism. And, of course, there is a curious mix of capitalism and socialism, in this pastoral view of familistic independence and profitability on the land.

And, of course, many of the miners through their unions anticipate industrial conversion from mining to high-technology employment or to some chemical industry. And there is a curious mix here as well. For these staunch socialist and communist unions have arrived recently at the point of suppressing their strikes so as not to give the province a bad name in its efforts to attract new multinational industries. In retrospect these last five years of anticipated drastic economic change had made strange bedfellows such as in prospect we might never have anticipated.

But the point is that old modes of manual being, and the feelings for circularity and redistributiveness of lifeway that rose out of them, have not disappeared—they have only lain dormant ready for a more propitious season, as it were, so as to spring up again ready to flourish.[17] Whether they will flourish or not is an open question. It depends on many forces. But, surely, long-term field research teaches us this lesson: that there is, at the very least, an ambidexterity in social life and that it is a mistake to think that the music of culture is played with only one hand in an increasingly dominant chord. There are always undertones and hidden harmonies and "old songs" ever ready to reassert themselves. For the anthropologist such melodies as are heard are sweet, but those unheard may be sweeter!

Toward an "Even-Handed" Conclusion: On the One Hand, But Then on the Other Hand

What we have tried to *grasp* here in retrospect, in this manual-mental interdigitation is something—it can only be something and not the whole thing—of the flow of culture that has over these twenty-five years been brought to our attention in these Asturian mountain villages. We anthropologists have long had the Heraclitean understanding that we cannot step into the same stream twice. And that fact—it is surely more than true for the stream of culture—is repeatedly brought home to us when we do long-term field research. And, of course, it is as true not only of the flow of culture but the flow in our own lives. For though we might pretend, like Heraclitus, that we stand in Archimedean fixity upon the bank and watch culture flow by, in fact we are carried along as well by the flow in ourselves and by the flow in our own culture as well as by the flow in that "other" culture that we seek to grasp.

As far as the flow in ourselves it seems evident, for example, that a young person's ethnography, the people the ethnographer talks to, the sense he or she will have of the life cycle, will not be the same as the ethnography written by someone of, as the French gently say, "uncertain age." But, also, as our fieldwork extends through the years we are caught up, or in the flow of the other. We become, ourselves, involved and made anxious or satisfied, depressed or hopeful, in short very partial, with the eddies, the backwaters, the progress towards a better life or away from one. The liquidity of it all disturbs the certainty of our understanding. And so if it is figuratively true that we cannot step into the same stream twice, even more so is it difficult to reach in and grasp anything that will not, in the end, run through our hands.

But yet, on the other hand and as part of our constant effort in this essay to be even-handed, one has to say immediately that there are certain things, ideas and images or memories of ideas or images of old lifeways, that are carried along in that flow in some deep undercurrent way and that can later come to the surface and be manifest again. So the complexity is that while we can never step into the same stream twice there is some principle of memory by which the stream itself does not forget and can later remember to reconstitute itself in former ways.

The recognition of the inevitable partiality of our work in ethnography is very much the tenor of our times and the mood of the post-modern ethnography of this decade. "Partial truths" are what we produce in our work, it has been argued forcefully.[18] Of course, that is something we have realized now for many decades. In the Spanish-speaking world (not to mention Derek Freeman's recent restudy of Margaret Mead), Oscar Lewis's restudy of Robert Redfield's Tepoztlán and Paul Friedrich's restudy of the same author's Tarascan work indicate fully the partiality of our investigations.[19] Such restudies show us the way that our work is relative to the particular place and time where we stepped into the stream of culture; and relative to our own particular personal the theoretical predisposition. They are relative to our particular place in the flow of personal time and, within our professions, our place in the flow of theoretical time. For theory is not more constant than culture though it seeks to embrace it and gain a permanent foothold within it.

In Iberian studies we have two notable examples of how time changes the circumstances of our fieldwork and gives us other perspectives. Julian Pitt Rivers's classic study, *The People of the Sierra*,[20] was undertaken a scant fifteen years after the conquest of the town by Nationalist forces in the Civil War and the severe repression of the Left that took place at that time. Yet it makes little mention either of that repression or of the important radical history of the town and the role of the anarchists there. This glaring omission in the view of Serran Pagan is a serious invalidation of the work![21] But it also is indicative of the authoritarian time in which the work was undertaken and, very likely, both the conservative political position and structural-functional theoretical interests of the author. What Spanish ethnography written under Franco—and some ethnographers have been forthcoming enough to indicate in the very title of their work the authoritarian framework of their studies[22]—would not have been different if undertaken after the dictator's demise?

One of the remarkable things about Jerome Mintz's *Anarchists of Casas Viejas*,[23] indeed, is that he obtained so much sensitive material objectionable to Francoist authoritarianism under the noses of the authorities. Of course, he was working at the tail end of that once iron-fisted regime when its grip on its subjects had greatly relaxed. But the point is that the data we get are so much conditioned by time and place. Though George and Jane Collier began work in Spain in the early sixties, it wasn't until after the death of the dictator that George Collier could develop what was only hinted at before—the oral histories and collateral material necessary to write an ethnographic history of the socialist movement in their town.[24]

It is perhaps an obvious enough point that social science undertaken under democracy is bound to differ from the social science, if any, that can be undertaken under dictatorship. Joseba Zulaika's *Basque Violence*[25] could not have been undertaken under Franco, but it is one among many recent studies—few or none as good—that treats Basque terrorism and treats it from many perspectives.[26] So politically the times are propitious for such variety of study though that does not mean we are free from politics and personal circumstance in our interpretations. We may not be bound hand and foot but we are not entirely unbound from time and circumstance.

There are those who, when reminded of the partiality of our studies, their place in the flow of time, lament the disappearance of both immutable scientific fact and the possibility of final validation of our work under the constraint of changing circumstance. But science itself has never promised certainty nor the eradication of ambiguity. Lawmakers in Washington often lament, so the story goes, the testimony of scientists before policy-establishing committees. So often their expert advice comes in the form of "Well, on the one hand, this is the nature and consequences of the problem at hand, but on the other hand, reassessing the data from another view, we get the following." "Legislators look for a one handed scientific expert" was the ironic title of an article in the *Congressional Quarterly*. Lucky we would be if it were only a matter of two hands. Most science is conducted with at least the tentacles of an octopus. And if that weren't enough there is the Kuhnian thesis in *The Structure of Scientific Revolutions*[27] that science progresses by thorough-going paradigm change such that the work done in one paradigm is fundamentally incommensurable from the perspective of the work done in the succeeding paradigm. Here not only do we have two hands but, in fact, the left hand doesn't know and cannot grasp what the right hand is going to be doing. If that isn't an arresting comment on the profound changes brought about by the flow of time, I don't know what is!

A Man's Reach Should Exceed His Grasp, or What's a Metaphor?

The full-stop conclusion of our paper is now at hand. And it is time to recall our epigraph taken from Warren d'Azevedo. He tells us that for men of wisdom among Gola, that is, for men of a "certain age," there is a duty attached to such retrospection as we have practiced here. Such men are expected to apply their accumulated memories to the solution of problems confronting the living present! In general terms, with this injunction in mind, we have argued that this accumulated wisdom is the wisdom of seeking the even-handedness, which implies the recognition of "partiality." As for "the problems of the living present" that this wisdom confronts, are they not the recurrent problems of dogmatism, absolutism, and bigotry? That is to say, are they not the problem of all the one-handed attitudes of history!

But I wish to emphasize that this wisdom, the wisdom of the knowledge of partiality embodied in even-handedness, has in this ethnographic essay arisen from the practice of trying to get in touch with those dexterities in which the people who have admitted us among them take pride. In this paper I have tried to follow some of the changes in these dexterities over a generation and their implication for the meaning world in which these people live and the meaning worlds, conceived in the simplest terms possible, linear and circular,[28] that they, together with those that provide them with their tools, have constructed.

The wisdom, such as it is in this approach, is to try and cease for a moment the loquaciousness of the academy—the elaboration of mental abstractions to which we are endlessly committed. The effort is to try to cease the loquaciousness of that professional discourse that has filled our heads before going to the field, that so often strains to assert itself into the local colloquial dialogue to which we are trying to become attuned and that very quickly engulfs and absorbs us once again when we return from the field.

In the ensuing silence of one hand clapping, as it were, we can perhaps sense the body's view of experience and meaning as these are bound up in its capabilities. We can perhaps come to sense the identity bound into the performance—or frustrations of performance—of these dexterous practices of which the body is capable. In the ensuing silence, perhaps, there may also come to us the wisdom of knowing a paradoxical thing—this sound of the one hand clapping—and that is the immediacy of knowing that despite our platonic hope of escaping to some archimedean point of enduring ideas, that we and our informants are together bound inescapably—bodily—into the flow of time in such a way that we can only discharge our ethnographic tasks partially, contingently! And yet, and yet on the other hand, there is something imminently present in immediacy and which follows close behind it. This is the preservative and sustenant and impending power of memory—memory of the enduring ideas and ideals in culture, here and now on the surface; there and then submerged or subterranean. So often these are memories that are tied into our bodies as memory is embodied, and which, amidst the flow of bodies, provide us with something more enduring to which we can recurrently return.

Beyond this even-handedness, this sense of proportion we apply in trying to understand time's flow is the wisdom of anthropological method—the wisdom of trying to grasp long-term change in culture by taking the point of view of those undergoing it. The cultures of cattle-keepers and miners in Asturias Spain are task-oriented cultures with impressive manual skills. With that in mind as well as the evolutionary argument of the impact of the hand's work upon the mind's thoughts I have tried to take the hand's point of view in the manual-mental coordination of human life. We have been in the grip of a master metaphor of rather unaccustomed presence in the academy but of great significance beyond it—the manual one—and we have set at the task of mastering our understanding of time's work in anthropological inquiry.

Of course, no metaphor or complex of related metaphors can speak to the entirety of human experience, much less the human experience of time. The reach of our experience always exceeds our grasp so that we endlessly put forth a succession and variety of imaginative figures of thought to try, at last, to grasp it. What we have chosen here, I firmly believe, is that set of manual metaphors, surely ingrained and conventional, indeed fundamental in our own language, which enables us to reach insightfully towards the experience over time of these cattle-keepers and miners as they struggle for task mastery in respect to circularity and linearity, accumulation and redistribution, dependence and independence. For these mountain cultures the manual is of proportionally greater interest and importance. In that sense the paradoxical experience of the passage of years *and* the return of older ideals is an experience of "time on their hands."

While there is a frustration, then, in anthropological fieldwork because we, like our informants, are bound by the proportionality of human existence and our own place in time, yet we can in some part escape that bondedness by long-term research. Over the long term we can get some sense not only of the contingency of things but, in response to that contingency, a culture's imaginative evocation of its always potential continuities. And I have sought to applaud that even-handed long-term research here.

Endnotes

1. J. W. Fernandez (1982) *Bwiti: An Ethnography of the Religious Imagination in Spain*. Princeton University Press, Princeton.

2. See the absorbing account of a Santiago pilgrimage by the anthropologist Ellen O. Feinberg (1989) *Following the Milky Way: A Pilgrimage Across Spain.* Iowa State University Press, Ames.

3. For a primary account of these semantic sources in the Indo-European languages see Hans Kurath (1921) *The Semantic Sources of the Words for the Emotions in Sanskrit, Greek, Latin and the Germanic Languages.* The Collegiate Press, Menasha, Wisconsin.

4. Mark Johnson (1987) *The Body in the Mind: The Bodily Basis of Meaning, Imagination and Reason.* University of Chicago Press, Chicago.

5. Janet W. D. Dougherty and Charles Keller (1985) Taskonomy: A Practical Approach to Knowledge Structures. In *Directions in Cognitive Anthropology,* edited by J. W. D. Dougherty, pp. 161–174. University of Illinois Press, Urbana.

6. This point is made by Charles Keller and Janet Dixon Keller (1990) "Thinking and Acting with Iron" an unpublished manuscript devoted to activity theory.

7. Johannes Fabian (1983) *Time and the Other: How Anthropology Constructs its Object.* Columbia University Press, New York.

8. For a persuasive colloquial statement about this distancing see Dennis Tedlock (1979) The Analogical Tradition and the Emergence of a Dialogical Anthropology. *Journal of Anthropological Research* 35:37–400. See also J. W. Fernandez (1985) Exploded Worlds: "Text" as a Metaphor for Ethnography (and Vice Versa). *Dialectical Anthropology* 10(1):15–26.

9. For a discussion for this impulse to escape Godelian circularity and ultimate inexplicability by jumping out of the system (JOOTSING) see Douglas Hofstadter (1984) *Understanding Understanding.* Scientific American Press, New York.

10. The phrase derives from my colleague Bernard Cohn and is employed by Richard Handler to describe the tendency of nationalist movements to define and know themselves and their nation as an object or entity. Richard Handler (1988) *Nationalism and the Politics of Culture in Quebec.* University of Wisconsin Press, Madison. See Chapter 1, "Meditations on 'la Fete' of November 15."

11. Godfrey and Monica Wilson (1945) *The Analysis of Social Change.* Cambridge University Press, Cambridge.

12. There have been in recent years, concomitant with a renewed interest in the body as social and cultural template, a whole series of books and articles seeking to revive or reinvigorate our attention to the place of the other senses in social life. For anthropologists it may have begun with Ashley Montagu's (1978) *Touching: The Human Significance of the Skin.* Harper and Row, New York. Most recently this renewed attention to the entire sensorium is seen in Paul Stoller's (1989) *The Taste of Ethnographic Things.* University of Pennsylvania Press, Philadelphia.

13. See the discussion of this raillery between generations of miners in J. W. Fernandez (1979) Syllogisms of Association: Some Modern Extensions of Asturian

Deepsong. In *Folklore in the Modern World,* edited by Richard Dorson, pp. 183–206. Mouton, The Hague.

14. Renate Lellep Fernandez (1990) *A Simple Matter of Salt.* University of California Press, Berkeley and Los Angeles.

15. Jane and Peter Schneider and E. Hansen (1972) Modernization and Development: The Role of Regional Elites and Non-Corporate Groups in the European Mediterranean. *Comparative Studies in Society and History* 14(3):328–350.

16. In terms of this paper, however, that is to say from the point of view of labor—from the manual point of view—the surplus value of the hand's production is still being alienated at an unacceptable rate by a distribution system still very much in the hands of an establishment little changed from the Franco years. For labor there continues to be, manifestly, distributive injustice in this new Spain and both our cattle-keepers and miners complain of it—though in different ways, and periodically—in the case of the latter—go out on strike about it.

17. I owe this metaphor of the dormancy of cultural ideals through time, several generations perhaps, and their coming to fruition in later more propitious circumstances to William Douglass's discussion of cultural ideals in "The Multiple Family Household Controversy: A Household Case" manuscript. See also J. W. and R. L. Fernandez (1988) Under One Roof: Household Formation and Cultural Ideals in an Asturian Mountain Village. *Journal of Family History* 13:123–142.

18. James Clifford (1986) Partial Truths. In *Introduction to Writing Culture: The Poetics and Politics of Ethnography,* edited by James Clifford and George Marcus. University of California Press, Berkeley.

19. Oscar Lewis (1964) *Life in a Mexican Village: Tepoztlan Restudied.* University of Illinois Press, Urbana. Paul Friedrich (1986) *The Princes of Naranja: An Essay in Anthrohistorical Method.* University of Texas Press, Austin.

20. Julian Pitt-Rivers (1954) *The People of the Sierra.* University of Chicago Press, Chicago.

21. Gines Serran Pagan (1980) La Fabula de Alcala y la Realidad Historica en Grazalema: Replantamiento del Primer Estudio de Antropologia Social en Espaa. *Revista Espaola de Investigaciones Sociologicas* 9(2):181–215.

22. Edward Hansen (1977) *Rural Catalonia Under the Franco Regime: The Fate of Regional Culture since the Spanish Civil War.* Columbia University Press, New York. Susan F. Harding (1984) *Remaking Ibieca: Rural Life in Aragon under Franco.* University of North Carolina Press, Chapel Hill.

23. Jerome Mintz (1982) *The Anarchists of Casas Viejas.* University of Chicago Press, Chicago.

24. G. A. Collier (1987) *Socialists of Andalucia: Unacknowledged Revolutionaries of the Second Republic.* Stanford University Press, Stanford.

25. Joseba Zulaika (1988) *Basque Violence: Metaphor and Sacrament.* University of Nevada Press, Reno.

26. In the province of Asturias the equivalent phenomenon, very difficult to address during the Franco era, was the October Miner's Revolution of 1934 suppressed by Franco himself as a general in command of Republican troops. Since the death of Franco there has been an outpouring of literature on the event and its antecedents and consequences. See Adrian Shubert (1987) *The Road to Revolution in Spain: The Coal Miners of Asturias.* University of Illinois Press, Urbana.

27. Thomas N. Kuhn (1962) *The Structure of Scientific Revolutions.* University of Chicago Press, Chicago.

28. For two insightful arguments on how far this simple dichotomy can yet take us in understanding a basic, enduring, and existential human dilemma of standing even-handedly before time's flow see Edmund Leach (1961) Two Essays Concerning the Symbolic Representation of Time. In *Rethinking Anthropology*, pp. 124–136. Athlone Press, London; and Stephen Jay Gould (1987) *Time's Arrow and Time's Cycle: Myth and Metaphor in the Discovery of Geological Time.* Harvard University Press, Cambridge.

Beginning to Understand: Twenty-Eight Years of Fieldwork in the Great Basin of Western North America

Catherine S. Fowler

As Malcolm Crick (1982:16) cogently observed a few years ago, all anthropology is "inherently autobiographical." That is, it is not so much *about* the other—other peoples, other cultures, other realities—as it is about the interplay between the field investigator and the other. That interplay starts for the investigator with the choice to pursue the discipline of anthropology in the first place—and the motives for that choice are probably about as varied as anthropologists. The next choices are of a place to study and of theoretical and descriptive interests within the discipline (although some of these choices are dependent at least in part on the academic fashions of the day). These choices are followed by ones involving a region and site for fieldwork; the choice of a topic for field research; and the choice of persons with whom to work.

But if anthropology is inherently autobiographical for the fieldworker, it is equally autobiographical for the native persons with whom one works. They, too, make a series of choices, the first being whether to allow the fieldworker entry into the community; that is, whether to let the proverbial camel put his or her nose under the tent. In times past, under the oppression of colonialism in various forms, communities often were not allowed to exercise that choice freely. Ethnographers were imposed upon them, more or less, as were various types of bureaucrats. This is less so today; as a result, some fieldworkers have felt the sting of rejection or the constraint of signing contracts specifying varying levels of community control over topics studied and results obtained. Later, in situations of true choice, native persons also choose whether to allow access to their households, and ultimately their lives. From the individual's perspective, choices are made as to whether to get involved or not, what to tell and how to tell it, and how to interpret what is told based on the person's experience. Motives may stem from a sincere interest in the particular topic as native scholars, the person's role/roles in the community (for example, as interpreters or protectors of the community to the outside world), or as a person seeking employment—some people may just need a job (Craig 1987).

But the interplay continues after the formal fieldwork is over, as many reflexivists have reminded us of late. It surfaces again when it comes time to write up the material. Choices then have to be made by the fieldworker as to the nature of the audience for whom he or she is writing (peers, bureaucracies, the educated public, the native community, or a combination thereof). One also decides how the material is to be interpreted (from particular theoretical positions), how to account for variation within the data base (the latter is one of the biggest problems faced by all, but one not often discussed), and what role to give those who provided the data (acknowledgment in a preface, formal consultantships and attributions, co-authorship). Decisions also need to be made as to what role the community/persons are going to have in critiquing the work. It has become quite common to give native communities review and comment periods in contract work done in the United States and Canada in applied anthropology, but it is less common with other written materials. A number of conflicts might be avoided with a little more attention to this matter.

Long-term fieldworkers and the communities and persons with whom they interact face additional decisions as to what will be their respective relationships after a particular project is completed. Not that either party necessarily knows in advance whether a relationship will actually be long term, but often the supposition is made by one or both that it will be. If one is anticipated by either party, some thought should be given to it early. Anthropologists often decline to be very candid about their field experiences except in the realm of anecdote. But if that is so, they are even less forthcoming about aspects of field exit and the maintenance of relationships through time. Those who do fieldwork in an area close to where they live need to think particularly about this aspect, as Joan Ablon (this volume) reminds us about problems with the choice of a field site in one's own community. However, the world is really a much smaller place than it was even twenty years ago, with telephones, telegrams, and even facsimile machines, so that this aspect of fieldwork requires more serious consideration by all. The level of long-term involvement and commitment, or better the lack thereof, was well expressed a number of years ago by a native consultant quoted as saying, "So you are an anthropologist—one of those people who come and live with us, act as our friends, but then leave us after all of that and all we ever get from you again is a Christmas card."

Given this view of anthropology as autobiographical from two perspectives—that of the fieldworker as well as of native persons—I'll now proceed to tell at least one side of another story; to try to account for my actions, activities, and motives over some twenty-eight years of intermittent experience among Great Basin Indian people, particularly Northern Paiute and Southern Paiute, and to a lesser degree, Western Shoshone and Owens Valley Paiute. This will be a biased account—more like a "just so" story—since we won't be able to hear from the other side. Unfortunately, most of the persons with whom I worked the longest are no longer living. But it would be quite presumptuous of me to think that for them my presence in their communities or lives was even of enough importance to record—should they have felt so compelled. Regrettably for the discipline, few native persons have reflected in print on these associations. We get brief glimpses in Don Talayesva's autobiography *Sun Chief* (Simmons 1942), in Triloki Pandey's (1972) "Anthropologists in Zuni," and from a few biting comments by Lakota Vine Deloria (1969:78) and Otomi Jesus Salinas (1975:71). Perhaps some day reflexivity of the type we are engaged in here may be an active part of native writing as well.

Given that this presentation lacks a second side, I will attempt to account for a few features of it by being a bit biographical—telling something of the lives of certain key individuals with whom I have worked through the years. In essence my long-term fieldwork has been with specific persons, and on specific topics, with some relationships spanning much or most of my field years. Also, with the exception of two to three three-month sessions, it has been more intermittent than the common ideal of anthropological fieldwork—intensive live-in situations of one to two years' duration. Rather, I have visited people for a day or two every month, or a week or two here and there, in some years fairly consistently, in others less so. But it has been through long-term acquaintance with specific individuals that I have learned, insofar as I am able at present, to contextualize what I know. And I am still learning from a variety of sources.

To begin at the beginning: I can't remember when I was not interested in North American Indians. As a grade school student, whenever a project came up in which we had a choice, I always chose something to do with Indian people—be it in art class, geography, or history. Not that our school was particularly oriented to teaching about ethnic diversity—as I recall it was not. Mostly I think I developed the interest on my own. But then I had not planned to make a career of this interest. I wanted to be a veterinarian. I kept that career goal in mind until my junior year in college.

The summer I was fifteen and again when I was sixteen, I had the rare opportunity to travel the American Southwest on two-week tours sponsored by the Girl Scouts. Twenty girls from all over the country each summer visited archaeological sites under excavation, as well as museums, national parks, and other points of interest. We also visited the Rio Grande Pueblo villages, Navajo homesteads, the Pueblo of Zuni, and villages on the Hopi mesas. It was my first opportunity to actually meet Indian people—the governors of Zuni and several Rio Grande pueblos were our hosts, as I later learned was their role—and to observe something of what I had been reading about for some time. I also immediately fell in love with the Southwestern landscape and more subtly, with the ethnic diversity in the region—Pueblo, Navajo, Hispanic, Anglo—with native languages as freely spoken as English. For someone from Utah with almost no personal experience with ethnic diversity, this was very important.

Our guide, or better, our mentor, for the summers was Dr. Bertha Dutton of the Museum of New Mexico. Bert was an anthropologist—I'd never heard the term before—and a formidable role model. She lectured to us in formal sessions on the culture history and ethnography of the Southwest. She quizzed us continually on what we were observing and what it meant. She seemed to know personally many of the Indian people we visited. Above all, she stressed to us that we should get educations and think of careers. We didn't have to become anthropologists, but we should become something. There are several of us "in the business" today, as well as in other careers because of Bert's encouragement and example.

I will not bore the reader with the details or reasons why I switched from preveterinary medicine to anthropology, other than to say that part of the decision had to do with the difficulties suggested to me of a woman doing large animal medicine, which would have been my choice. In my junior year at the University of Utah, I switched to anthropology. Warren d'Azevedo was at Utah that year, and I retook, at the urging of the department chairman, the course in introductory cultural anthropology from him. His lectures on his African fieldwork were the most memorable parts of the course, particularly how he and his wife and two children had lived for two and a half years in a remote Liberian village, and of all the people they had met, and what they had seen and learned. It was a personalized anthropology, an approach that I much enjoyed as a student but suspect I am not very good at as a teacher. I later took courses in North American and Great Basin Indians from Warren, and participated in a seminar on Great Basin cultures. In addition to the seminar pointing to a field direction for me, it also introduced me to Don Fowler, my partner for twenty-six years.

I paralleled my interests in anthropology at Utah with interests in biology—undoubtedly a hold-over from the veterinary medicine interests. I took botany, zoology, and ecology, most of which focused on the Great Basin as that was the regional emphasis of the department. Gradually, the two fields began to come together.

In my senior year I was given my first field opportunity through work on the Glen Canyon Project—a massive archaeological salvage venture funded through the National Park Service and designed to recover archaeological, historical, and biological data from the area about to be inundated by the lake created by the Glen Canyon Dam.

I had been hired by Jesse Jennings, chair of the department at Utah and director of the project—on Warren d'Azevedo's recommendation—to do what is now called ethnoarchaeology. I was to attempt to find out how Southern Paiute people had used the land in the project area in the historic period, and as far back as they could remember. The data were to be as site specific as possible. I was to take people who were willing to go with me to the area and have them indicate places they knew, especially old camping sites. They also were to interpret what was on the ground for me.

That was how I first met Grandma—although I certainly did not call her that then—one spring day in 1962. I had come to Cedar City, Utah, to ask what she and her husband knew about southeastern Utah, and especially the area in and around Glen Canyon. I explained all of this to Grandma and Grandpa and about ten other curious family members and friends who had assembled for the occasion. Our first meeting proved to be brief. As we looked at maps in the kitchen that afternoon, I learned my first two ethnographic lessons, one specific and one general. First, Great Basin Indian people, at least the older generation, only talk about what they know from first-hand experience—from having been raised in an area and thereby acquiring the knowledge and hence the right to comment on it. Second, and related to the theme of this series, that ethnography involves relationships among persons. It did not take long to discover that neither Grandma or Grandpa knew about the country of concern to me—they had been born way west of there, and, although they had seen it and were related to people from that region, they were not from there. Grandpa said: "You want to know about this country over here sometime, you come back." Grandma was more pointed. She said as I was leaving, "You come back sometime. $1.00 a word." I remember thinking to myself: "Did she really mean $1.00 a word? How can I afford that? Maybe she was only kidding." Grandpa had seemed so nice. Grandma was tougher: she was a woman of power, and she knew her worth. She was putting me on notice that if I wanted to work with her, she would decide the terms.

I did not see Grandma and Grandpa for a few years after that. I did go on to work with other Southern Paiute people on the Glen Canyon Project, principally two older men who had been born and raised in the "right" country and thus knew it from first-hand experience. From them, and particularly from being with them in the country they knew so well, I began to learn something of the detailed knowledge they possessed of flora, fauna, microhabitats—of ecology. I learned how to find water—other than by knowing where it was to begin with—and a host of other things about the land and resources. We visited old pinyon-gathering camps, hunting and habitation sites, springs, dance grounds, race tracks, recreation sites, and much more (Sweeney and Euler 1963). I recorded as best I could (I had not had any linguistic training) the many native place names for geographic features, as well as the names of animals, birds, plants, lizards and insects. Our mutual interests in flora and fauna, and my newly awakened interest in ecology—they already knew about the interrelatedness of life and land— proved to be a good meeting ground. I knew enough to ask some more or less intelligent questions. They knew a great deal about the subject matter and were interested as well. They understood less my interest in their old camping places and what they contained. They had not consciously thought much about that before or what it meant. They had little trouble finding the exact spot of some event that had occurred fifty or sixty years before, or in reading the subtle signs of occupation on the ground—some darkened earth, a small pile of stones. But interestingly, there was little overt sign of their presence on the landscape. In fact, their impact appeared to be so slight that without their guidance, one would never have known that they had been there at all. This was a lesson I have carried with me to the present in my wonderings about how to deal with the interface of archaeology and ethnography in the Great Basin.

Something else became abundantly clear as we neared the end of that first field project—that I and the persons who were teaching me were not looking at some pristine or aboriginal situation. The individuals with whom I was working had all been born after white (Mormon) settlement of the region. The habitation sites they knew were near towns where their parents had done wage work. They could not remember a time when they did not have horses, although their parents had told them there was such a period. Interestingly, they could remember a time when the country was better off—the washes were not so deep or wide, the sagebrush not so dense, seed and root plants were closer at hand. Thus, in order to deal effectively and accurately with the sites we visited, I would have to consider history—ethnohistory and environmental history—the impact of eighty to one hundred years of non-Indian influences on the land and its peoples.

Until that time, my training in anthropology at the University of Utah had been principally in general anthropology with an emphasis on ethnography—ethnography of the ethnographic present—that time just prior to contact and disruption of lifeways by European societies—at least that is how I remember it. But then that was also the ethnography that interested me the most and still does. I remember upon returning to the university purposefully taking a course in contemporary North American Indians, in which I learned something about the Bureau of Indian Affairs, the several levels of Indian law, and a number of less interesting things. Somehow this gave me the "before" and the "after" reference to what I had learned in the field, but no middle. D'Azevedo's seminar on Great Basin Indians had some ethnohistoric content. He also had employed me that previous summer to work on a bibliography of Washoe sources—many of which were historical (d'Azevedo 1963). I had gathered some ethnohistoric sources for the Glen Canyon Project before going to the field, but obviously I had to have more in order to make any sense of what had happened. I'd also have to take more ecology courses to learn about environmental history. At the time, Walter Cottam, one of the leaders in that subfield of biology, was teaching at the university; I took courses from him and read, among other things, his influential monograph "Is Utah Sahara Bound?" (Cottam 1947) on the environmental impact of grazing of Utah's rangelands and forests. What he had to say dovetailed nicely with what the Southern Paiute gentlemen had been telling me. At least some things were beginning to fit together.

I finished my part of the Glen Canyon Project with a paper on the environment of Southern Paiute country, including some indication of how it appeared to have changed through time. The paper (Fowler 1966) was incorporated into a larger monograph by Robert Euler on Southern Paiute ethnohistory, wherein he talked about some of the reasons for the changes in people's lifeways I was observing in the field. Euler was an established scholar with much more experience than I in ethnohistory and much more capable of accomplishing the job that needed doing.

I married and left Utah in 1963 for the University of Pittsburgh. Having not completed my Master's degree at Utah, I was strongly urged to start over on several of the basics. Unfortunately descriptive linguistics was not offered that year, something that I definitely needed and wanted. But I was able to take a language and culture class from Edward Kennard, a distinguished ethnologist and fluent speaker of the Hopi language of Arizona. Many of the points Kennard made about the necessity of linguistic training to do adequate fieldwork hit home. These included a quote from his mentor, Franz Boas, to the effect that we as anthropologists often presume to probe the innermost thoughts of a particular people without so much as a "smattering of their language," something that should not be. I also remember reading with a great deal of interest several papers in the emerging field of ethnoscience, including Charles Frake's (1962) influential paper on the methods of ethnoecology. Why not take a more serious look at native views of the environment and its interrelationships and their taxonomies of plants and animals? I intended to try it as soon as we returned west. When Don finished his Ph.D. coursework at the end of that year, and Warren d'Azevedo offered both of us jobs at the University of Nevada, Reno, we did return.

Warren had come to Reno the year before at the behest of Wendell Mordy of the Desert Research Institute to start an anthropological research program focused on the Great Basin. All of Don's field interests were in the Desert West, as were mine. The academic department Warren founded, at first combined with sociology, was bright and new, and the university seemed to want to build in desired directions. The university also had no nepotism rules, an exceedingly important factor for us. Sans degree for a second time, I went to work for the Desert Research Institute in the unit then called the Center for Western North American Studies (Warren's Great Basin focus) and Don went into the sociology/anthropology department.

I finally had the opportunity to take some descriptive linguistics courses in those first few years at Nevada. Wayne Suttles, well known for his work on the Salishan languages of the Northwest Coast, was in the department. Bill Jacobsen, who had completed his doctoral dissertation on the Washoe language of the Great Basin, was newly hired in the English department. Sven Liljeblad, distinguished Swedish scholar, who had worked among Northern Paiute and Shoshone speakers for some twenty-five years by then (by now over fifty years), was a visiting professor. From each of these individuals I was able to take general and specific linguistics or Native American language classes that focused my interests in the discipline and also made me, I hope, a much better fieldworker. Linguistic anthropology has remained one of my major areas of concentration in teaching and research since that time.

It was during Wayne Suttle's field linguistics class that I met another person, who along with Grandma and others, would be an important teacher about the native world—Harry Sampson. Mr. Sampson, now for some years deceased, served as a native language consultant for the class, and we learned to transcribe and analyze his language, Northern Paiute. Mr. Sampson was a graduate of Stewart Indian School, a printer by training (by then retired), and a founding member of the Reno Musician's Union. He was also a devoted student of his own culture and language, having served as interpreter and consultant to anthropologists Willard Park in the summers of 1933 to 1940, and Omer Stewart in 1939, and as interviewer and interpreter for WPA botanist Percy Train in 1934–1935. When Joy Leland and I began further work on Northern Paiute ethnobotany with Mr. Sampson, we were in for a surprise. Not only did he know the Northern Paiute names and uses for a myriad of plants, he also knew their scientific names far better than we did. Mr. Sampson had kept his own field notes during the WPA study and he consulted them during our further investigations. It was with Mr. Sampson that Joy and I first tried work on ethnobiological taxonomies (Fowler and Leland 1967). He grasped the concepts readily, and we worked through several versions with him. We also employed him as an interviewer with other Northern Paiute speakers, gathering texts and dialogues on plants and animals as he saw fit. We then spent considerable time working through the materials and transcribing and translating them with him. We also worked with other persons, including several elderly women at Pyramid Lake. In all, however, Mr. Sampson played the primary role. His level of knowledge of the natural world was superior, and our many field trips to gather plants were always adventures as well as major learning experiences. Although I am sure our naivete caused him to chuckle on more than one occasion, his sincere interest in the subject matter always carried him through. Although we paid him for the laborious tasks of interviewing and translating, there were several occasions when he would not accept money because of his own interests and deep honesty—he had reached the level of his social security allowances for the period and would have to report any extra income. In terms of his own motivations, the data were very important, and he wanted very badly for them to be written down and preserved. Unfortunately, I am sure Joy and I disappointed Mr. Sampson, as had Willard Park before us (Fowler 1989), by not publishing the data we gathered. Our only publication from that work was a paper on method, written for our colleagues, and not for the community. Regrettably, Mr. Sampson was not properly credited, following the fashions of the day, which rarely spoke of the important role played by native persons in data gathering and interpretation.

In 1967, I spent three months back in Southern Paiute territory, working with several individuals, including Grandma. This work was funded by the University of Utah through a grant from the Doris Duke Foundation. The project was done in the milieu of the beginnings of ethnic consciousness-raising—an attempt to gather history from native perspectives. Although the project was still oriented in many ways around Western/Anglo concepts of history, with events and dates, we also inquired into native concepts of historical time and events and tried to match the two. I also used the opportunity to continue ethnobiological inquiries with Grandma and Grandpa, and again we went to the field to collect plants, animals, and place names.

During that summer, and the next few summers that I had available for fieldwork, between working for others and continuing coursework at the University of Pittsburgh for a doctorate,[1] I worked quite intensively with Grandma and also with Grandpa. Grandpa and I, and one of his daughters with whom I became very close, wandered the hills of southwestern Utah searching for all we could find of the past and present natural world. Given that Grandma was busy raising yet another complement of children (she had given birth to nine of her own and was now raising various grandbabies), she rarely accompanied us on those forays. But, whenever we returned home, she was always anxious to see what we had found. Although she initially put me on notice that her work would cost $1 a word, her own curiosity as to what we were finding soon took over. Grandpa did not know plants nearly as well as she, and we both had to have her participation. It was he who talked her into it. I recall many occasions when we returned with the day's harvest and spread it before her on the kitchen table. She would say, "Well what have you got for me today?" And her face would slowly brighten, as if she were seeing old friends—plants with their inherent foods and medicines from days long gone—times of work and pleasure in preparing meals from native foods, also long gone. She told me on several occasions, "These weeds are our life. They make us grow good. Not like the things they get today in the store. This is good food. You get lots and we eat good."

Grandma's toughness remained on several occasions as well. Sometimes when we disappointed her, she would say about our harvest, "What kind of Indians are you? Don't you know nothing? This is no good for nothing." Gradually our friendship grew through repeated visits and repeated queries, most of them targeted for me in concepts of the natural world. She started referring to me to the rest of the family as her "white daughter," largely I suspect because of what I was learning. Our friendship also may have grown because of my continued relationship with her daughter—we have remained close through the years. Gradually my discussion with Grandma, and Grandpa before his death in 1971, expanded to persons and events from the past, and how the old people used to live all phases of their lives, from birth to death. Our inquiries went more into general ethnography, into all phases of the life she once lived or had heard of from her parents. In terms of my own fieldwork, including with a number of others, that is also where my interests remained for several years. Although I have stayed in Grandma's household on many occasions throughout the years, my field notebooks contain very little about contemporary Southern Paiute life. My work with Grandma was specific, dealing with times past. My presence in her household and my interactions with her daughter and other members of her family were personal. I have never taken notes on this, nor would I write about it. For better or worse, my fieldwork is quite compartmental- ized.

It has been my personal relationships with the family, however, that also have caused me to write little about what I have learned from Grandma be- yond my dissertation and some short articles (Fowler 1972, 1986; Kelly and Fowler 1986).[2] A number of years ago, her daughter, I am sure out of cu- riosity about what our conversations might lead to, said to me one day: "I hope you will never write anything that will hurt my mother and father. I would not forgive you if you did." Her statement caused my first reflexivity. How could things from the past hurt Grandma and Grandpa? At first I could not imagine that they could. Those days were gone, and much of the knowledge of them had gone as well. Wouldn't people be sincerely inter- ested? Maybe they wouldn't even read the materials, as anthropologists al- ways had written principally for each other until then. But then the field was beginning to get into trouble for this and was increasingly under attack for not considering its impacts on native communities. This was happening worldwide, as native scholars began to read more and more of what had been written about them—often with disbelief and even disdain. Vine De- loria (1969) had recently published *Custer Died for Your Sins: An Indian Manifesto,* in which he proclaimed many anthropologists as public enemies of Indian people. What was it they thought they were doing, he wrote, coming to Indian reservations each summer, learning about Indian ways, publishing books for each other, without any consideration of the native persons or communities, the contemporary problems they faced, or any attempt to sincerely help them in modern life? Maybe what I was doing could hurt Grandma and Grandpa. Perhaps the community would get angry with them for having sold out, telling me things that I had no business knowing. How could I be sure? The safest bet was not to say or publish anything. Also, what I was learning was not doing them any particular good, in the practical sense. The Southern Paiute had been terminated from federal control in 1956, and they had not fared well. Poverty was severe, housing and educational levels were worse. But I was ill-equipped to deal with any of that. I had no training that I thought would do them any good at all.

I did continue to visit, however, and to telephone, and to maintain my friendships. My visits became shorter, and my conversations with Grandma more general. I still gathered a few plants for her, on my own after Grandpa passed away. Notebook entries were less frequent. I watched for evidences of activism within the community—AIM (American Indian Movement) or other major movements. Although there were none, I kept a low profile. I might have stopped going to the community altogether had it not been for my personal relationships.

In the early 1970s I became interested in museum studies, particularly studies of Great Basin material culture gathered in the last century or early in this one. My primary interests were still in the old ways, so approaching them through material culture and through the editing and publication of the field notes of others from times past seemed worthwhile. Given that the published ethnographic record from the region was at this time also slim, and not based on lengthy fieldwork, it also seemed wise to improve that record in as many ways as possible. Don and I had worked on the notes of John Wesley Powell, famed nineteenth-century Colorado River explorer, a year or two before (Fowler and Fowler 1969, 1971). As I started teaching at the University of Nevada, Reno, I began working on the field notes of Willard Park on the Northern Paiute of western Nevada, gathered in the 1930s. I received a grant to study the material culture collections he made, to be used as illustrations for the proposed monograph. The more I saw, the more I became convinced that museums were treasure troves of data of considerable importance to understanding the past. Social anthropologists had abandoned the study of material culture some decades before, but then I had never thought of myself as a social anthropologist. I was a Boasian ethnographer if I was anything. Boasians had done a great deal with material culture, but none of them had worked on Great Basin collections. Museum collections seemed to speak more eloquently than did the notes made by their collectors of the intricacies of subsistence—fishing, hunting, gathering—and also of a number of other aspects of culture. I visited several museums over the next few years, often with Don as my photographer, doing comparative studies of Northern Paiute, Southern Paiute, and Shoshone material culture. The more I saw the better I was able to contextualize older field notes and to understand the data on the natural world I had obtained through fieldwork (Fowler and Fowler 1981). I also became active in teaching in the university's interdisciplinary museology program, an interest I maintain to the present.[3]

Although my active fieldwork with Southern Paiute people had gone into partial dormancy, I began to work again with Northern Paiute people in the mid 1970s. Through the talented amateur anthropologist, the late Margaret (Peg) Wheat, I met Wuzzie George of Fallon, Nevada, another exceptional person with whom I maintained close ties for several years. Mrs. George was remarkable in many ways—a native ornithologist and a particularly keen observer of the natural world. She had been raised by her maternal grandmother in the small settlement of Stillwater, and, together with her grandmother, had daily collected duck eggs and ducklings, gathered plants in the marshes, deserts and uplands of the Stillwater Range, and hunted small mammals in these same localities. She was very close to her father, a well-known bird hunter. She was a basket maker, and skilled in making sagebrush bark clothing, building cattail houses, making tule duck decoys, and many other things (Fowler 1990; Wheat 1967). Her husband, Jimmy George, had been a well-known native doctor, who had cured an estimated 1,000 people throughout western Nevada and eastern California in his roughly forty years of active practice. Mrs. George had accompanied him frequently when he went doctoring and acted as his interpreter to the patient's family and friends. She was a true believer, a person of high intelligence, although her formal classroom education had been less than three months. She was very knowledgeable in the ways of her ancestors and keenly interested in sharing her knowledge. She would often say about our note taking or our tape recording, "You put him on paper," or "You put him in machine," as she was thoroughly convinced that what she knew was passing from the scene. Each generation, I am sure, thinks the next one is "going to the dogs" and not taking proper interest in the past. But Mrs. George, as were Mr. Sampson and Grandma, was quite convinced of it. Each of them liked to remember the past, to be asked questions that brought back fond memories. To be caused to think about all of that brought pleasure. Peg, Mrs. George, and I also had some good times and a lot of laughs as we wandered the desert in Peg's Volkswagen bus or on foot. When we were joined by Sven Liljeblad, who had worked with Mrs. George intermittently since the 1950s, we had even better times, since he was fluent in her language. Together we recorded songs and stories, and I learned even more about the natural world.

Although Mrs. George seemed to enjoy all of these activities, she did feel the sting of community criticism, especially when Peg's book *Survival Arts of the Primitive Paiutes* first appeared (Wheat 1967). Several of her friends accused her, and later Peg, of making lots of money. Neither was the case. Peg and Wuzzie's relationship survived, as did their relationships with other persons. But obviously many people, including Mrs. George, were not clear that a book would be the result of their conversations, and they were even less clear that such a publishing venture was unlikely to make money. Now the book is highly valued by many Indian people.

In 1978, Mrs. George had a stroke, and our period of intensive fieldwork regrettably began to draw to a close. We were able to complete a film, *Tule Technology,* featuring some of Mrs. George's skills, through the Smithsonian Institution's Office of Folklife Programs (Fowler 1990). Mrs. George still loved to see her birds, so we continued to take her on short trips about the marshes or bring her to sit by the Carson River so that she could watch them feed. She was buried on a bitter winter day in 1985, in her 105th year. No one will ever again know a fraction of what she knew or experience life as she did.

By the late 1970s, several native communities in the Great Basin had begun experimenting with cultural and language study programs, sometimes with federal funding, sometimes with tribal monies. People in Cedar City, as well as in western Nevada, began to ask me what I might know that could be of help. At last there seemed to be a community interest and, more importantly, a need for the types of data that I had been gathering. The need became a little overwhelming. It was then that I wished I had published more, rather than having to dig through my field notes or through my library to fulfill each request. Maybe I had been too cautious. When I looked at the data that were actually available in published sources that Indian people might be able to use, as opposed to the more esoteric theoretical and methodological ramblings for our colleagues, I could find little. It was just as well that several young Indian people were interested in doing their own interviews, as there was not a great deal of published material they could synthesize. I contributed what I could to workshops on writing native languages, doing oral interviews, and so forth. But most of the programs fell on hard times, either for lack of sustained funding, lack of consistent interest, or lack of trained personnel. I remain convinced that had federal or tribal funds been appropriated for curriculum development and teacher training well before anyone went into a classroom, most would have fared better. But budget cycles seemed not to allow for that. Everyone had to show results quickly, or no more support was forthcoming. The few programs that have had an impact in the region have been more modest efforts, moved slowly, and trained their personnel in advance.

As these interests began to grow, I also began to do more work with Grandma, by now in her nineties, partly at the request of her daughter. "Why don't you talk to Grandma like you used to anymore?" she queried. "She always seems better when you visit and ask her things. I don't know what to ask her. She just gets mad at me." True, Grandma did get mad at her own children. She somehow felt that they should know these important things, even though they had not lived them through experience as she had. She would tell them stories, as had been the teaching methods long ago. But it was hard for her to describe other things to them that they should have experienced first-hand. "You just don't pay attention," she would say. This is the dilemma of many young Indian people today who really do want to learn. They cannot play the naive observer, quite as I was able to do. In many senses, I got a precious gift from Grandma, Grandpa, Wuzzie George, and Harry Sampson. Young Indian people have to be willing to learn by doing, as was the old way. And, unfortunately, skilled teachers of those old traditions are now few. As one of Grandma's granddaughters recently remarked to me, "When I was young all I wanted was life in the fast lane. Not this old stuff. Now I know I have to be someone my children will look up to, and I have to learn. I am trying hard, but it isn't easy. And who will teach me?"

What I reviewed with Grandma in the last few years are the unpublished field notes of yet another Great Basin anthropologist, Isabel Kelly. Kelly worked in all Southern Paiute areas, including Grandma's area, in the 1930s (Kelly 1932–33, 1964). Using Kelly's notes as prompts, Grandma and I explored even more historical areas of past Southern Paiute life, including aspects of that all-important period of transition from Anglo settlement to the time of Kelly's recording. What has been most instructive about all of this to me is the realization that Kelly, too, was not working with pristine or aboriginal conditions, even though, she, as had her colleagues Julian Steward and Willard Park, presents the data with the implication that they represented an earlier period. By exploring with Grandma details of the lives of persons with whom Kelly worked—where they lived, what they did for a living—as well as her memories of that period, I can better understand the responses Kelly obtained and better interpret them.

The same is true of data from yet another project, an ethnography of the Stillwater Northern Paiute, based on my data as well as those gathered on tape by Peg Wheat over many years (Fowler 1992). These taped interviews have certain advantages that not even my work on the Kelly materials with Grandma can match. I can listen and re-listen to the responses made by Wuzzie George to specific questions put to her. Because I knew her well, I feel I understand far better what her answers really mean—when miscommunications have taken place, when people have properly understood as well as misunderstood her responses. Although I, too, have made extensive tape recordings of people through the years, I now wish I had all my data on tape, as I can see in my own notes places where I suspect I misunderstood or misinterpreted but was not fast enough to put more than a question mark. Those will do me no good now, given that Wuzzie George, Harry Sampson, and Grandma are gone. Grandma died in 1989, thus bringing to close our long relationship. She was somewhere near her 100th year.

Also within the past few years, I have moved somewhat reluctantly into the modern era, with studies of the potential socioeconomic and cultural impacts on Great Basin Native Americans of massive federal projects such as the MX missile and the Yucca Mountain Nuclear Waste Repository. Although I still prefer working with older people on older topics, these individuals and topics are now pertinent to contemporary questions—how to best preserve native rights and native lands. Armed with data on past, as well as contemporary, land use, and coupled with existing environmental legislation (American Indian Religious Freedom Act, National Environmental Policy Act, Archaeological Resources Protection Act, etc.), and in partnership with young as well as older tribal members, we are at least attempting to get some messages across. This is not an easy role for me, as I have had to learn in many situations to advise but not to be surprised if the tribe or individuals go in totally different directions. Sometimes they are absolutely right. Sometimes, from my perspective, they are wrong. But it is their fight, not mine, although I might feel quite strongly about some of the particular issues involved. I remain somewhat pessimistic about all of these endeavors, however. Native Americans in the Great Basin, as well as elsewhere, need to win a few of these battles against highly political decision-makers, or the war will soon not be worth fighting.

In retrospect, after twenty-eight years, as the title of this article indicates, I think I am beginning to understand something about the Great Basin Native American world. What I think I understand has largely come through long-term and continued involvement with persons, and with data gathered from various sources—fieldwork, archives, museum collections. In all, the long-term association with people has been the most rewarding. It is they who have helped me most to contextualize what it is I think that I know. By knowing individuals, I can better understand and evaluate their responses as well as the responses of others I don't know as well.

But there are another set of relationships that also have been important. They are the collegial ones. It has been especially important for me to have had Warren d'Azevedo as a colleague these many years—to be able to bounce ideas and problems off him—to utilize his fertile and insightful mind. Also, I owe a great debt to his wife, Kathleen, who without doubt knows people and the complexities of human relationships in and out of the field better than any of us. And to my other colleagues, some already named—Joy Leland, Sven Liljeblad, Bill Jacobsen, Peg Wheat, members of my department, and my husband, Don, I also owe intellectual debts. They, too, have been partners in the research.

Long-term relationships in fieldwork are not without difficulties. In long-term relationships, especially when the people with whom you work are already elderly, you unfortunately also must watch the slow, painful process of their personal deterioration. Ultimately, you witness their deaths. You reach a point in your fieldwork when you can no longer gather data from them as they are unable to give any longer. You ask yourself, "Why didn't I ask this or that, why didn't I do more or visit more often? Why don't other persons, their family members, other tribal members realize that these people are repositories of knowledge that can never be recovered? Why is the television the center of the household when it should be an elder?" The answers to these and many other questions are exceedingly complicated, and I guess in the last analysis, we outsiders, as well as family and community members, merely do what we can, learn what we can.

Lest I sound too pessimistic about the course of Native American culture change in the Great Basin, or stress too much the changes from the then of the nineteenth century, which has been my interest, to the now of the twentieth century, I need only think of Grandma's funeral, or, better, funerals in the summer of 1989. Her first funeral was an all night sing, a traditional mourning ceremony, conducted by an elderly gentlemen with a sharp, clear voice which he sustained in traditional song cycles with only a half-hour break for thirteen hours. He was backed up by five other singers from all over Southern Paiute country. All of Grandma's female family members helped to send her spirit on by respectfully dancing her clothing, pictures, and other possessions back and forth during the singing. Even granddaughters who prefer "life in the fast lane" fully participated. Small children slept, played, and on occasion appeared to be watching intently. Speeches were given in Grandma's language, to some persons who probably did not understand, but who paid attention anyway. Others were given in English, but the intent was the same. Grandma's second funeral was in the Cedar City Mormon Church, with the Bishop presiding. The church was filled with persons from the community, Anglo and Southern Paiute, who came out of respect for her. Nearly one-third of those in attendance—

roughly one hundred people—were immediate family members. Grandma left a living legacy as well as an intellectual one, and neither will soon fade from our midst.

As for me, I feel even now more keenly the obligations to get out some of the materials gathered from all of these individuals, but in a format that makes sense to the native communities, not just to my peers. I will continue to write some things that are probably of little worth to them, but I hope these can be balanced with some that are. Perhaps then the true nature of what has been our joint enterprise will be better evaluated and better understood.

Endnotes

1. I returned to the University of Pittsburgh in 1967 to complete a year's residency for the Ph.D. But until that time, my job had been as a research assistant, compiling bibliographic materials for the Center (Fowler 1970). The job allowed for some fieldwork, that done principally with Harry Sampson in conjunction with Joy Leland. I also taught in the Continuing Education Division of the university.
2. Another factor in this, perhaps, is that the record I had been able to compile was fragmentary—not monographic—and I did not understand fully what it meant historically or how to best present it.
3. In the early 1970s, I held a half-time appointment in the department of anthropology—the fate of many women of my generation in dual career marriages. (I was not also raising children, however, an additional factor in many women's career trajectories.) Under these conditions, there was little money or time apart from teaching for other than local fieldwork.

References Cited

Cottam, W. P.
1947   Is Utah Sahara Bound? *Bulletin of the University of Utah* 37:1–40. Salt Lake City.
Craig, C. G.
1987   Jacaltec: Field Work in Guatemala. In *Languages and Their Speakers,* edited by T. Shopen, pp. 3–58. University of Pennsylvania Press, Philadelphia.
Crick, M. J.
1982   Anthropological Field Research, Meaning Creation and Knowledge Con-

struction. In *Semantic Anthropology*, edited by D. Parkin, pp. 15–37. Association for Social Anthropology Monograph 22. Academic Press, London.

d'Azevedo, Warren L. (editor)

1963   *The Washo Indians of California and Nevada*. University of Utah Anthropological Papers no. 67. Salt Lake City.

Deloria, Vine

1969   *Custer Died for Your Sins: An Indian Manifesto*. Macmillan, New York.

Fowler, C. S.

1966   Environmental Setting and Natural Resources. In *Southern Paiute Ethnohistory*, edited by R. C. Euler, pp. 13–31. University of Utah Anthropological Papers no. 78. Salt Lake City.

1972   Comparative Numic Ethnobiology. Ph.D dissertation, Department of Anthropology, University of Pittsburgh, Pennsylvania.

1986   Subsistence. In *Handbook of North American Indians*, vol. 11, *Great Basin*, edited by W. L. d'Azevedo, pp. 64–97. Smithsonian Institution, Washington.

1990   *Tule Technology*. Smithsonian Folk Life Studies no. 6. Washington, D.C.

1992   *In the Shadow of Fox Peak: An Ethnography of the Cattaileater Northern Paiute People of Stillwater Marsh*. U.S. Fish and Wildlife Service, Portland, Oregon.

Fowler, C. S. (compiler)

1970   *Great Basin Anthropology: A Bibliography*. Desert Research Institute Publications in the Social Sciences and the Humanities no. 5. Reno, Nevada.

Fowler, C. S. (compiler and editor)

1989   *Willard Z. Park's Ethnographic Notes on the Northern Paiute of Western Nevada, 1933–1940*. University of Utah Anthropological Papers no. 114. Salt Lake City.

Fowler, C. S., and J. Leland

1967   Some Northern Paiute Native Categories. *Ethnology* 6(4):381–404.

Fowler, D. D., and C. S. Fowler

1969   John Wesley Powell, Anthropologist. *Utah Historical Quarterly* 37:152–172.

1981   The Uses of Ethnographic Museum Collections: Some Great Basin Examples. In *The Research Potential of Anthropological Museum Collections*, edited by A. M. Cantwell, J. B. Griffin, and N. A. Rothchilds, pp. 177–199. Annals of the New York Academy of Sciences 376.

Fowler, D. D., and C. S. Fowler (editors)

1971   *Anthropology of the Numa. John Wesley Powell's Manuscripts on the Numic Peoples of the Great Basin, 1868–1880*. Smithsonian Contributions to Anthropology no. 14. Washington, D.C.

Frake, C.

1962   The Ethnographic Study of Cognitive Systems. In *Anthropology and Human Behavior*, edited by T. Gladwin and W. Sturtevant, pp. 72–93. Anthropological Society of Washington, Washington.

Kelly, I. T.

1932–33 Unpublished Field Notes, Southern Paiute. Manuscripts in C. S. Fowler's possession.

1964   *Southern Paiute Ethnography.* University of Utah Anthropological Papers no. 69. Salt Lake City.

Kelly, I. T., and C. S. Fowler

1986   Southern Paiute. In *Handbook of North American Indians,* vol. 11, *Great Basin,* edited by W. L. d'Azevedo, pp. 368–397. Smithsonian Institution, Washington, D.C.

Pandey, T. N.

1972   Anthropologists at Zuni. *Proceedings of the American Philosophical Society* 116:4:321–37. Philadelphia.

Salinas, J.

1975   On the Clan of Anthropologists. In *The Human Way,* edited by H. R. Bernard, pp. x–xx. Macmillan, New York.

Simmons, L. (editor)

1942   *Sun Chief: The Autobiography of a Hopi Indian.* Yale University Press, New Haven (reprinted 1978).

Sweeney, C. L., and R. C. Euler

1963   *Southern Paiute Archaeology in the Glen Canyon Drainage: A Preliminary Report,* pp. 5–9. Nevada State Museum Papers no. 9. Carson City.

Wheat, M. M.

1967   *Survival Arts of the Primitive Paiutes.* University of Nevada Press, Reno.

Years and Careers
William A. Douglass

I begin by noting my personal and professional debt to Warren d'Azevedo who convinced me that you can go home again. I was born in Reno and did my undergraduate work in Spanish literature at the University of Nevada. At the time there was no anthropology department. Rather, anthropologists Mary Sellers and subsequently Arnold Strickon held appointments in sociology and were allowed to teach an anthropology course or two each semester. Their classes were my first exposure to the discipline that was to become my vocation. While on a junior-year-abroad program at the University of Madrid, I audited courses in the human geography of Spain. This convinced me to pursue graduate studies in social anthropology with the intention of returning to Iberia for field research. I eventually settled upon the Basque country, and between 1961 and 1963 I conducted field studies in two Spanish Basque villages.

Meanwhile, the University of Nevada launched the Desert Research Institute (DRI) in 1961. One of its four components was to become the Center for Western North American Studies with the mission of investigating the human dimension of Great Basin ecology. A team of consulting anthropologists—Fred Eggan from Chicago, Robert Heizer from Berkeley, and Omer Stewart from Boulder, Colorado—was brought in to help define the specific research agenda for the new center. Among their many suggestions was a plan to create a Basque studies program. This was in recognition of the fact that Basque sheepherders had been present in the American West for over a century, yet their role in the region's economy, ecology, and history was but poorly understood. Since no other American university had expressed an interest in the Basque Americans, they seemed to present a unique research opportunity for the nascent institute. The choice proved to be doubly fortuitous since, unbeknownst to its proposers, America was poised on the brink of a national fixation with its ethnic diversity. The projected Basque studies program was well timed to anticipate the outbreak of the "roots" phenomenon and the explosion of ethnic studies within American academia.

In 1963 Warren D'Azevedo came to Reno, hired jointly by DRI and the University of Nevada, Reno, department of sociology. In part he was to shape the Center for Western North American Studies and he was convinced that its success depended upon creating a viable anthropology department on the Reno campus. This became his first priority; however, the destinies of the center and the department were intertwined and remain so today.

My involvement began in 1965 when Warren d'Azevedo and Wendell Mordy, the founder of DRI, approached me with a job offer to start a Basque studies program. I had yet to complete my dissertation, and I must confess that I was ambivalent about returning to my hometown and undergraduate institution. Given my first-hand knowledge of the lack of anthropology in Reno a scant few years earlier, I found it difficult to believe that there was now a full-blown department. It was Warren's enthusiasm and vision of the future that made all the difference in a personal and professional decision that I have never regretted.

As I now turn to a discussion of the nature of long-term anthropological research I would first introduce a caveat. I expected that the contributions appearing before mine would simplify my task. They would break ground and I would climb upon their broad shoulders and peer over the horizon, all the while anticipating that mine would in turn provide the platform for the next contributor. In this fashion, and through our cumulative wisdom, we might have reached new heights in understanding the anthropological enterprise. At the very least we might have created a totem pole worthy of the *National Lampoon* or *Mad* magazine!

I no longer find the totemic imagery to be appropriate, however. I now realize that the commonalities in conducting social anthropological research far outweigh the differences. I would therefore invoke another metaphor to describe our collective task in this volume—that is, I would liken it to being handed a kaleidoscope. Each of us will hold it up to the light and give a twist, thereby creating a different pattern, but within the limits imposed by the same component chips. I could, as did Professor Ottenberg, discuss the interaction between myself and my informants as we both aged while attempting to cope with the rapidly changing world. Indeed, it was originally my intention to do so. However, I am afraid that would simply make his points with different anecdotes. I have decided, therefore, to view years and careers differently, indeed as an heuristic device through which to discuss certain developments within the field of anthropology and its institutionalization as an academic discipline. In this regard, I have three particular twists on my own career kaleidoscope that I shall explore.

First, unlike most social anthropologists, who work in Third World field settings, I have conducted my research in Europe. Second, long-term research for me did not mean a return to my original field sites. Rather, it entailed application of my knowledge of Old World cultural patterns to the study of the European emigrant diaspora worldwide. Third, unlike most anthropologists, my professional duties have focused more upon program building, administration, and research than upon teaching.

From the outset the study of cultural otherness was the hallmark of the anthropological enterprise. For armchair analysts like Morgan and Tylor, missionaries, travelers, and colonial administrators provided the cultural exotica, usually wrenched from context, that informed their grand evolutionary schemes, which pointed towards that culmination of the human endeavor known as Western civilization. After Malinowski, field research in non-Western settings became the methodological sine qua non of the discipline and the unavoidable *rite de passage* for its aspiring practitioners. It is only recently, then, that the anthropological purview of First World settings, particularly Europe and the United States, has gained qualified acceptance within the discipline. In part this is a simple expedient, a response to the dual conditions that much of the non-Western world no longer welcomes Western anthropologists on the one hand and that funding for anthropological research of any sort has diminished on the other. We, therefore, now have a situation in both Europe and the United States in which aspiring anthropologists sometimes finance their own field studies, which for practical reasons are then conducted within driving distance of their home institutions. While ameliorating somewhat, there is still a feeling within the discipline that such studies are not quite legitimate, that they are a compromise of the ideal, which is to mount a full-scale anthropological expedition in some remote corner of the globe.

To what can we attribute this reticence to regard First World settings as legitimate venues in which to conduct anthropological research? I believe in part it stems from the rather uninteresting, tacit jurisdictional agreement with our sister disciplines in the social sciences. Stated baldly and simplistically, the anthropologist who targets, say, urban America is trespassing on sociology's turf. Of greater philosophical interest, however, is the broader implication of this jurisdictional competition, namely, the fact that anthropology, harkening back to its intellectual roots, purports to study cultural others, whereas a study of urban America ostensibly targets our cultural selves.

Actually, while the urban American example makes a point, it does not reflect accurately the true thrust of the anthropological incursion into First World research. Rather than addressing mainstream Western culture, we have tended to dwell upon its more exotic eddies and backwaters, reflected in the concern with cultural enclaves within Western societies represented by certain immigrant and ethnic groups, religious sects, unassimilated native peoples, and socially marginal and countercultural groups.

In the case of Europe this assumes geographical expression in that the majority of European anthropological studies concentrate upon the Celtic fringe, island cultures, and the southern and eastern countries. It is not accidental that one of the earliest and, arguably, most influential European ethnographies was Julian Pitt-River's (1954) *The People of the Sierra*. For the young, Oxford-trained English aristocrat, Andalusia represented a degree of cultural otherness perhaps best captured by the dictum (attributed to Alexandre Dumas) regarding Spain that "Africa begins at the Pyrenees." To this day Hispanists represent the largest bloc within the ranks of Europeanist anthropologists, followed closely by Italianists, Hellenists, and Lusoists. Indeed, the southern bias is so pronounced that it has given rise to a whole new subfield, denominated Mediterranean studies, which has its own conferences, journals, university chairs, and polemics.[1]

If, from an Anglo-American perspective, the Mediterranean Basin may be regarded as the least Western expression of European culture, anthropologists working in its constituent countries have further refined the quest for cultural otherness. Clearly, I was attracted by the fact that the Basques represent an inexplicable, non-Indo-European cultural enclave within Iberia, a people manifesting a serological profile differing radically from that of surrounding populations and speaking a language that is unrelated to any other human tongue. As a social anthropologist I was not prepared to address the mystery of the origins of the Basques, but the conundrum certainly added to my personal fascination with the culture. It has proven beguiling for nearly a dozen other social anthropologists as well. Andalusia, too, has drawn its share of anthropological attention, as have the gypsies and such marginal groups as the transhumant, pastoralist Pasiegos of Asturias.

The second geographical expression of the quest for cultural otherness is our village-study approach. With a few notable exceptions, Europeanist anthropologists have focused upon rural rather than urban settings (Boissevain 1979). Within the rural hinterland, true to the legacy of *People of the Sierra,* more studies have focused upon mountain dwellers than upon the inhabitants of the seacoasts or the plains.

If social anthropology is currently racked by reflexivity, for Europeanists the reassessment of mission turns in part upon the appropriateness of the dominant little-community approach to our subject matter. The reasons why Europeanist anthropologists opted for a little-community focus are complex. In part they are intertwined with the emergence of peasant studies within the discipline as a whole. One need only read the works of Robert Redfield (1953, 1960) and George Foster (1960) to appreciate the extent to which Europe informed the field (peasant and peasantry are, after all, European concepts). At the same time our understanding of European peasant culture draws upon a comparative perspective regarding the nature of folk societies around the globe. I would argue, however, that the Europeanist fixation with remote, rural field settings is equally due to the nature of the anthropological perspective.

Anthropologists first turned their attention to Europe in the late 1940s and the 1950s, a period in which structural-functionalism was the dominant theoretical paradigm within the discipline. As graduate students we were trained to regard participant observation as *the* anthropological method, and its purpose was to gain a holistic overview of a particular culture. The approach was honed for and upon the study of the South Seas island or the African tribal segment.

As anthropologists began to address peasant cultures, the village provided a close analogue, a seemingly *manageable* unit for conducting a holistic field study. To be sure there were practical as well as theoretical problems with the approach, since it was not as plausible to treat the little community as a social isolate. Indeed, by definition that which distinguished peasant from primitive culture was the former's complex embeddedness within wider social structures. Hence, the peasant village was a part society, representative of the folk within a folk-urban continuum. Still and all, when studying the folk or peasant dimension of Third World countries, it did not seem too farfetched to treat the little community as a bounded, self-contained entity, at least for heuristic purposes. It also seemed reasonable to regard it as representative of a dominant or characteristic social and cultural reality. Thus Pul Eliya (Leach 1961) seemed an apt expression of Ceylonese culture while Chan Kom (Redfield and Villa Rojas 1962) encapsulated Yucatan's culture.

The same could not be said, however, for Europe. There, by the mid-twentieth century, it was debatable whether any village community could be regarded as sufficiently remote, either geographically or socially, to admit application of the social isolate paradigm. Conversely, even if such units could be identified they were likely to be so tangential to contemporary national reality as to call into question the relevancy of their study at all. Consequently, within the ranks of Europeanist anthropologists there is considerable debate over the appropriate research agenda, with one strong faction arguing that we must abandon our village studies altogether or become trivial (Boissevain 1979).

The little-community approach of Europeanist anthropology is beset by another dilemma as well. More than any other research setting, Europe posed particular intellectual challenges to our discipline. The two symbols of European culture are the plow and the book. The book represents both a penchant for record keeping and the institutionalization of the quest for knowledge. In practical terms this meant that every European community, no matter how remote its setting and insignificant its size, is situated in a conceptual time frame that may encompass several centuries of written records and in conceptual space that embraces regional, national, and even international networks. Neither by predilection nor formal training were anthropologists prepared to deal with these realities. Accustomed as we are to ignoring history altogether, or equating a few legends, myths, and the recollections of village elders with a community's past, most of the anthropological works on Europe have incurred the criticism of incorporating shoddy or simplistic historical knowledge.

And who are our critics? Our competitors, of course. For it is in the European setting that the anthropologist runs head-on into the entire panoply of established academic disciplines. Indeed, in turning to Europe we are returning to our intellectual roots, for in a very real sense Europe launched anthropology. A reading of Tylor's (1871) *Primitive Culture* or Frazer's (1890) *Golden Bough* reveals the extent to which an interest in European mythology and folk customs provided a comparative frame of reference for the founders of the discipline as they extended their purview to other world cultures.[2] This baseline European evidence was derived from the works of philologists, folklorists, classicists, archaeologists, ethnologists, physical anthropologists, historians, and others. The upshot is that, in framing a research problem in the European setting, the anthropologist is a late entrant into an arena dominated by established sister disciplines whose practitioners range from whole university departments, to well-established and well-regarded free-lance scholars and autodidacts whose decades of attention to local traditions make them far from dilettantes. When the anthropologist plunges into these crowded waters with limited language and archival skills, and with the intention of spending a year conducting participant-observation fieldwork prior to making holistic pronouncements about a community and, by extension, a culture, there is enormous potential for naivete and commitment of serious error of both fact and interpretation.

Lest I make too strong a case against the possibility or relevance of conducting meaningful anthropological research in the European context, and thereby repudiate most of my own efforts, let me state that I do believe we are uniquely situated to make a contribution—but only if we are prepared to pay our dues, and the price can be daunting. Let me illustrate by enumerating the methodological challenges posed by a study that I conducted in 1972–73 in southern Italy, in the town of Agnone in the region of the Alto Molise.

Until the early twentieth century, Agnone was an administrative, commercial, artisan, agricultural, and educational center of considerable importance. As the only town of any size (about 12,000 inhabitants in the mid-nineteenth century) in the Alto Molise, Agnone had its own hinterland of dependent villages. By the 1870s the region was characterized by extensive transatlantic emigration, a movement that continues down to the present. This, coupled with post-World War II migration to nearby urban centers, the industrial areas of northern Italy, and neighboring Common Market countries, has depleted the population of the Alto Molise. Today Agnone has about 6,000 persons and has largely been eclipsed as a significant urban place.

Given the magnitude of its decline, Agnone seemed to be an ideal place in which to examine my main research concern, which was the causes and consequences of emigration in south Italy. The question, as framed, is inherently historical and, as such, has been broached by a number of other investigators, employing such analytical devices as push-pull models and network theory to study patterns of chain migration between sending and receiving areas. However, in the case of Agnone there was an intriguing historical question that would not be ignored. According to nineteenth-century contemporary accounts, transatlantic emigration from the Molise *began* in the town.

To attempt to account for this fact was to pose historical questions of a different order of magnitude. It no longer sufficed to simply invoke the relative ecological and economic deprivation of south Italy, the region's tradition of political alienation and social atomism, and its longstanding history of social injustice as explanations for the propensity to emigrate. To be sure, at some level these and other generic factors were at work, but in and of themselves failed to account for Agnone's precocious role within the south Italian migratory movement. Rather, what was required was consideration of what made the community unique, in at least some respects, within the south Italian experience.

I concluded that certain features of Agnone's feudal heritage and its responses to the abolition of the feudal system predisposed the community to become one of the few bastions of nineteenth-century liberalism in south Italy. This, in turn, created the bases for pronounced social and political alienation in the ranks of the peasant and artisan classes, which, by the second half of the nineteenth century, began to manifest itself in a propensity for emigration. Such conclusions were gleaned from extensive archival research and embraced primary documentary sources dating from the fifteenth century down to the present, with a smattering of earlier evidence.

Rather than a scarcity of information, I was confronted with a bewildering wealth of sources. In Agnone itself there were two excellent libraries, one housed in the parish church of San Emidio and the other in the town hall, each maintained by a knowledgeable and dedicated scholar. Both were rich in primary source material, some of which dated from the Middle Ages. Each contained civil and ecclesiastical documentation, including such items as the records of former monasteries and convents, the town's fifteenth-century statutes and ordinances, and a mid-eighteenth-century household census listing the family structure, occupational makeup, assets, and liabilities of each domestic group. One of the libraries had complete runs of the several newspapers published in Agnone during the late nineteenth and early twentieth centuries. Each of the town's seven parishes had its own archive. The town hall had records dating from the early nineteenth century to the present, including vital statistics, census material, tax rolls, and the proceedings of the municipal council. There was also an extensive published literature of Agnone, including several personal memoirs and monographs by both nineteenth- and twentieth-century local historians. Indeed, the community had its own intellectual traditions, contributing a playwright, a theologian, and several pedagogues of Italian letters.

Relevant documentation regarding the town was scattered widely in ecclesiastical, state, and private archives located throughout south Italy and beyond. The operative languages of the research included Latin, Old Italian, Old Spanish, French, and modern Italian. It was also necessary to acquire certain paleographic skills.

What all of this meant was that I returned from the field with more than the standard set of anthropological field notes. Rather, my physical and intellectual baggage included two suitcases of handwritten and photocopied documents, generated by four field assistants, and over one-hundred rolls of microfilm taken with a portable microfilmer. Upon my return to Reno, despite the fact that I had limited teaching duties, transcription and prelimi-nary analysis of these data required five years. While other research interests intervened, I was never disassociated with the project for long, yet it was not until 1985, or some twelve years after the field research, that I pub-lished a book entitled *Emigration in a South Italian Town: An Anthropological History* (Douglass 1984). While I had no idea of what I was getting into, in retrospect I can see no other satisfactory way of framing the Agnone re-search. By the same token it will stand as a cautionary note regarding the peculiar demands that European anthropological research can make on both years and careers.

My second twist of the kaleidoscope refers to the fact that my long-term research has not entailed a periodic return to my original field sites, the two Basque villages of Murelaga and Echalar. Rather, I have applied the insights gleaned from my earlier Basque research to the study of the Basque emi-grant diaspora worldwide. The same could be said of my work in Italy.

Indeed, there is a sense in which I have spent more than a quarter of a century playing out the internal logic of a research design that I both pro-duced and of which I am a product. As noted earlier, because of my expe-rience with Old World Basque culture I was offered the position of coordi-nator of Basque studies at the University of Nevada. At the same time it was clear that the Desert Research Institute's interest in Basques centered on their impact as sheepherders upon the ecology of the Great Basin.

In my early years I traveled throughout the American West collecting oral histories from elderly informants, attending Basque festivals, and en-gaging in participant-observation by living periodically in Basque hotels and sheep camps. While this provided considerable standard social anthro-pological evidence of Basque immigrant adaptation in the American West, the analysis of which I could inform with my personal understanding of the immigrants' Old World cultural background, it became apparent that a crit-ical piece of the puzzle was missing. Basques had been emigrating for at least five centuries to four continents. Consequently, their movement to the American West was but one facet of a process that embraced enormous temporal depth and geographic breadth. I despaired of truly understanding the decision of a Basque emigrant to select Boise, Idaho, as a destination without understanding why the same individual rejected Buenos Aires, or the industrial city of Bilbao in his own homeland for that matter.

Consequently, I joined forces with my colleague Jon Bilbao, a historian by training, and we extended our research purview to the better-established Basque colonies of several Latin American countries. It was this comparative framework that allowed us to define what was truly unique about the Basque experience in the American West (Douglass and Bilbao 1975).

My next step was more fortuitous than foreordained. By the early 1970s, in part due to the Basques-in-the-New-World project, I had a growing interest in the theory of human migration. I was tempted to return to my original field sites in the Basque country, in part out of a feeling of nostalgia for persons and places scarcely visited in ten years. However, after having conducted more than three years of field and archival research in the two tiny communities, I doubted whether a fourth year would prove truly productive. I would argue that there is a point of diminishing returns in anthropological field research, and I was beginning to sense that I was at that juncture with respect to Echalar and Murelaga. It was, therefore, with somewhat heavy heart that I decided to look for another field site in a European locale characterized by massive transatlantic emigration.

Southern Italy loomed as both a logical and practical choice. For more than a century the area was one of the continent's prime seed beds of emigrants. In terms of its land tenure, family organization, and attitudes toward household, community and physical labor, south Italy provided major contrasts to Basque society. It therefore promised to provide significant variations upon the emigration theme.

There were other reasons for choosing a south Italian field site that were more personal than professional. My knowledge of Spanish promised to make the task of learning Italian easier. At the time Peter Benedict was teaching in the anthropology department at the University of Nevada, Reno. Peter and I were graduate students together at the University of Chicago. He had conducted fieldwork in a Turkish town and shared my interest in migration studies (Benedict 1974). His father was from the village of Pizzone in the Italian south, the family still owned land there, and Peter was anxious to combine anthropological research with a search for his own roots.

After a reconnaissance by car of several remote regions of southern Italy, we framed a joint project that was to center upon the town of Agnone, a community within an hour's drive of Pizzone. Peter subsequently withdrew from the study in order to become the director of the Ford Foundation's social science program in Turkey, and I ended up undertaking the Agnone study on my own. Parenthetically, I would note that there is almost always a personal side to the selection of field sites, a point that is underdeveloped in the literature regarding the nature of anthropological research.

I have already discussed some of the peculiar intellectual and methodological challenges posed by Agnone. At the same time, it was there that I was infected by the germ of my next field study. While in the Basque village of Murelaga in the early 1960s I had interviewed a few individuals who had worked as contract laborers cutting sugarcane manually in North Queensland, Australia, recruited by the sugar industry and the Australian government. In the mid-1960s the harvesting was mechanized, abolishing the cane-cutter profession. Some of the men had remained permanently in the sugar districts, others had resettled in Australian cities, notably Sydney and Melbourne, while most had returned to Europe.

In describing their lives in Australia, the Basque returnees emphasized an Italian influence. It seems that near the turn of the century Italians were the first Europeans to cut sugarcane in the tropics and had come to dominate most aspects of the industry, even acquiring many of the farms. Italian was therefore the *lingua franca* of the barracks where the cutters were housed, and all of my Basque informants had developed some fluency in the language. In the Alto Molise and Abruzzo I encountered returned emigrants who also had cut sugarcane in Queensland, and I even met a few individuals who *knew* my Basque informants from Murelaga.

I was therefore presented with a unique opportunity. Most immigration monographs begin with a chapter on the migrants' Old World background, usually stitched together from a reading of secondary sources. The body of the work then focuses upon the migrants' adaptation (or lack thereof) to the host society. Implicit, if not explicit, is the notion that they arrived with cultural baggage derived from their Old World background and that this somehow influenced or conditioned the assimilation process. I was presented with an intriguing opportunity to test this assumption. I had conducted anthropological field research in the two European sending areas and was therefore not a captive of other investigators' interpretations of the Old World settings. The experiences of both the Basque and Italian recruits were remarkably similar. Both were derived from rural backgrounds, both manifested similar educational and socioeconomic profiles before emigrating, both entered Australia in identical circumstances, even, in some cases, sharing the same employers and housing. Finally, the demise of manual harvesting forced both groups to opt for a new future, whether in Australia or Europe. In short, the circumstances were about as close to a controlled laboratory experiment as one is likely to encounter in an anthropological field-study situation. Therefore, in 1980 I conducted field research in North Queensland. I also surveyed a cohort of twenty-five Basques and twenty-five Italians who remained in the sugar districts and twenty-five of each who had resettled elsewhere in Australia. The following year I interviewed similar cohorts of returned migrants in the Basque country and in south Italy.

I am still preparing the results of the study for publication. For present purposes, however, the point is that the long-term anthropological study need not entail progressively deeper and deeper penetration into the cultural reality of a single field site, a kind of peeling back of the layers of an onion until closure is effected by using up the core. Rather, in the case of my studies of the Basque and Italian emigrant *diasporae,* each phase itself became an aperture, a window upon a new, yet linked cultural reality the study of which was informed by a common, yet cumulative, theoretical thread.

Lest I sound too purposive or prescient, however, let me now give a third twist to the kaleidoscope. A noted Spanish social historian, Julio Caro Baroja (1968), once wrote a book entitled *El Señor Inquisidor y Otras Vidas por Oficio,* which might be translated as *The Lord Inquisitor and Other Lives by Definition.* In it he argues that there are certain professions in which the behavior of the incumbent is preordained—institutionally predetermined. I believe there is a sense in which this applied to my career once I opted for an appointment at the Desert Research Institute. It is worth discussing some of the implications of that decision, particularly since the subsequent crunch in the academic job market has forced many anthropologists to seek such "soft-money" positions rather than standard teaching appointments.

For the teaching academic occupying a tenure-track post, research and publishing are part-time activities scheduled for early mornings, late afternoons, and evenings, weekends, and summers. Given the pressure of other career demands there is a built-in penchant or incentive to rework familiar material. In the case of anthropologists this may well lead to the long-term field study entailing return visits to the same field sites and extended contact with key informants. In fact, this penchant so worried Evans-Pritchard (1951:76) that he felt compelled to exhort aspiring anthropologists to conduct fieldwork in at least two distinct cultures, reasoning that in order to become a rounded professional one had to have a comparative perspective that transcended simple reading of published ethnographies. Indeed, within academia there is institutionalized recognition, reflected in the system of sabbatical leaves, of the dangers of intellectual introspection. It is the purpose of the sabbatical to allow otherwise harried and buried professors the breathing room either to bring a major piece of research to successful conclusion or to retool by undertaking a new research initiative.

If, however, one casts his or her lot with a "soft-money" organization, such as the Desert Research Institute, the pressures of imperatives shift. By definition you are forced to become an academic entrepreneur. Ideally you have the potential of enjoying maximum intellectual freedom and near total flexibility regarding your research goals. De facto your freedom is limited by your capacity to fund your own activities. Failure to do so can quickly lead to rather arbitrary assignment to team projects or even to dismissal. You are therefore vulnerable to external agendas, and particularly to the research priorities of the public and private granting agencies.

There is, therefore, a qualitative difference between seeking a summer stipend or sabbatical support to pursue one's research interests and trying to fund a whole career by means of grants. If you are engaged in the latter there is an ever-present danger of intellectual and even ethical compromise. The situation is rarely black or white, however, and, contrary to pregnancy, it is possible to become just a little bit compromised. By this I mean that most people working in a research institute setting are pursuing some sort of mixed strategy that permits them to survive when between grants. Most are sufficiently successful at this juggling act so as not to lose sight of their priorities. Also, in fairness to the administrators of most research organizations, the produce-or-perish standard is rarely applied ruthlessly. Rather, it is more common for unsupported staff to be carried on discretionary funds for at least a year or two.

The main point I wish to make is that the soft-money-support syndrome imposes upon the investigator certain rules of its own, rules that have decisive implications for an anthropologist aspiring to long-term research. Rule one is that your project must be ambitious. That is, it is in both your interest and in that of the institute to frame a relatively expensive, multiyear study. You are thereby relieved from the onus of proposal writing and the psychological worry over job security; the institution is rewarded by substantial indirect cost recovery, which is its prime source of financial flexibility. The alternative of trying to fund yourself with a series of small grants is inefficient and risky, both from the individual and institutional standpoints. Rule two is that it is much easier to fund a new initiative than to retrace your steps. Agencies might give you a few thousand dollars to spend a summer back in your original field site looking at some new problem; they are much less likely to give you $100,000 to return there for several years. A third rule is that granting agencies fund research rather than writing. This means that over time one is likely to amass volumes of data, the analysis of which must be subordinated to the time demands of proposal preparation for yet another original research project.

While I like to think that a large measure of personal predilection shaped my career agenda, in truth I recognize that I also have lived one of Caro Baroja's lives by definition, determined at least in part by the operation of the three rules of soft-money survival. I have never regretted my approximately ten years at the Desert Research Institute nor do I regret leaving it. The life of the soft-money researcher may be likened to that of the professional athlete. It is glamorous while it lasts but it really is a young person's game.

Having been a player, I am left with a certain legacy. There are, of course, the filing cabinets crammed with data that will take the rest of my life to analyze. There is also a certain perspective regarding the anthropological enterprise, both as it is viewed by the wider society and in terms of its internal organization. At the risk of sounding overly cynical, I think it is worth raising some of these points.

The organization of research funding ultimately reflects our society's priorities. During the 1960s and early 1970s America had a brief romance with the social sciences; indeed there were a few years in which anthropology was the ascendant social science, touted as the corrective to the Western bias within our sister disciplines. Whatever the reasons, and they are complex, the romance has soured. For a brief period it seemed possible for anthropology to occupy a privileged position within the nation's research agenda. In retrospect I believe this led to self-delusion even in the best of times. There were, after all, only a handful of agencies that ever funded our efforts and the commitments were never of a magnitude to provide us with indefinite continuity in settings like the Desert Research Institute. Society wants to cure cancer, probe space, invent machines, control (and then clean up) the natural environment; despite our protestations our efforts are regarded by most of our fellow citizens as a curiosity or a luxury. Ultimately, our lot is more likely to be cast with philosophers than with physicists, a not altogether intolerable fate but not a particularly lucrative one.

At the present time, reflexivity rages within our discipline, triggered in part by the Third World's rejection of First World practitioners of an allegedly imperialistic and paternalistic profession (Clifford and Marcus 1986; Marcus and Fischer 1986). Our pain and guilt are exacerbated by the fact, with a few exceptions, that anthropologists are well-intentioned and altruistic, at times even to the point of naivete. What I would argue, however, is that there is another dimension to our predicament that has received much less attention. Not only have we lost our entree to many of the societies that have hosted our research, we also have lost much of our mandate within the society that sponsored it. Over the past ten years we have made a virtue of deconstruction, which is to say that our former penchant for grand theory and what at least some now denounce with considerable disdain as scientism, has been replaced by near intellectual anarchy.[3] We no longer invoke organic or mechanical models of society; we question whether it is even possible to comprehend cultural otherness, let alone communicate its essence adequately to our audience. In short, we now exalt the complexity of the human condition and are leery of attempts to reduce human behavior to a few discoverable principles. Who would deign, let alone dare, to predict the future predicated upon our analyses of the present and the past? In short, the greening of anthropology has proceeded apace and we are now humanists.[4]

To illustrate the point there are the contents of our publications. A recent issue of *Current Anthropology* has an article by Roger Keesing (1989) entitled "Exotic Readings of Cultural Texts" and a short comment by John Bousfield and John Davis (1989) posing the question "What if Sophistry is Universal?" An equally fresh *American Anthropologist* features an article by

Erve Chambers (1989) entitled "Thalia's Revenge: Ethnography and Theory of Comedy," which reviews eighteenth-century English satire and the place of comedy in Western intellectual traditions. Then there is the issue of *Man* that features an article by Ralph Bulmer (1989), "The Uncleanness of the Birds of Leviticus and Deuteronomy," which effects an anthropological analysis of certain passages of the Old Testament. There is also an article by Daniel A. Segal and Richard Handler (1989) entitled "Serious Play: Creative Dance and Dramatic Sensibility in Jane Austen, Ethnographer."

To read much of the soul-searching and debate that brought us to this juncture is to be told that it was a natural process, a combination of evolving awareness and deepening understanding of our strengths and limitations as a discipline. I am afraid that for a veteran of the soft-money wars like myself much of this discussion comes across as purist to the point of being simplistic. I can't help but be struck by the coincidence that the former major single source of funding for social anthropological research, the National Institute of Mental Health, essentially turned its back on the discipline. The National Science Foundation's commitment remained static and its priorities have begun to shift away from social anthropology to physical anthropology and prehistory. Meanwhile, the National Endowment for the Humanities broadened its guidelines to encompass anthropology. Is it therefore surprising that our penchants, not to mention our proposals, have acquired a less scientistic overtone? Move over Derrida!

Thus far I have been discussing the consequences as an individual researcher of my decision to join the staff of the Desert Research Institute. There was, however, a whole other dimension to the commitment that raises issues regarding the long-term relationship between an anthropologist and his subjects. I refer to the fact that I was brought to Nevada to start the Basque Studies Program. Actually, it is probably more accurate to state that I was charged with inventing the program since neither my employers nor I held strongly preconceived ideas about its content. What was clear was that the effort should acquire an anthropological orientation reflecting, at least in part, the funding priorities of granting agencies in the late 1960s. At the same time it was evident that the Desert Research Institute's interest in the Basques was their impact as sheepherders upon Great Basin ecology. My decision to study the Basque sheepherder of the American West therefore derived more from an institutional imperative than from personal predilection. Had I accepted a standard teaching position elsewhere I suspect I would never have studied the Basques of the American West. Conversely, it is likely that I would have pursued my European Basque interests more assiduously since, indeed, I had a competing job offer from Morton Levine of Vassar College, who also had conducted Old World Basque field research. Morton's work focused upon the prehistory, prehistoric art, and physical anthropology of the Basque country. He had the support of Margaret Mead and the American Museum of Natural History to create a Basque studies program with a very different focus from the one that was eventually established at the University of Nevada, Reno.

There was another reality that was perceived, but dimly, in the initial stages of our program building, but which ultimately profoundly influenced its direction. At Vassar College and the American Museum of Natural History, a Basque studies program would have remained exclusively research oriented. In Reno the very geographic setting placed it squarely at the center of Basque settlement in the American West. This meant that not only were we enmeshed in our research context, we were also confronted with a constituency.

Therefore, from the outset the Basque Americans placed certain demands upon our fledgling organization. Did we plan to teach the language? Would we do so through correspondence courses? What does the grandfather's last name—Bastanchury—mean? Can you tell me what happened to his brother Michel who came to the United States in 1878 and was never heard from again?

Then there was the growing fascination with Basque culture among the wider public. In 1957 Robert Laxalt published his critically acclaimed novel *Sweet Promised Land,* the story of his father's life as a sheepman in the American West. The book was an instant success and its impact operated at several levels. It gave the nation its first insight into the Basque American experience. For Nevadans in general it became a point of pride, an alternative image for a state ambivalent about its glitzy reputation. For Basque Americans the book triggered ethnic pride, an ennoblement of a sheepherder heritage, which had previously been down-played when not denigrated.

In 1959 Basque Americans held their first public festival in Sparks, Nevada. During the early 1960s, festivals and Basque social clubs proliferated throughout the American West. Indeed, this activity generated part of the stimulus for founding the Basque Studies Program, which, in turn, provided the Basque American experience with its scholarly credentials. Consequently, from the outset the program functioned in a public arena. It regularly received requests for lectures about the Basques that ran the gamut from Boy Scout troops and Rotary clubs to other American universities.

There was, of course, a serious scholarly dimension to the program as well. In part this was facilitated by another fortuitous, or at least external, factor. Spain was in the throes of the Franco dictatorship and the Spanish Basques were its most implacable foes. It was therefore impossible to organize formal Basque studies in the Basque homeland itself. This conferred upon our fledgling program both a unique opportunity and responsibility. For the first decade of its existence many European Basque scholars and institutions regarded the Basque Studies Program as a beacon, a bastion, indeed a safe haven for a beleaguered culture. In 1968 Jon Bilbao joined our staff. His role as the author (Bilbao 1970–81, 1985–87) of the standard bibliographic work in Basque studies made Reno the clearing house for Basque scholarship worldwide. Jon's extensive bibliographic ties made it possible to create here, within an astoundingly short period of time, a world-class Basque library, which itself became a magnet for Basque scholars from throughout the United States, Latin America, and Europe.

To meet the demands of all these constituencies the Basque Studies Program rapidly evolved dimensions that transcended the Desert Research Institute's research orientation. We established a newsletter for Basque Americans; created a publications series within the University of Nevada Press; instituted courses on the Reno campus in Basque history, anthropology, language, and literature; and established study-abroad programs in the Basque country for American students. Consequently, in the mid-1970s the Basque Studies Program was transferred from the Desert Research Institute to the University of Nevada, Reno, where it remains today.

For my present introspective purposes, the point to be made is that the Basque Studies Program became my vehicle for addressing the anthropologist's personal dilemma of his ongoing relationship with the persons and culture that attracted his attention in the first place. Simon Ottenberg (this volume) discussed in depth the parallels between his personal development and the dizzying pace of change in African Afikpo society. As he became older he became an elder, his earlier published work serving as Afikpo culture's written charter, its repository of traditional knowledge, as it postured itself to face the twenty-first century. Given the nature of the societies we study, coupled with the incredible changes they have experienced in recent times, practically any anthropologist whose years and career span a quarter of a century or more is likely to echo Ottenburg's sentiments.

I certainly can with respect to the Basques. The rural society I had studied in the early 1960s is a world that has all but disappeared and the awareness of it now persists in part through the acquired knowledge and cumulative effect of the Basque Studies Program's nearly quarter of a century of existence. Indeed, this is so much the case that it might be said we are now producers of the very culture that we purport to study. If we consider, for example, some of the interesting research questions surrounding the persistence of spoken Basque in the American West it is difficult to factor ourselves out of the equation. We provide Basque Americans with courses in the language and are a main vehicle facilitating their stays in the Basque homeland. Our study-abroad programs now have alumnae sprinkled throughout the Basque communities of the American West. In many cases they have assumed a leadership role within the local Basque club or dance group, which permits them to advocate Basque language instruction. We recently developed and published a Basque-English dictionary (Aulestia 1989; Aulestia and White 1990) and a Basque grammar for English speakers (King 1994). These publications promise to become the medium for introducing *Euskera Batua,* of the Unified Literary form of the language, into the American West. *Euskera Batua* was developed quite recently by the Basque Academy and is now the main vehicle of expression in the mass media of the Basque country. Most of the Basque emigrants to the American West left Europe before the introduction of this speech form and are therefore not conversant in it. In short, our studies of the persistence of spoken Basque in the American West and the evolution of its form must take into account the Basque Studies Program's impact upon the preservation of Basque culture in the Basque American community. This becomes, then, applied anthropology of a special nature, removed from the economic and medical issues that inform most attempts at practical application of anthropological expertise.

As I contemplate my years and career with regard to my original and abiding interest in the Basques I am both gladdened and saddened. It has been a privilege and a wonderful adventure to be associated with the successes of the Basque Studies Program. At the same time by riding that particular horse I have become more of a purveyor than student of the culture. In the process I have all but lost touch with the young graduate student who once had the time and energy to hike Pyrenean trails in order to visit every family in two remote villages. I no longer merit the compliment that I once cherished. Salvadora, an elderly tavern-keeper, used to laugh and tell her customers, "If you want to learn something about Echalar ask Guillermo; he even knows the mice here by their first names!" Last May I returned to Echalar for my first visit in ten years. Salvadora no longer recognized me. I am not sure she should have!

Finally, at the risk of becoming maudlin or at least sounding cranky I would conclude with a few observations about the state of the debate within contemporary anthropology. While I recognize our past sins and understand the need for self-confession and collective reflexivity, both as belated acts of atonement and ostensible bases for some sort of new beginning, I cannot help but be somewhat nostalgic for the good old days. I refer to the time when ethnography was conducted with pride rather than apology, and anthropologyland, to steal a metaphor from Bernard Cohn (1980), was divided into feudal fiefdoms in which Warren d'Azevedo could be the Baron of Gola, Simon Ottenberg Count Afikpo, and I the Duke of Basque. To be sure it was a fantasy world, resting precariously upon the fiction that one observer, and an outsider at that, could gain a comprehensive overview of a whole culture. It encapsulated the arrogance inherent in the notion of "my people" and the assumption that by undergoing the physical and psychological stress of a field stint among them one had somehow earned the right to be their interpreter, apologist, and even cultural gatekeeper. However, as with other ages of chivalry in different times and places, there was a code of conduct in feudal anthropologyland that was not altogether unattractive. Like the quest for the Holy Grail the search for ethnographic knowledge was an individual journey. There was, however, a sense of common mission that determined the research agenda, namely, the almost sacred charge of documenting the variety of the human experience at the time when many cultures faced extinction.

The ethnographic report became our sacred text, deriving its authority from what Geertz (1988) recently has called the act of "I-witnessing." That is, authority was authorial, stemming from the account of an observer converted through the act of observation into *the* expert witness. Each of the fiefs within feudal anthropologyland had its text that was not to be trifled with. We need only recall the reaction that greeted Oscar Lewis's (1951) restudy of Tepoztlán, which called into question the accuracy of Robert Redfield's (1930) original analysis of that Mexican town. Even those who conceded that Lewis was probably right were at least mildly outraged by the act. Lewis was in clear trespass and thereby in violation of an unwritten code that reserved a preserve to each of the lords of feudal anthropologyland. To a degree Lewis never quite recovered from the stigma, which made him a bit of a pariah among his peers. Perhaps his crime was to engage in reflexivity before its time.

Given the choice between the world according to Redfield versus the world according to Lewis I would linger in the former. I fear, however, that this is unrealistic since anthropologyland has come of age, making those of us who were trained in the old schools of ethnography as anachronistic as the primitive and peasant cultures we studied. We can retool or retire. For a person my age this is not an altogether pleasant prospect since I am too young to retire and too tired to retool.

As I grapple with this personal dilemma I am not left totally devoid of a sense of mission. For I, too, am becoming an elder within a particular culture, the culture of anthropology. It is not coincidental at this acerbic stage in our discipline's soul-searching that we are beginning, as in this volume, to take another look. Which is to say that there is a correlation between our discipline's current muddled vision of its future and a growing propensity to contemplate its past. This is perhaps most evident in another trend within our journals, which is to publish in-depth sketches of individual anthropologists. At times framed in an interview format while at others in that quintessential humanistic document—the biographical sketch—many of our elders have been asked to divulge the past, assess the present, and speculate about the future, using their own years and careers as the medium. To cite but a few examples such notables as Maurice Bloch (Houtman 1988), Claude Lévi-Strauss (Augé 1990), Raymond Firth (Parkin 1988), Eric Wolf (Friedman 1987), and P. E. de Josselin de Jong (Fox 1989) have been queried. A 1934 interview with Marcel Mauss (Murray 1989) was exhumed. Sol Tax (1988) was asked to write an autobiographical memoir, while the careers of Frederica de Laguna (McClellan 1989) and Meyer Fortes (Drucker-Brown 1989) received biographical treatment. To some this may seem an exercise in self-indulgence or the diversion of eclipsed persons; however, I would argue that the very future of anthropology hangs in the balance.

Endnotes

1. Contrast, for example, Boissevain (1979), Davis (1977), Gilmore (1982), Herzfeld (1984), Llobera (1986), Pina-Cabral (1989).
2. In so doing they were simply emulating sixteenth-century European scholars who sought to bring the behavior of newly discovered cultural others into some sort of logical perspective. According to McGrane (1989:22): "These practices and beliefs became intelligible because they were seen in a relation of repetition, of analogical repetition, with the Ancient Greeks. And, reciprocally, the seemingly invincible strangeness of the Greeks became less alien, less incomprehensible, insofar as it could be related to the practices and customs of the inhabitants of the New World. The alienness of the pre-Christian past became suddenly familiarized in simultaneity with the alienness of the extra-Christian present."
3. There may, however, be signs of an impending (the inevitable?) backlash. At the 1989 annual meeting of the American Anthropological Association one of the best-attended sessions was entitled "Anti-anti-science: A four-field critique of the work of science-bashing anthropologists" (Eades 1990:15)!
4. The distinction between scientific and humanistic anthropology should not be overdrawn since both tendencies have been, and continue to be, inherent in the discipline since its founding. Indeed, one paradigm for writing our intellectual history is to treat particular eras in terms of the temporary ascendancy of one of these tendencies over the other. More than a quarter of a century ago Eric Wolf (1964:88) underscored the difficulty of disaggregating anthropology into its scientistic and humanistic elements by noting, ". . . anthropology is . . . less subject matter than a bond between subject matters. It is in part history, part literature; in part natural sciences, part social science; it strives to study men both from within and from without; it represents both a manner of looking at man and a vision of man—the most scientific of the humanities, the most humanist of the sciences."

    A decade ago, or when anthropologists by and large were still learning to spell, rather than practice, hermeneutics, two major figures peered over the horizon, as it were, to speculate about the immediate future of the discipline. At the time sociobiology was fashionable, though neither would-be seer believed it to be anthropology's future direction. Rather, for both the issue turned more upon the old conundrum of the relationship between anthropology and the humanities. Paul Bohannan, in his 1979 presidential address to the American Anthropological Association, predicted that the future lay in the direction of the policy sciences. Reviewing anthropology's prospects in a post-colonial, nuclear age beset with major environmental problems, his address, entitled "You Can't Do Nothing," was an appeal for personal and professional engagement. He envisioned a new applied anthropology in which anthropologists would not just join the ranks but would assume a leadership role amongst the policy sciences (1980:519–520). Regarding the humanities he noted: "The humanities, by and large, are in a completely different realm of discourse from the social sciences—the insights of one can often illuminate the other, and the data of one can be used as fodder for the other. But that is not the point. They are not in any sort of epigenetic relationship."

Meanwhile, in Reno during the 1979 annual fall lecture to the Humanities Council of the State of Nevada, Clifford Geertz (1980:178) posited the diametrically opposed view that: "The golden age (or perhaps it was only brass) of the social sciences when, whatever the differences in theoretical positions and empirical claims, the basic goal of the enterprise was universally agreed upon—to find out the dynamics of collective life and alter them in desired directions—has clearly passed. There are too many social scientists at work today for whom the anatomization of thought is wanted, not the manipulation of behavior." For Geertz (1980:168) anthropology was becoming (and would become) interpretative rather than mechanistic and axiomatic in orientation. He noted: "The recourse to the humanities for explanatory analogies in the social sciences is at once evidence of the destabilization of the genres and of the rise of 'the interpretive turn,' and their most visible outcome is a revised style of discourse in social studies."

Published in *The American Scholar* as "Blurred Genres: The Reconfiguration of Social Thought," Geertz's piece was both seminal statement and harbinger of developments within the discipline during the 1980s. By the same token for Geertz the blurring of genres was no panacea. Indeed, he (Geertz 1980:168–169) was prescient when noting: "All this fiddling around with the proprieties of composition, inquiry, and explanation represents, of course, a radical alteration in the sociological imagination, propelling it in directions both difficult and unfamiliar. And like all such changes in fashions of the mind, it is about as likely to lead to obscurity and illusion as it is to precision and truth. If the result is not to elaborate chatter or the higher nonsense, a critical consciousness will have to be developed; and as so much more of the imagery, method, theory and style is to be drawn from the humanities than previously, it will mostly have to come from humanists and their apologists rather than from natural scientists and theirs. That humanists, after years of regarding social scientists as technologists or interlopers, are scarcely equipped to do this is something of an understatement. Social scientists, having just freed themselves, and then only partially, from dreams of social physics—covering laws, unified science, operationalism, and all that—are hardly any better equipped."

In retrospect one finds Geertz's predictions more accurate than Bohannan's in characterizing anthropology in the 1980s. However, as a Hegelian (and cynic) I suspect that Bohannan may yet enjoy "delayed gratification."

References Cited

Augé, Marc
1990   Ten Questions Put to Lévi-Strauss. *Current Anthropology* 31(1):85–90.
Aulestia, Gorka
1989   *Basque-English Dictionary.* University of Nevada Press, Reno.
Aulestia, Gorka, and Linda White
1990   *English-Basque Dictionary.* University of Nevada Press, Reno.
Benedict, Peter
1974   *Ula: An Anatolian Town.* Brill, Leiden.
Bilbao, Jon
1970–81 *Eusko Bibliographia (Enciclopedia general illustrada del Pais Vasco; Cuerpo C).*
        10 vols. Editorial Aunamendi, San Sebastian, Spain.
1985–87 *Eusko Bibliographia, 1976–1980.* 3 vols. Servicio Editorial Universidad del
        Pais Vasco, Bilbao, Spain.
Bohannan, Paul
1980   You Can't Do Nothing. *American Anthropologist* 82(3):508–524.
Boissevain, Jeremy
1979   Toward an Anthropology of the Mediterranean. *Current Anthropology*
        20:81–93.
Bousfield, John, and John Davis
1989   What if Sophistry Is Universal? *Current Anthropology* 30(4):517–518.
Bulmer, Ralph
1989   The Uncleanness of the Birds of Leviticus and Deuteronomy. *Man*
        24(2):304–321.
Caro Baroja, Julio
1968   *El Señor Inquisidor y Otras Vidas por Oficio.* Alianza Editorial, Madrid.
Chambers, Erve
1989   Thalia's Revenge: Ethnography and Theory of Comedy. *American Anthropologist* 91(3):589–598.

Clifford, James, and George E. Marcus
1986   *Writing Culture. The Poetics and Politics of Ethnography.* University of California Press, Berkeley.

Cohn, Bernard
1980   History and Anthropology: The State of Play. *Comparative Studies in Society and History* 22(2):198–221.

Douglass, William A.
1984   *Emigration in a South Italian Town. An Anthropological History.* Rutgers University Press, New Brunswick.

Douglass, William A., and Jon Bilbao
1975   *Amerikanuak. Basques in the New World.* University of Nevada Press, Reno.

Drucker-Brown, Susan
1989   Notes toward a Biography of Meyer Fortes. *American Ethnologist* 16(2):375–385.

Eades, Jerry
1990   Power, Paradigms and Poverty. *Anthropology Today* 6(2):15–16.

Evans-Pritchard, E. E.
1951   *Social Anthropology.* Cohen and West, London.

Foster, George M.
1960   *Culture and Conquest. America's Spanish Heritage.* Viking Fund Publications in Anthropology 27. Wenner Gren Foundation, New York.

Fox, James J.
1989   An Interview with P. E. de Josselin de Jong. *Current Anthropology* 30(4):501–510.

Frazer, James George
1890   *The Golden Bough: A Study in Comparative Religion.* Macmillan and Co., London and New York.

Friedman, Jonathan
1987   An Interview with Eric Wolf. *Current Anthropology* 28(1):107–118.

Geertz, Clifford
1980   Blurred Genres. The Reconfiguration of Social Thought. *The American Scholar* 29(2):165–179.
1988   *Works and Lives. The Anthropologist as Author.* Stanford University Press, Stanford.

Gilmore, David D.
1982   Anthropology of the Mediterranean Area. *Annual Review of Anthropology* 11:175–205.

Herzfeld, Michael
1984   The Horns of the Mediterraneanist Dilemma. *American Ethnologist* 11:434–454.

Houtman, Gustav
1988   Interview with Maurice Bloch. *Anthropology Today* 4(1):18–21.

Keesing, Roger M.

1989   Exotic Readings of Cultural Texts. *Current Anthropology* 30(4):459–479.

King, Alan R.

1994   *Basque Grammar: An Introduction to the Language.* University of Nevada Press, Reno.

Laxalt, Robert

1957   *Sweet Promised Land.* Harper and Row, New York.

Leach, Edmund R.

1961   *Pul Eliya. A Village in Ceylon.* Cambridge University Press, Cambridge.

Lewis, Oscar

1951   *Life in a Mexican Village: Tepoztlán Restudied.* University of Illinois Press, Urbana.

Llobera, Joseph R.

1986   Field Work in Southwestern Europe. Anthropological Panacea or Epistemological Straitjacket? *Critique of Anthropology* 6(2):25–33.

Marcus, George E., and Michael M. J. Fischer

1986   *Anthropology as Cultural Critique. An Experimental Moment in the Human Sciences.* University of Chicago Press, Chicago.

McClellan, Catharine

1989   Frederica de Laguna and the Pleasures of Anthropology. *American Ethnologist* 16(4):766–785.

McGrane, Bernard

1989   *Beyond Anthropology. Society and the Other.* Columbia University Press, New York.

Murray, Stephen O.

1989   A 1934 Interview with Marcel Mauss. *American Ethnologist* 16(1):163–167.

Parkin, David

1988   An Interview with Raymond Firth. *Current Anthropology* 29(2):327–341.

Pina-Cabral, Joo de

1989   The Mediterranean as a Category of Regional Comparison: A Critical View. *Current Anthropology* 30(3):399–406.

Pitt-Rivers, Julian

1954   *The People of the Sierra.* University of Chicago Press, Chicago.

Redfield, Robert

1930   *Tepoztlán—a Mexican Village.* University of Chicago Press, Chicago.

1953   *The Primitive World and its Transformations.* Cornell University Press, Ithaca.

1960   *The Little Community/Peasant Society and Culture.* University of Chicago Press, Chicago.

Redfield, Robert, and Alfonso Villa Rojas

1962   *Chan Kom. A Maya Village.* University of Chicago Press, Chicago.

Segal, Daniel A., and Richard Handler
1989   Serious Play: Creative Dance and Dramatic Sensibility in Jane Austen, Ethnographer. *Man* 24(2):322–339.
Tax, Sol
1988   Pride and Puzzlement: A Retro-Introspective Record of 60 Years of Anthropology. *Annual Review of Anthropology* 17:1–21.
Tylor, Edward Burnett
1871   *Primitive Culture: Researches into the Development of Mythology, Philosophy, Religion, Art and Custom.* J. Murray, London.
Wolf, Eric R.
1964   *Anthropology.* Princeton University Press, Princeton.

Reflections on Fieldwork with Little People of America: Myths and Methods

Joan Ablon

George Foster has said, "writing is the price that anthropologists pay to do field work." That certainly is the case for me. As I look back on more than twenty-five years of field research I realize this has been the most important element in my life, and, in fact, I tend to divide my life into epochs in terms of the field populations I was studying at various times. I have worked with a total of eight populations now. This paper has provided me the opportunity for a bit of primitive analysis of some of the trends in my professional development. I will be writing here about personal, immediate, and nitty-gritty issues and concerns, most centering on my work with dwarfs, or little people, over a twelve-year period, 1976–88.

My first fieldwork experience was as a student in a small highland Mayan village in the state of Chiapas, Mexico. The bulk of my research has been urban, however, chiefly in the San Francisco Bay Area. Since I began my dissertation research with relocated American Indians in the Bay Area in 1961, I have felt that the subjects I studied had to be of significance for assisting with some of the many problems of American society. That is why I chose an urban thesis project and subsequent research despite my thirty-year love affair with Chiapas and Guatemala. My mentor at the University of Chicago, Sol Tax, early imbued in me a necessity for *helping* as well as *learning,* the two goals of his action anthropology philosophy. Although I have not been able to formally operationalize an "action program" as Tax conceived it, I have always considered myself basically an action anthropology protégé. Urban anthropologists were rare when I began my dissertation in the early 1960s. In fact, when I handed in the first three chapters to my committee at the University of Chicago, one member of the committee asked me if perhaps I should consider switching to sociology, because, he stated, the anthropology department had never had an urban thesis before! And indeed I understand that mine remained the only one for almost twenty years.

I have studied relocated American Indians, alienated Black teenagers, and Samoan migrants. I also have worked with Irish Catholic families, some of whom had severe alcohol problems. This led me to the study of alcoholism and family life, as well as to Al-Anon Family Groups, a support system for families and intimates of alcoholics. My papers were pioneer efforts in each of those fields. This was the fun, of course! As I look back I see that a connecting conceptual link between these various study areas has been marginality, difference, and in some situations, social stigma. The stage had been set for a study of dwarfism.

I suppose there was a time when I did not know one dwarf, and I could remember only having seen two or three in my life. Now I can hardly remember that time. I have many close friends who are dwarfs. I attend meetings with dozens and even hundreds of dwarfs. I have a network of little people I visit over the whole country.

How did I get involved in a study of dwarfism? Through serendipity, another central element of my life—through the luck of meeting a family with a dwarf child. I am a great believer in chance happenings. These often lead us to important subjects for study—subjects that we had never thought about before. In a population I was studying in San Francisco, there was a family with a dwarf child who belonged to Little People of America. My curiosity about that organization led to my request to attend a monthly chapter meeting. The meeting was of unusual interest to me, and I was welcomed in a most gracious manner by the members. I found my research interests rising to the many possibilities for investigation. I found only one article, then some ten years old, in the scientific literature on the organization of Little People of America (Weinberg 1968). My request to do a study was met with enthusiastic cooperation. The study of dwarfism and of a self-help or support group for dwarfism constituted a unique opportunity for me to wed a number of disparate research concerns: (1) the social experiences that persons with stigmatized health conditions undergo; (2) the impact of chronic illness and disability on family life; and (3) the role of social support systems and therapeutic self-help groups in maintaining health and mental health in contemporary society. These subjects are all of the greatest significance in the lives of many millions of persons in our population today, yet relatively little has been written on them compared to the more physical aspects of illness, which have been copiously examined in medical and clinical literature. Likewise few anthropologists have examined these issues, although they are all very appropriate for the field of medical anthropology in which I work.

Clinical definitions of dwarfism typically include persons 4 feet 10 inches and under. There are more than 100 types of dwarfism, differing in etiology and physical characteristics. Estimates of the number of dwarfs in the United States range widely, but the figure of 100,000 is cited frequently (Weiss 1977).

The range in variation in physical types of dwarfism among the members of Little People of America is extremely broad. The majority of members exhibit some type of skeletal dysplasia or bone disorder. Most skeletal dysplasias produce persons with disproportionate short stature, that is to say, the limbs are not of expected size proportionate to the torso and head. If you recall dwarfs you may have seen on the street or with whom you are acquainted, they are most likely achondroplastic dwarfs. Achondroplasia is the most commonly occurring form of dwarfism and is characterized by an average-sized head and torso and disproportionally short arms and legs. Proportionate dwarfs, those that in common parlance are often called "midgets," usually lack the growth hormone. "Midget," however, is considered a derogatory word by most dwarfs, referring to those little persons often exploited in the past by side shows or the like.

Dwarfs typically have normal intelligence, and although some individuals experience specialized physical problems, most dwarfs generally are able to engage in a similar range of occupations as average-sized persons (a term many dwarfs prefer to "normal"). The barriers to normative lifestyle expectations that exist for most dwarfs are generally social rather than logistical. Attitudes of potential employers, school and workmates, and the general public often serve to set dwarfs apart as distinct kinds of functioning persons and to create lower expectations of general ability or special levels of performance than for other people.

Little People of America (LPA) is a nonprofessional self-help organization with a membership of some 5,000 persons—dwarfs and their families. Members come from many walks of life and represent a variety of economic and educational levels. Little People of America is a remarkably energetic organization that sponsors activities on local, regional, and national levels. The major event of the year for most LPA members is the national weeklong convention, currently a gathering of 700 to 1,000 dwarfs and their families. During this week there are a great many social, recreational, and educational events. For little people, this week is somewhat analogous to "Sady Hawkins Day," if you remember that quaint cultural custom out of the *Little Abner* comic strip. It is the one occasion of the year to meet and mingle with other little people, and to form close relationships, and to even find a spouse—if you are lucky. Obviously you have to work fast, and this parameter sets the tempo for the week.

Over a twelve-year period I attended almost every local event held in my area, many regional meetings, and also eight national conventions held all over the country. I published two books, *Little People in America* (Ablon 1984), focusing on the life career of adult dwarfs and the impact of the organization of Little People of America on their lives, and *Living with Difference* (Ablon 1988), a study of average-sized families with dwarf children. These are essentially the only scholarly books available on the social dimensions of dwarfism. In 1987 I was presented an honorary life membership in LPA. Thus, I will continue to be involved with LPA, but I see my role now as an interested friend and member of the organization, not as conducting on-going research. For the past three years, I have been engaged in another study, which I will discuss later.

Why did I work with little people over so many years? The basic reason was that the administrative tasks connected with my position as rotating chair of the medical anthropology program at my university for about half of that period cut so heavily into my research and writing time that I could not complete the various dimensions of a complex one-person study or the write-up of data before 1988. Medical center faculties have an eleven-month year, not a nine-month year. Thus, research, and writing time in particular, is diminished.

Another reason I tarried, I must admit honestly, is because I was having such a good time! The organization of LPA and individual members were immediately welcoming from the first time I attended a meeting. The local and national presidents were very open to my study, and individual members were most gracious about responding to my requests for visits. Very quickly I had more invitations for visiting than I could accept. In most instances my interviews were conducted over dinner or luncheon tables.

Thus I was given continual positive feedback by the friendliness of members. Also, three plaques were presented to me by the organization. The first, a beautifully inscribed desk set, was presented at a local awards banquet after about two years into my research, long before members saw any serious or tangible sign of publications. The second plaque came several years later, probably after the publication of my first paper. The third plaque commemorates the lifetime membership, and, like the others, was a surprise, presented at the national awards banquet in Philadelphia in 1987. After it was announced, one person was appointed to drag me up to the stage, knowing that my inclination was to hide under the table. Many members know that I do not like to appear before large groups. I have been told that they perceive this as related to a general modesty about my research and my professional status, a characteristic that has been attractive to them. This brings us to the subject of personality.

I am basically a very outgoing and friendly person, and this has helped me in most of my fieldwork settings. Many LPA members became friends very quickly. Much of what I have to say today deals with the professional and personal implications of strong friendships with informants. Fieldwork may become exceedingly more complex because of these personal issues.

The Significance of Friendship

Strong friendships carry their own burdens of responsibilities as well as joys. Anthropologists have traditionally maintained strong friendships with informants and certainly this is one of the unique features of our methodology. On this issue Foster and Kemper (1974:3) have stated:

From the beginning anthropologists formed close ties with the people they studied, and almost all anthropologists . . . have written affectionately about their key informants, some of whom became lifelong friends. Anthropologists quickly realized that the best and most accurate data come from persons who like and trust them. Hence, "establishing rapport" came to be an anthropologist's first assignment upon arriving in the field: to search out the most knowledgeable individuals, present oneself to them in a plausible and empathetic role, and make friends. . . . Today, in cities as in rural areas, most anthropologists retain this basic philosophy: good rapport with good friends, trust and confidence, and abundant conversation over long periods of time.

It is certainly easier to be a "lifelong friend" of an informant in a city in Mexico or Asia, however, than of one who lives a few miles away. The implications of being "good friends" with informants in urban areas where we live have not been explored nor experienced by many anthropologists over a longitudinal period. How do such friendships affect fieldwork? There were many little people whom I saw weekly or monthly over many years, and in time I regarded them as highly individualized friends as well as informants. (In this situation there were not the extended holidays from one another that academic anthropologists and their informants usually have.) My interest in my informants was based on my professional and personal concern about events in their histories and contemporary lives, as well as their futures or destinies. Their very different personalities and personal backgrounds both simplified and complicated the task of defining the commonalities of experience in their life careers that could be attributed to their dwarfism and the societal responses to it.

Reciprocity

Concerns about reciprocity became more immediate for me. The responsibility for helping was a tangible goal I thought about a lot. And I do believe that the books resulting from my research have contributed to the betterment of little people. The organization of LPA itself has bought more than 2,500 of these books, which have been sold to members and interested professionals. Many members bought five or more copies to give to relatives and friends, or to their physicians or public library.

For the LPA perspective, I asked two of my chief informants, both past national and local officers, if they felt there were any changes in LPA as a consequence of my presence in the group. Both felt that my work has helped individual members and families to look at themselves and their children more objectively, and to step outside of the organization and see LPA as it compares to other organizations. They say, in fact, for all its problems, LPA still "isn't doing too badly." Further, they feel that the existence of my books detailing the structure and functions of LPA as an organization has given the group more "clout" by making the medical community and social welfare agencies more aware of the organization. If indeed these have been some of the consequences of my work, then I feel the goals of my research have been realized.

The friendship and affection that I have for LPA members also has created for me even more than the usual ethical concerns about the fallout resulting from my research. A major issue in this regard has been the consequences of publication. During the last twenty years, anthropologists have acknowledged and anticipated the fact that their publications about populations in the developing world might be read and utilized positively and productively by those populations. When your informants live only a few miles away, however, and might walk into a bookstore and be greeted at the door by a book about themselves, or they might see interviews about themselves with the anthropologist on television, the issue of publication becomes immediately critical.

Simon Ottenberg (this volume) discusses problems around the disclosure of secret or sacred materials. A primary concern I have had in my research has involved a related issue. What about "dirty linen," materials that my informants might consider to be negative or to portray them in a bad light?

I decided, I suppose somewhat arbitrarily along the way in those twelve years with LPA, that I would not publish materials that my informants or I would consider to be "dirty linen." Some of my considerations were based on their history and some on my own. Through the centuries dwarfs typically have been portrayed as mythical creatures with especially good or magical, or especially bad or evil, attributes. I felt that the chief goal of my research was to normalize dwarfs, to move them out of the category of mythical creatures. For example, in my first book (Ablon 1984:7) I wrote:

Imagine a life of difference: not total difference, but partial difference. You are a thirty-year old man with a wife and a child. You have a good white collar job, and you own your own home in a pleasant suburban neighborhood. You have two cars. You were born in this country and speak English well. You have the average amount of formal education. But you will always be different. You are a dwarf.

And later:

A specific intention of this work is to demystify the nature of dwarfs. *The dwarf is not the elfin figure of folk tales nor is he or she the nonhuman creature of the video game who lives in a cave. The dwarf is the operator of a computer who at this moment is unraveling the problems of your health insurance for you, or charting a safe return for the plane that carries you through the skies.* Dwarfs are ordinary people who bear the burden of a physical difference, and more importantly, a symbolic difference that our society seldom allows them to forget.

Dwarfs have received more than enough bad publicity through history. I was determined not to publish anything that would continue a tradition of depicting them as deviant or weird. My work likewise would not be voyeuristic about their physical difference.

Now, from my own history, in my work on alcoholism and American family life in the seventies, I wrote a number of papers explicating characteristics of the Irish-American Catholic family system that appeared to be related to problematic drinking in the families I studied. There was great professional interest in these papers. I received hundreds of requests for reprints from clinicians and other professionals in this country, Canada, and Europe. I likewise received considerable positive feedback about their clinical usefulness. Nonetheless, I emerged from that experience unhappy with detailing the family "dirty linen" of a population.

In contrast, my work with Al-Anon Family Groups, carried out in an overlapping period, provided me with a feeling of delight that I could share the knowledge of a remarkable, yet at that time little known, nonprofessional therapeutic modality with the professional world. Everything I learned about Al-Anon was positive. I emerged from these two experiences in the late seventies having made a decision that, since I was in a position to choose the subjects I studied, I would choose positive ones and not publish negative materials that my informants might be ashamed of. This decision in itself might render my work humanistic rather than scientific, but so be it.

The implications of this decision were played out in several issues during my study of LPA. I chose not to emphasize some of the negative political maneuverings of some officers of the organization. I dealt with such behavior through what I deemed to be a reasonable analysis of why LPA officers might be more inexperienced socially and politically than the average-sized population due to their exclusion from many opportunities in the general society. For example (Ablon 1984:166–167):

The opportunity to learn the simple give-and-take inherent in the operational procedures necessary for the running of a club is also a significant aspect of the LPA social arena. . . . for many little people, this form of social interaction may be relatively new to them. Many have *not* had the opportunity to experience the common give and take involved in negotiations of planning social events, balancing small budgets or treasuries, and especially of being in leadership positions. . . .

Some members comment on the social immaturity of others, that they bicker over small items, or that they complain a lot about little things. These characteristics may reflect a paucity of experience of just this kind of organizational give-and-take and also reflect the coping pattern often developed by some dwarfs as described by subjects—that of not complaining about inequities and bad deals handed to them at work or in business matters for fear of losing jobs or business opportunities that were won with difficulty in competition. Thus, in the company of peers of similar stature, and thus similarly disadvantaged in the larger world, one can complain loudly without reprisal. Again, this specialized social arena of LPA meetings offers a unique opportunity for learning social skills, another dimension of the process of normalization.

By determining not to resort to voyeuristic reporting, I did not emphasize sensational aspects related to my informants' dwarfism. A situation arose that activated this determination. The manuscript of my first book was sent to a highly respected anthropologist for review. One of his chief concerns was that I had not included any detail about the sex lives or drug experiences of my informants. I was astounded by this. Yet my concerns about getting the manuscript published also enveloped me. I spent several weeks working on a new chapter that would include data on sex and drugs. I interviewed several informants specifically on sexual behavior at the annual national convention where hundreds of young adults hungry for normal sexual experimentation congregate. As I put together the new material I realized more and more that parents who could learn about LPA through this book might be frightened away by this subject and decide not to bring their children to the convention. If they were to attend, these children most likely would encounter their first opportunity for true egalitarian relation-

ships there. In some cases this contact with LPA could be crucial for turning around their lives. Most monographs I was familiar with do not necessarily include details of people's sex lives or drug habits. Why should a
book on dwarfs include these? Do their physically different bodies titillate
our prurient interests? I decided to junk the new chapter.

A second editor accepted the book without my revising so much as one
page. The book has been highly successful with little people who have embraced it as a fair, accurate, and non-exploitative description of varied aspects of their lives and experiences. I am told that the book has brought
many new members to LPA.

In another situation dealing with my second book, *Living with Difference,*
which is about average-sized families with dwarf children, I felt considerable anxiety about including several accounts by parents of their initial
highly negative reactions to the fact of their child's dwarfism and their likewise negative first impressions of other dwarf children. I do believe that I
procrastinated in the completion of this manuscript because I was so fearful
of the reaction of adult dwarfs to the knowledge that some of the parents
(now such good friends of theirs) had had these negative responses. Because
the number of families in the area of study was limited, and everyone knew
that I was interviewing within this pool of families, I feared I would make
all of the families suspect and jeopardize their friendships with the adult
dwarfs in the local chapter. On the other hand, both parents and professionals whom I queried advised me that I should publish these negative reactions so that new parents who read the book and who have experienced
such thoughts will realize that reactions of this kind are normal and common. I decided to include the accounts.

I always show drafts of my work to several informants before I publish
anything. It is the best manner of checking the validity and reliability of my
data. In this case I dreaded the comments of informants, fearing they would
seize on this issue. Sure enough, two persons immediately pointed to the
quotations on that very page that dealt with responses of parents. They expressed shock that the responses had been so negative. This was their only
concern about the entire 300-page manuscript! Nonetheless, they too felt
that the negative feelings should be expressed and independently suggested
deleting some of the most extreme negative statements. (This was helpful to
me because I often tend to be so literal about quotations that I regard them

as all-or-nothing inclusions.) I did, however, retain some of the negative expressions of emotion to make the point. I never received any further comments on this issue from LPA members or other readers after the book was published.

The necessity of asking informants to review my manuscripts is an obvious and crucial one for me. I regard them as my partners in this endeavor. They pass judgment on what I have accomplished and they point out omissions. They keep me honest and, I hope, accurate. My informants provide the "voices" to speak for little people. In my view, my writings on little people also constitute a critique of a society that cruelly stigmatizes them and of a medical system that has so often failed them. Perhaps in this sense I *am* publishing dirty linen—that of the medical world!

During the past decade my interests and my writing style have become much more applied. I am interested in gathering detailed descriptions of problematic lifeways specifically to urge and help to enable clinicians and others to provide more comprehensive and effective services for the people I work with and to demystify these populations for the general public. My writing has less jargon and in fact, I have been told, has become much clearer, often aimed at the intelligent layperson as well as the practitioner or theoretician. For example, many of my dwarfism publications have been utilized extensively by nonprofessional parents of dwarf children.

Physical Difference

Anthropologists and others who travel to culturally distant places often comment about "culture shock". In my fieldwork this has translated into "physical difference shock". One of the processes I have written about in my work with little people deals with the significance of a kind of physical mirroring shock for little people when they attend an LPA function for the first time. Most dwarfs emphatically state that before coming to LPA they denied their dwarfism both to themselves and to others. For example, they avoided any encounters with other dwarfs they might have met by chance on the street. Said one informant, "If I saw another dwarf I would go around the block to avoid him." Informants acknowledged that they were short, but never that they were dwarfs.

When they came to their initial LPA social events they were forced to look at themselves clearly for the first time. I wrote (Ablon 1984:163):

The shock of seeing so many other little people precipitates the process of accomplishing a cognitive restructuring of the self-image—the acceptance of self-identity and physical identification of being a dwarf—deviance avowal [sociologists have talked about the process of deviance *disavowal*]—and from this may follow a successful benefiting from the varied dimensions of social interaction and the sharing of logistical and medical strategies in LPA. But perhaps even more significant are the implications for freeing the person in his or her total interactions in the average-sized world to experience life on all levels more casually and happily.

What about my own physical difference shock? Somehow I quickly became accustomed to being with little people. This could be because of my long-standing conceptual interest in physical difference as a research subject. The one time I really experienced a reverse short stature shock was after I attended my first LPA national convention in Portland in 1977. The organization literally took over a medium-sized hotel, and for a week I rarely left the hotel and the 500 dwarf participants. There also were few average-sized family members there. When I checked out and entered the Portland airport to return to San Francisco, I remember my puzzlement and surprise when I suddenly realized that I was surrounded by all these people who seemed really enormous.

During my years in LPA I became acquainted with many profoundly short little people, some of whom have rare types of dwarfism that are manifested in unusual proportions and mobility limitations. Very quickly I saw them only as individuals with their special personalities and talents, unique in the same way that all of us are unique individuals. Their physical traits only entered my consciousness if we discussed medical problems or if others stared at them when we were together.

Perhaps because of my frequency of social contact with so many physically different people, I apparently absorb very easily what might be shocking for others. In fact, while writing this paper I became aware of the significance of physical difference shock for me in contexts other than LPA. My current research is with individuals and families who have neurofibromatosis (NF), a neurological genetic disorder. This condition became known to the general public only in recent years through the book entitled *The Elephant Man* by Ashley Montagu (1971), and the play and film inspired by that book. It is now recognized that the Elephant Man did not have NF, but is posited to have had a much more severe condition called Proteus Syndrome. I interview many informants who would generally be considered to be physically deformed because of numerous bodily tumors or extreme scoliosis, which may visibly distort the spine. As I have become accustomed to these kinds of physical difference, the arbitrary nature of the physical criteria for beauty stands in bald relief. Further, the primacy of the media in rigidly defining cosmetic prescriptions for beauty is apparent. One of the goals of my research is to utilize anthropological approaches to analyze and address such issues.

Personal Issues

I attempted to get an LPA perspective on some of the issues I have been talking about by asking two informants if *they* had noticed any changes in me during the years of fieldwork with LPA. The first responded, "yes." She thought that I had changed. She felt that in *our* anthropological sense of acculturation, I had taken on many of the expectations and customs of the group. She gave a number of substantive examples.

The second informant, a philosopher and problem-solver, stated that he did not think I had changed noticeably since I was doing a study that I had a natural affinity for, observing social activities and interviewing, listening many hours to people talking. He said, "You loved every minute of it and it showed. In fact," he continued, "it reinforced what you were like anyhow so you became even more so the way you are!"

I would like to close by considering some of the more personal issues of urban research. In our own urban areas we are very vulnerable to the scrutiny of our informants. Our own personal visibility is greatly increased. Our informants want to know how much money we make, where we live, who we live with, what our social life or sex life is—and they will certainly ask us. Furthermore, they, living close by, may utilize our own methodology of systematic observation to cross check *our* answers to *their* questions.

There is the issue of value conflicts with informants, which may not be as burning when one is far afield because the conflicts here may deal with our own contemporary political and ethnic problems. Racism and conservative values may be more apparent and repugnant to us here than when equivalent values appear in a society remote from our own personal world, especially if we have been activists in working for social reform, as have many anthropologists.

A consideration that becomes more significant with time is the accretion of numbers of informant-friends who still desire and expect us to maintain our relationships and be present for important social events in their lives— these same events that were at one time critical for the gathering of our data, and for which we ingratiated ourselves into their lives.

If indeed one major aspect of reciprocity that we have to offer is our friendship and attention, how can we shrug this off when we move on to study other groups? The fact that such new friendships are made and cultivated on our work time is no justification for dropping our relationships from past projects as we move on to others. Yet, when our personal social hours are so limited, how can we afford to multiply our friendship obligations over the years of changing field projects? This is indeed a personal dilemma, and I have experienced it as both a married and single person. In either case, time becomes even more of a tyrant than it ordinarily is.

In closing, I will reiterate that when the anthropologist is miles away from home, he or she is able to avoid a great many personal and professional issues of fieldwork that may become particularly crucial factors when he or she works in their home communities in their own culture. Indeed, I think such issues should be discussed to help both students and faculty decide the kinds of projects they wish to undertake in their careers, and to consider the distancing or lack thereof that is characteristic of the anthropologist-informant relationships of alternative fieldwork modalities and geographic choices. One could conceivably avoid some of the professional and social issues I have discussed, which may appear to be burdens above and beyond the normal problems of fieldwork. In the field of medical anthropology, this issue may be more important than in some other areas because of the sensitivity of the issues we often study. Projects more typical of survey-research modes or strictly formal interviewing in hospitals or institutions will preclude the kinds of intimate relationships that field anthropologists have traditionally maintained in small communities. For me, however, the richness of these latter relationships have their own unique, personal rewards, which far outweigh the problematic aspects of urban field research.

Acknowledgments

The dwarfism research described in this paper was supported by NSF grant no. BNS-7618402. The neurofibromatosis research is currently (1990) funded by NSF grant no. BNS-8819633.

References Cited

Ablon, Joan
1984   *Little People in America: the Social Dimensions of Dwarfism.* Praeger Publishers, New York.
1988   *Living with Difference: Families with Dwarf Children.* Praeger Publishers, New York.
Foster, George, and Robert Van Kemper
1974   *Anthropologists in Cities.* Little Brown, Boston.
Montagu, Ashley
1971   *The Elephant Man: A Study in Human Dignity.* E. P. Dutton, New York.
Weinberg, Martin
1968   The Problems of Midgets and Dwarfs and Organizational Remedies: A Study of the Little People of America. *Journal of Health and Social Behavior* 9:65–71.
Weiss, Joan O.
1977   Social Development of Dwarfs. In *Proceedings of a Conference on Genetic Disorders: Social Service Intervention,* edited by W. T. Hall and C. L. Young, pp. 56–61. Graduate School of Public Health, University of Pittsburgh, Pittsburgh.

Afterthoughts

Warren L. d'Azevedo

In 1989 I was asked by Don Fowler and Don Hardesty to name some of the persons I thought provided the most congenial personal and professional association over the years and for whom I reserved a special regard. When I set about to comply, the spontaneous first listing was both surprising and instructive. It quickly sprouted to incorporate about sixty individuals among whom were colleagues who had been mentors, compeers, former students, and other good geniuses of a wide range of age, talent, and disciplines. Actually, I suppose I had expected there to be more but, except for a few added by sudden recollection later, this was the compass of it.

After correcting for those no longer living or who might find my suggestion of mutuality presumptuous, the list was reduced by about one-half. But my handlers proposed even further culling. The roster should include only anthropologists and, in particular, those who might be disposed to take part in a series of lectures marking my transition to emeritus status, and who shared with me a bent for prolonged involvement with the peoples encountered in early fieldwork. There was also a proviso (about which I could pose no reasonable complaint) that the areas of specialization should exceed my preoccupation with Africa and the western Great Basin region of North America. When this was done, I was now down to little more than a dozen names.

So this was the potent residue of a lifetime of enriching alliances within my chosen vocation! Not quite half of the original roster contained admired associates now dead, while about a quarter were excluded by discipline or by research orientation. Most of the remainder were younger than I, a fact inducing me to reflect on the hypothesis that one measure of advancing years might be subjectively derived from the ratio between the number of significant others still living and those retired irrevocably to memory. The only sop to such doleful computation would be to discover that one has acquired as many viable peers and youthful associates as have been lost to private reminiscence and the vicissitudes of history. Having exceeded seven decades of treasured existence I count myself lucky on this score.

My tenuous optimism in the face of the fortuity of good fortune has been given a gratifying boost by what was done here on my behalf. All those who came forward to do this thing—the organizers of the lecture series, the editors and authors of the essays assembled in this book—are colleagues who in one way or another have influenced my life and thought. All are some years my junior and all began their careers at an earlier age than I. Moreover, all have been more productive of published works and, as friends and virtual mentors of longstanding, they have nourished me with their substance. It would seem that the moment is apt for the invocation of Bacon's paradox; for I am a survivor of a callow time, while *they* are my elders in this most ancient and modern of epochs.

What pleases me most about what is written in this book is how each of the authors has managed to imbue with new life certain old themes and concepts of our discipline. I have never been at ease with the designation "fieldwork," or even "the field." To say that one has "gone to the field" and that to have gone again and again to some remote place of privileged inquiry constitutes "long-term fieldwork" are increasingly irksome usages. They no longer mean what we intend them to mean, yet we seem to be stuck with them as artifacts of an earlier perception of our calling.

There was a time when anthropologists of whatever stripe or degree of conviction "went out" to some separate place or places where, during episodic sojourns, they strove to become participant-observers among another kind of people representing yet another kind of human culture. Though the beholder and the subject both were participants in the encounter, it was the former who appropriated the authoritative voice while the latter was the fount of the exotic polyphony to be recorded and interpreted. And, though this information was garnered from individual persons, these persons were in the final analysis transmuted into "a people" or "a culture" properly distanced in time, space, and sensibility from the world of the spectator. By the rules of conventional exposition, all that was truly human and mutually affecting in such an extraordinary communion of strangers was suppressed as irrelevant or digressive. All the players, including the interlocutor, were given masks to wear in a performance scripted by the professional stranger to be presented before a distant and scarcely imaginable audience. In this process the life-giving torrent of fresh impressions and self-reflection were usually edited out and relegated to moments of cathartic revelation among friends or to neatly framed anecdotes for the edification of students. Either way, the anthropologist not only had relinquished his or her own personhood but also robbed the other major players in the collaborative drama of ethnographic research of their real identities.

I am not one of those, however, who think that the great store of ethnographic study accumulated in the past must be considered severely compromised because of its failure to meet every new-found standard of judgment employed in hindsight by modern revisionist critique. Without it we would have little left to go on, nothing substantial to salvage or deconstruct except perhaps the accounts of travelers, adventurers, or the sensational disclosures of popular media. There would not have been that intrepid vanguard, which for the better part of a century chipped away at the wall of ethnocentrism and complacency dividing the so-called Western from the non-Western world. What was done was revolutionary for its time and circumstance, as much so as any of the concurrent advances of knowledge in the major sciences. The explosion of Euroamerican enlightenment concerning the global distribution of human inventiveness, or the complex diversity as well as correspondences among peoples and their cultures, was accompanied by epochal discoveries in human evolution and prehistory—including those studies of our primate kin that are sweeping away the vestiges of the androcentric fallacy. To trivialize these accomplishments as the flawed products of a hegemonic civilization in the throes of totalizing its worldview is to dissipate the momentum required to move on with as much power to disclose and comprehend the changing reality before us. Burning bridges to the rear does not ensure either an astute choice of roads ahead nor any greater degree of free agency.

There is in some quarters the apprehension that anthropology, as a discipline at least, is about to self-destruct by internal fracturing and a crisis of identity among its members. Disquieting as such portent may be to many whose status and employment depend upon a professional label, it should be pointed out that the current torment of reflexivity and doubt is hardly more severe than the periodic agonies of personal reassessment propelling most persons into maturity, or those paradigmatic shifts in worldview that have driven our leading minds to accept such heresies as a terrestrial genesis exceeding five-thousand years. It seems to me that the anthropological disposition, by whatever name and whether as discipline or insistent orientation, is likely to be around a good while longer. The intrinsic allure of its subject matter and the proliferous disorder of its professional structure give it an adaptive advantage somewhat on par with the human imagination itself. But if, as some say, the poor rupturing discipline has had its day we can indulge the prospect that the fertile compost of its decay will have nourished every other intellectual project of our era.

The correlate of this domestic ferment is the fact that most of the world—the earthly throng of all those *others*—once seen and defined largely through *us*, is raising a multitude of independent voices in a common parlance of intercultural inquiry and disputation. Disquieting and even scandalous as this has been to some, it is proving to be a potent corrective to the problematic aspect of our gaze. We are becoming the *outside* while they are looking *in*. This reversal in the line of scrutiny is a violation of the privacy and immunity long taken for granted in the intellectual fastnesses of the so-called Western world, and may account, in part, for the post-colonial (viz. "post-modernist") malaise distracting many in the academy. Where once one could sally forth to gather the trophies of "the field," returning in due time to ponder and write in the protective custody of one's own kind, the very legitimacy and authority of such venerable undertakings is now challenged or discredited.

But the onslaught is coming not only from out there. It is erupting right in here, on the hallowed turf of this most consolidative of nations where enclaves of diverse peoples are clamoring for parity and uncompromised recognition of their identities. Those who lament what they perceive to be a globalization of homogenized culture and the passing of human diversity might well take another look. New and changing cultures are proclaiming their presence all around us and everywhere. There seem to be at least as many outsides—within and without—as ever before and a spate of fresh vantage points from which to view and find entrance to them. In such a milieu the anthropological perspective promises to become ubiquitous.

In order to apprehend these new dimensions of diversity, students of human culture must come to grips as never before with the motivations and qualities that incline them to so ambiguously defined a pursuit. More than ever before the anthropologist is obliged to become a self-conscious instrument of knowing. It is the whole person who perceives and interprets, not some skilled automaton programmed for specific inspection, recording, gleaning, and divulging. Moreover, this person has a history, an individual involvement of body and experience that conditions at any moment in time what is seen, heard, felt, or remembered.

It seems inconceivable that professed students of others should ever not have taken so profound a matter into account. This distancing, this enormous lacuna in consciousness that now has become a subject of our critique, is also the void that has separated us from those we strive to know. The impersonal observer witnesses and transcribes a faceless world of impersonal others, devoid of communion or genuine humanity. If such a plight were to continue without remedy the time may soon be upon us when we have become the hapless participants in a new technic of virtual ethnography. A cosmos of illusions will be at our fingertips, generated and manipulated by a keyboard in the comfortable seclusion of offices and homes. No need for a travel itinerary, immunization shots, enduring inconveniences, establishing rapport with pesky natives or wrestling with obdurate data. All can be simulated to our liking. And when the *other* is able to do it, too, the awful symmetry of the new medium will be confirmed. Old cultures will reveal their secrets on command and new cultures will blossom like hothouse hybrids on the computer screen. Communication and knowledge will be self-contained, transcribed, and instantaneously retrievable. And when our inevitable disenchantment erodes the power of the game, even the most massive infusion of data could not breathe life into its texts.

The most potent antidote for this malady of disengagement is the shock of recognition that occurs when the observer also becomes the observed.

Almost instantly both parties in the transaction of intercultural inquiry are afforded at least a glimpse of one another as having a genuine existence as living, changing beings in a world of change. There is an irony here, however, in that most anthropologists have actually experienced this enlightening effect while living among the people they are studying. Yet it is rarely sustained over long absences. Unless activated by continuous involvement it eventually subsides into the recesses of private nostalgia where it languishes unexpressed and dissociated from the sanitized arena of published research.

It was not so long ago that personal accounts of doing anthropological fieldwork, or being an anthropologist, were relegated to a separate genre along with biography (for example, life histories of others), autobiography (as told to a researcher by an other), or even ethnohistory (time-depth through oral tradition and archival materials of and about others). With rare exceptions such work was not considered directly relevant to the aims of ethnography and was treated, rather, as a literary supplement containing occasional insights of problematical merit or utility. Only a few anthropologists—with varying degrees of cogency—ventured these modes of exposition and risked the indictments of subjective humanism, psychologizing, or a spurious historicity.

The debarment of the observer as a person from the field of observation, while sustaining the requisite posture of objectivity in a social science endeavoring to avoid identification with humanistic studies rather than the authoritative natural sciences, restricted anthropology to a narrow vision of its subject matter. At the same time, descriptions of how to do ethnography were unaccountably rare. The few textbooks strove to present an organized and cumulative review of the development of theory and empirical knowledge in "the study of man," and occasional outlines of cultural materials served to codify for the researcher the rapidly expanding categories of elements that standard ethnographies might be expected to address.

As late as the 1950s, when I was a graduate student, I do not recall that there was any serious attention given to field method. Other than for anecdotal references to the importance of participant-observation, the techniques of establishing rapport and the observer's status, or dealing with that exotic vocational ailment called cultural shock, there was little guidance for the actual procedures of acquiring and evaluating data. To be sure, one must be heedful of adequate sampling and the value of cross-cultural comparison, but the grubby arcana of alien encounters with intelligent beings of another culture, or the dawning awareness that the neat mandates of a preconceived "problem" or "project" might be inapplicable to the reality at hand, were a part of the ordeal of initiation left to the aspirant to endure alone. One read and re-read ethnographies—classic and the current—seeking models of exposition and direction through the labyrinth of interpretation. Mentors who could be eloquent and persuasive in matters of theory and the results of ethnographic research were remarkably unforthcoming about their personal experience in the field or the details of how they worked. It was as though all the vital drudgery of the essential task itself as well as the intimate astonishment of unforeseen awarenesses were secluded in some mysterious preserve far from prying eyes, inquisitive competitors, or seekers after first causes.

What was missing for many of us was explanation of that creative and singular process by which an individual whose work and intellectual authority we admired came to see and comprehend what had been experienced on the ground-level of discovery. We wanted to know who the real person was who had gotten from here to there, and whether we ourselves could manage to do it. Biographical information on major anthropologists—apart from the oral tradition of intramural lore—was confined exclusively to depiction of professional attainments and scholarly contribution. Our role models were devoid of personal life and thought, yet we yearned to emulate their lofty achievements or bask in their grace. We also accepted the initiatory charge to learn how it was done by going out and doing it. Moreover, anthropology—in the academy, at least—seemed assured of its mission in science, and deemed its efforts to be cumulative and progressive.

Not until the 1960s, after I had carried out my first field projects and had begun to teach, do I recall becoming aware that some breakthrough was taking place. Out of nowhere, it seemed, manuals and full-length discussions of fieldwork method and principles were appearing as though responding to some general urgency or demand. Field schools and team research projects were attracting renewed interest, and curriculums of departments made way for relevant instruction. Mainstream anthropology was kindled by new theoretical orientations and critical appraisal of its mission. But on the periphery something more subtle was happening. Here and there the voices of anthropologists as persons could be heard among their voluble fellows. I do remember the almost clandestine eagerness with which some of us had greeted the publication of such thirst-quenching works as *Return to Laughter* and *In the Company of Man*. The moisture of life was seeping from the aquifer, and the climate was ripe with germination and promise. All the while, however, historical contingencies were shaping the future.

A major shift in anthropological perspective had begun to occur during the first two or three decades following the Second World War. The world seemed to have become smaller and more dense. Maps once dominated by the primary colors of Western hegemonic interests acquired a crazy-quilt of hues and subdivisions almost beyond the limits of the cartographer's craft. Views from the moon and the digital processing of satellite imaging revealed a lonely, vulnerable planet on which human beings and their works were reduced to invisibility. Down on earth populations swelled and competed for resources. The terrifying technology of destruction unleashed by a militarized science raised the specter of human extinction on a scale never before imagined, while rampant industrial pollution and the reckless exploitation of the environment threatened the existence of all life. At the same time, Western assumptions of rectitude and privilege were being challenged from within and without by anti-colonial struggles, wars of national liberation, and by crumbling illusions that exposed the nakedness of benevolent empires and capitalist democracies. A worldview fortified by centuries of assurance of the ascendancy of Western science, technology, and social values was riddled with doubt, and a civilization seemed on the verge of dissolution.

Symptoms of disenchantment spread through the intellectual denominations of the Euroamerican world as a rising chorus of unfamiliar voices questioned the credibility of received wisdom. Conventional aims and procedures of knowing—in fact the very possibility of knowing—were subjected to merciless critique. Tremors of change already had begun to affect the thinking of anthropologists as early as the 1960s. The world was rapidly becoming a vastly different place than it had appeared to be a short while before. Being a citizen of a Western society no longer granted the prestige or impunity that once attended those who went about where they chose to go. Even when returning to work among those who had once welcomed or tolerated them, they might now meet suspicion and rejection. The crucial activity of fieldwork itself was becoming an embarrassment as anthropologists were increasingly called into account for the legitimacy of their errand and its relevance to those who were the objects of investigation. The questions were painfully deep and explanation inadequate.

One effect of this predicament has been a rapid erosion of what was once a shared conviction about the coherence of the discipline and the unity of its aims. Its vaunted "holism" shows signs of fracturing into four, eight, sixteen or more subfields, each labeled as a kind of anthropology no matter how attenuated from a mythical progenitor. In some quarters there are rumblings of defection into independent disciplines or mergers with what used to be called "related fields." As for sociocultural anthropology—once the hallmark of a more integrated profession—one hears whispers that it may have had its day. Wars, exploitation, corruption, impoverishment, and bitter recrimination have so transformed whole regions formerly visited and studied that many have retreated from the direct engagement of field research while others found themselves drawn willingly or inadvertently into partisanship. Some took refuge in the notion that such projects were becoming moribund in a world of globalized culture and "vanishing natives." For others the thrust of ethnographic work became in the final analysis a critique of their own culture, its arrogant complacency and misguided uses of power. Still others discovered the lodestone of metaphysical truths and separate realities ostensibly profaned by their positivist fellows. And others, still, embraced the virtual realism of fiction and its unfettered constructions.

In the mainstream corridors of the academy the effects of this diffusion of interests and aims—though somewhat constrained by institutional precedents and the emoluments of privilege—have produced a degree of creative dispersion and successive waves of novel vision that would have confounded our predecessors even more than it does us. Methodologies and theoretical approaches abound ad interim, coming in and going out of fashion as rapidly as any consumer-oriented society could wish for. Ideology subsumes ethnology, and the demand for innovation relegates much of what was produced even a fraction of a generation ago to near oblivion. Little wonder that students also are bewildered, and that the best of them are becoming more critical of the profession as a career vehicle than their professors are of its intellectual content. They see a vocation whose membership has multiplied well beyond the capacity of the beleaguered academy or other relevant public institutions to absorb those seeking employment. Funds for training and travel are scarce. Uncertainty is aggravated by the apparent lack of public interest and the diminishing status of university departments of anthropology.

Not only does the viability of the discipline appear to be in question but it has lost much of its glamour—except, perhaps, for archaeology, prehistory, and primate studies where the promise of rugged adventure and tangible discovery still beckons. Without the lure of the field as a laboratory of research into the human condition, and a shared conviction that something of inestimable importance is to be found there, what remains but disputation and critique about what others once ventured to do?

I have always felt that the young in general, and those on the verge of institutional commitment in particular, are grounded in the starkest of realities. They often have a keen sense of the contradictions facing them in the established order, and what the odds might be. This perception was reinforced at the 1992 annual meeting of the profession in San Francisco where I and a small group of "senior" members were invited to participate in a discussion organized by the National Association of Student Anthropologists. The scope of the announced topic and its charge were awesome:—"The Old and the New in Anthropology: Six Students Question Six Senior Anthropologists, Trying to Resolve the Controversies of the Past 50 Years." Contrary to expectations, the room and the adjoining hallways were overflowing with young people from universities throughout the country. They seemed more serious and intent than most panel audiences at large meetings. I had some misgivings about whether I was adequately prepared for the onslaught, even though I had spent some time conscientiously reviewing what I thought to be the major issues in theory and practice I had encountered over four decades of professional life. There was a moment of panic as I realized that, as a senescent survivor of the vocation these young people were just entering, I was among those whose careers had progressed through the predictable stages of what seemed to be a more stable time. What did I really know of their concerns, and how competent was I to deal with their sharply honed facility with the language and concepts of current inquiry? I steeled myself for recriminatory and father-killing debate, but had no stomach for it.

The proceedings, however, took a quite different turn. We senior members of the panel were not asked either to elucidate or defend the past but, rather, were being solicited to offer guidance through the chartless landscape of the present. There was none of the confrontational posture one had learned to anticipate in student bullsessions, or the emulous disputation of seminars. The mood was the more disquieting one of respectful and anxious waiting for a message. It soon became clear that we seniors flanking the podium were not about to be pilloried as feckless representatives of a failed enterprise, or the providers of decontextualized footnotes to the grand texts of a neocolonial, capitalist, new world order. Nor were we to be flailed with the scourge of post-modern redemption or its epistemologic scalpel. In fact, reference to hyphenated post-isms was strangely absent, an omission about which I felt a bit of disappointment because I had hoped to affirm a positive assessment of some promising new directions ascribed to that ambiguous category.

Little of my defensive pedantry or wary reading of the text had any direct bearing on what eventually transpired at the meeting. The issues raised were disarmingly practical and straightforward, but nonetheless vexed. Their gist was a troubled complaint about the discipline, its teaching, and its status. Some described departments in which there are as many insular approaches advanced as there are faculty, where professors are seldom in their offices or even in their classrooms, and so absorbed in their own projects that they have little time for students except the chosen few ardent followers. Scarcely any are dedicated teachers and it is rare to find anyone willing to talk about what anthropology really is. One struggles to find a niche, but the message seems to be—make what you can of it and leave us alone. Where are the mentors?

Then there were the questions directed to the panel of elders on the dais. What had it been like to be an anthropologist when we were young? Did we think we were engaged in something worthwhile—and why? Why had we chosen to become anthropologists rather than physicists, biologists, sociologists, historians, professors of English, or merely investigative journalists? How did we decide where to do fieldwork and how did we get there? Did we believe there would be jobs and a secure future awaiting us? Did we actually know our mentors and work with them? What were they like? What were we like?

Removed from context, as I have done with these questions, one could construe them as argumentative or sardonic. But that is not how it was. The young people crowded into that conference room were notably grave for a gathering of graduate students. They had come to this place from major universities apparently in earnest anticipation of a forum where they could air their concerns. Clearly, they had not come to debate theory or to reenact the battle of the Ancients and Moderns. They were on neutral ground, and communicating on a most basic level of shared distress. It was serious business.

There were moments during the proceedings when I had thought that we elder guests were being positioned as a bridge between a wistfully contrived golden age of certitude and the uncentered present. At other times it was as if we were a mere backdrop or sounding board. Possibly it was that our assigned generational status and distancing from the local arenas of their academic struggles posed no threat of reproach, no need to be scrupulously on one's mettle. Whatever the heart of the matter, our role was privileged and our brief comments were accorded deferential attention.

I do not think my colleagues felt any more assured than I that our responses were as adequate or relevant as we might have hoped. One or two of us tendered eloquent appeals to the ethos of anthropology as we saw it. Others told lively anecdotes of successful teaching experiences or encounters with memorable mentors and facilitators. Some made useful suggestions for coping with the alienating situations that had been depicted. And I recall remarking at one point that if anthropology is so disenchanting, and if many departments actually were like those described, I wondered how any but fools or those possessing extraordinary valor would want to become anthropologists today. It would seem to require a degree of self-motivation and tolerance of risk not many of my generation would have been able to muster under similar circumstances. It would seem that only individuals of uncommon determination and a sure notion of what they wanted to do were likely to persevere.

As I spoke I became uncomfortably aware that I was engaging in a lame, if not patronizing, dodge. I had missed the mark. These young people had not come there merely to ventilate discontents or to rationalize inaptitude—and certainly not to be lectured by those they had invited. What I had missed was the elusive undercurrent of entreaty that had surfaced during the discussion. They were seeking *example*, not injunction. I realize in hindsight that these students were expressing a need to apprehend anthropology as a *practice,* and to make connection with those they believed to have made an avowed commitment to the profession as a way of life and a course of action in the world. I am not sure of the extent to which any of us senior respondents met that tacit request, but I do remember that interest was most intent when we spoke of ourselves, our personal experience and viewpoints. *We* were the actual subject.

This encounter with a group of aspiring students in my discipline has contributed much to what I have been writing here. It alerted me to the possibility that every litany of discontents, every exhortation to amend our understanding of what we are about may contain within it the kernel not only of what I had missed in that exchange but of what has been missing in anthropology. That fertile yet uncultivated seed may be what I referred to earlier above as the frankly subjective and autobiographical dimension of practice. Its germination has been slow but insistent over the past few decades. As I have mentioned, in the 1960s and 1970s (when fieldwork still held a central place in anthropology) a new and belated attention was being given to methodology. A surge of writings began to appear dealing with the *craft* of anthropology. They were welcome signs that the profession was facing its responsibility as an accountable science of the human condition in a changing world. But there was also during this time an outpouring of writings that revealed a new and sensitized awareness of the ethical aspects of research, investigator-informant relations, and the moral dilemmas of engagement. This increasing self-consciousness was a response to a rapidly changing and complex social reality, and to the compelling necessity of a deeper comprehension of role and mission. There can be little doubt that this period marked a turning point in how anthropology as a profession viewed itself. The way was opened to a new resolve about what could and should be done. An initial task was the reforging of the investigator into a self-correcting instrument of observation—a reflective stranger.

Over the past twenty years or so, a signal and problematic effect of these fundamental shifts in anthropological perspective has been to propel many of its practitioners into a state of acute introspectiveness. Quandaries concerning the relevance, authority and future of the discipline have become dominant preoccupations, and the discourse of some appears so attenuated from the parent field as to be indistinguishable from other scholarly pursuits. I do not think that this trend can be faulted in itself, nor does it portend the aimlessness and atrophy that has been referred to as a crisis of identity. It should be noted that the vigorous proliferations of subdisciplines in anthropology are nevertheless explicit expressions of facets of what the discipline has always claimed as its forte. Elements of the original charge live as long as anthropologists call themselves by that name.

Notwithstanding all these advances, regressions, and millings about, there is still something missing at the core, something whose absence I detected at the student gathering and which, if invited to take its proper place in our colloquy and our literature, might restore a measure of the authority and inner assurance we search for. Even if we had the temerity to think that our discipline was posing most of the right questions and coming up with a goodly share of right answers, we could not dismiss what is for us a lingering unanswered question. That question is not what anthropology *is* but a more incisive one that cuts to the root: What and who are anthropologists and why do they do it?

We have countless life histories and autobiographies of those *others,* recorded in the field and reconstructed in absentia, but scarcely any of equivalent value for those who recorded and authored them. And though ethnographic writing has become increasingly personalized in recent years —often to the point of engulfing the objective situation—much of it employs a piecemeal reflexiveness intended to illustrate some particular therapeutic renovation of an ethnographer's sensibilities. At its best, however, this attention to the dynamics of fleeting interreactions has enhanced the power and credibility of what is observed and has illumined interpretation. The observer comes into focus as a sentient being.

But more is required to balance the dyadic equation than the insertion of revelatory glosses into the scholarly text. For when all is said and done, neither we, on the one side, nor the original donor of substance, on the other, have access to the kind of information that can transform the one-dimensional image of the ethnographer into an approximate person. That information is the missing dimension, the essential component of the genuine reciprocity we claim to be seeking in the cooperative process we call fieldwork. It is almost precisely the same kind of data we find so edifying for our understanding of the role of individuals in other cultures—the personal history, if you will, or the reflections of an individual responding to the request for a resume of those significant events and experiences that have shaped a life. No small matter, one might say. Yet we have elicited reams of them in our notebooks from which we have gleaned the memories of others for gratuitous riches given to us and taken away by us with no thought of requital in-kind.

That there is a hankering for reciprocity in this regard is not difficult to confirm. I doubt that there are any ethnographers who have not experienced one or more of those interruptions of interview sessions in which the respondent manages to execute a turnabout in the direction of inquiry. In actuality, it may have happened more frequently than we recall, for one tends to develop perfunctory answers to such intrusions and to move on as quickly as possible to the task at hand. I am thinking of the countless moments in which I have been made aware that my hosts in another culture are as curious about me as I am about them. Why should they not want to know what brought me to that place so far from my home, where I have no local kin, no visible patrons or means of support, no clearly comprehensible mission?

In rural Africa, if one hopes to enjoy the hospitality of villages and towns, one had better be prepared for the introductory query, "What is your business here and who sent you?" But that is not the end of it, for as one proceeds one is subject to the inquisitive and often wry probing reserved for all strangers no matter how amiable or accommodative. Why have you come all this way to study us? How would *your* people deal with me if I went to your country on the same business? How do *your* people eat, sleep, dream, make love, marry, train children, respect their relatives, deal with witches, fight, die? Who are *your* ancestors, and what god do *you* pray to? What will you do with all we are telling you here? Although I never got to be quite at ease under such reversals of scrutiny, I did learn to cope with them by appeal to a repertoire of explanations that had proved to be useful. I also came to realize that what I felt was not too different from what they had endured with my relentless intrusions. Actually, the direct approach of my African associates was far less unnerving than the tacit caution and deeper obligation one often meets among Native Americans where the unspoken but nonetheless insistent issue may be, "What kind of person are you?" It occurs to me, however, that the most lasting and rewarding associations formed over four decades in my two regions of research involve individuals with whom I was able to sustain a mutually gratifying level of dialogue and trust. They are friends who know as much about me as I do about them, and it is from them that I have learned much about myself.

I do not believe it is at all incongruous to suggest that what one discovers about reciprocity under these conditions might also apply to relations among anthropologists, their students, and members of their cultures. The question of who and what we are and how we see ourselves is a crucial and neglected subject in our discourse. Over the past several years a small but welcome step toward meeting this want has been the series of interviews or "conversations" with leading anthropologists carried intermittently in the pages of the journal *Current Anthropology*. For those who have followed these elicited memoirs, there is bound to be a renewed sense of appreciation for what the discipline is and what it means to become an anthropologist. All at once the profession begins to come alive with real people of vastly different backgrounds and personalities finding their ways to the work they want to do. Their brief reflections should be brought forth from obscurity and assigned as required reading in any course on the history of anthropology and the personal dimension of its charge. They provide some example, some insight into intention and practice, and there is an unrequited hunger for it.

An even longer step in this promising direction has been taken by seven of my contemporaries whose essays are collected here. As I read what they have written I was astonished to discover how little I actually had known about them—each an individual of singular temperament and life experience who had been a friend and colleague through a good part of my own life. In these reflections they were revealing to me and others something rarely glimpsed in scholarly work or professional association. Here were frank and deeply considered words disclosing the contingencies, the decisions, the commitments, the self-evaluations, and intimate opinions that define the course of individual growth and achievement. Whether specifically intended or not, these essays are disquisitions on practice.

As I read, I also became aware of a subtly pervasive and resonating theme running through them all, a quality that might well be a diagnostic trait in the character of those who have experienced prolonged and purposeful involvement with peoples of other cultures, and whose lives and thought have become so intertwined with those others as to constitute an integral element of identity. In essence, it embodies the creative plight of cultural marginalization, of being both an outsider and insider in one's own world while irrevocably linked to another. It also poses a moral dilemma; for the anthropologist, as ethnographer, is always to some extent an elective alien estranged by circumstance and proclivity from customary fealty to any dominating worldview while, at the same time, enmeshed in the language and meanings endowed from childhood on.

The voice of Nazif Shahrani strikes a clear and poignant note in these pages. Born and raised an Uzbek, a Muslim, and trained as a social scientist in American universities, he depicts the irony of his status as "a native anthropologist." Not only did he relinquish his early religious convictions but, as an ethnographer of his own people addressing a Western audience, professional credibility required that he avoid assuming the "native insider's view." Apparently the privilege of speaking for the insider is reserved for the authoritative *Other,* for it seems "only the outsider can pretend to do that!" Thus we are made aware that Shahrani's marginality is multidimensional, and that coping with it may present difficulties seldom faced by his colleagues. He is both the *we* and the *other* of our discourse, but we are also the *Other* of his. Consequently, a multiplicity of commitments and perspectives informs his ingenious conception of "the field" as the inclusive arena of one's "discipline," one's "cultures" of orientation, and the culture in which "fieldwork" is done.

The remarkable aptness of this insight led me to consider that each of the authors in this book (if not all anthropologists) have lived out their professional lives *in the field,* and what they have written here are personal assessments of sustained transcultural experience in just such a frame. In one way or another each takes stock of the exigencies of personal history and the attributes that shaped his or her separate trajectory—what William Douglass refers to as "years and careers" as he ponders the "accident" of his long involvement with the Basques; the tendency in time to become identified with the culture one proposed to study objectively; the problems of career maintenance, program building, and routinization. With disarming candidness Joan Ablon asserts that the underlying purpose of her work has been "to de-mystify the nature of dwarfism." It troubles her little that anthropologists like herself might be considered to occupy "a marginal, interstitial space" in the discipline. When asked what is anthropological about her "applied" and "partisan" approach, her response is forthright—"life history, how individuals have lived, coped and changed in a culture and society." She is especially regardful that her work has value to those she studies, and she does not think that, once committed, one can ever withdraw from "the field."

From another vantage point, Robert Winzeler recalls that he once was somewhat fearfully taken for a headhunter by a group of Melanau, in contrast to the Iban who were bemused by the general European preoccupation with headhunting. As a people proud of their history, in which warfare and ritual head-taking were endemic, albeit incidental to a complex heritage, the Iban deride the distortive focus of inquisitive aliens. In this context Winzeler remarks that anthropology must be wary of being perceived as "the science of the strange," or as the pursuit of "the bizarre seen through the lens of respectability." The intellectual and emotional involvements of repeated and intensive study among peoples of another culture preclude this derangement by compelling attention to the course of lives and to changing conditions and adaptations. Thus his interest in problems of ethnohistory and ethnicity alerts him to potentially rewarding lines of new research into the rapidly transforming world he studies. Why is it, for example, that the modern Dayaks of the forest are striving to apprehend their past while the coastal peoples are trying to forget it? These and other absorbing queries are what have brought him again and again to Malaysia. He also admits to a strong attachment to the region as the place he likes most to be.

For James Fernandez the subjective accretions of life in the field endure because of "the preservative power of memory in our body." He avers that our abstract concepts have their roots in bodily metaphor, in the task-mastery and handiwork by which we learn and communicate with others. From this memory, expanding in scope over time, we derive our sense of the flow of culture. Fernandez asks of himself whether during his early sojourns among the people he chose to study he could ever have imagined what the world would now be like for us or them. Could he have envisioned a socialist Spain or the Africa of today? Yet as the bonds of mutuality with others extend over the years, our memory deepens and we are less likely to be confounded by the unforseen. What once seemed true was only partially so, and relative to time and place.

Those thoughts reverberate in me, as well, as I think of the vigorous Gola societies in which I once lived and worked, but now decimated by Liberian civil wars, or when I recall the destitute Washoe people of the 1950s, ignored and slated for cultural extinction, but now proclaiming nationhood and self-determination as a unified tribe on the remnants of their ancient lands. My memory informs me that not only would such eventualities have been deemed highly improbable four decades ago, but that I would not now care to harbor a guess about the state of things a decade hence. If hindsight is indeed superior to foresight, as received wisdom instructs us, one must conclude that our task is clear: to observe and experience the emerging present as responsibly as possible so that our collective memory contains an accurate account of the past for the future to interpret. Anthropology can be more, but no less than this.

Similar reflections on time and change permeate Catherine Fowler's moving account of affinity with her "native mentors" among the Northern Paiute. She writes that her interest has always been in specific individuals and that, regardless of what is being investigated, ethnography is ultimately the product of relations between persons. The longer those relationships are maintained the deeper are the ties and responsibilities. The death of two old people with whom she had formed a close bond over many years—her virtual grandparents—and the successive passing of other treasured elders, each an irreplaceable guide into a disappearing language and lifeway, were profoundly affecting events that overwhelmed her at times with the pathos of bereavement and cultural loss. All around her, nevertheless, were the tenacious cycles of family life—the children, and now the grandchildren of those remarkable old ones among whom she has been given the roles of special friend, a kin, and recorder of memories. As these young people awaken to a revival of tribal heritage, she is sought after for past knowledge and feels the anguish of not having learned and written more. She wonders whether she is prepared to face the realities of change as it unfolds for them, and how the fragments of their past culture will survive and mutate into the future. As for what brought her to anthropology as a vocation, she says that she wanted to be a veterinarian in her youth, and then a museologist, but that an early trip to the American Southwest and a stint on a major archaeological project led her to Native American ethnology. What followed is, in the words of an esteemed elderly scholar, "a coherent life of feeling and commitment."

In a deeply considered exposition, Simon Ottenberg affirms the view that "personal emotional involvement is the stuff of anthropology," and refers to his decades of engrossment in Africa as "my changing dialogue with the Afikpo." This long and intimate association has imbued his reflections with a keen appreciation of transience. He speaks of being astonished on each visit among the people he has known at the vast changes that have taken place since he saw them last. But these changes also are marked by the deaths of friends and surrogate relatives at a rate far greater than at home. The changing world is an uncompromisingly mortal one. Ottenberg notes the possible hazards of long-term study of the same people, for it may nurture an unwitting intellectual nostalgia for the past, a compassionate urge to become an advocate or defender. Yet he attests to an abiding concern about the effects of his writings on how the Afikpo are perceived. The ethnographer, after all, is often an inadvertent shaper of history, or a patent revisionist whose veracity should be called into account. His colleagues will acknowledge, however, that his summons to Nigeria in 1988 to be gowned as a "junior elder" was a confirmation of accountability and valued entrance into local history that all of us would cherish as a consequence of our own work.

But he, too, asks why one goes into anthropology in the first place. For him, as with many others, the answer is located in early life. When I read that he associates the attraction Afikpo village life had for him with a childhood among beloved close relatives in a small Swiss village, I felt a pang of empathy. I was reminded that I wanted one day to begin a memoir for my children with the line—"My maternal grandmother was a Swedish peasant who spoke in tongues, and my paternal great grandfather was an Azorean whaler." At the age of six or seven I imagined that I was the only one of my grandmother's resolutely Americanizing descendants who cared to comprehend her pentecostal art; and, later, I had to go to sea to find my way into anthropology—the only discipline I could have tolerated or, perhaps, the only one that would have tolerated me. I think that when Ottenberg suggests that many of us are motivated by a yearning for a lost ethnicity, he is on the mark. If one probes far enough down, the luminous moments of fateful arrivals and departures can be rediscovered.

My selective reading of the essays in this book is, of course, very much my own and thus subject to the skew of entrenched humors and fixations, a privilege apparently granted me in this instance. There is a great deal more to this rich lode than what I have mined for my present use, but each reader will find a different vein and strike a claim. To me, the prize was a confirmation of my longstanding opinion that anthropologists are of a special breed—especially those who have lived *in the field* a better part of their lives. For them, what once may have been exotic or alien in cultural diversity becomes familiar and reassuring: so-called culture shock gives way to the elation of discovery within expanding frontiers of reciprocity. In the long term, this kind of learning generates transformations that conjoin the persons and meanings of another way of life with the self as the subject of a vitalizing inner dialogue.

Now lest I be charged with suggesting that our profession is a sanctuary for an elect, let me state again that I do not believe the transcultural perspective to be an exclusive endowment among anthropologists but is an attribute of particular individuals who may be found in any walk of life in any society. However, it is through anthropology as we profess it—and especially in the practice of ethnography—that this orientation is tempered by "the handiwork and task-mastery" of a discipline devoted to its employment and elucidation. My thesis in these pages has been that the more we know about its practitioners as participants and students in the world as it is, the more we clarify our resolve.

And one last afterthought: I would like to believe that time and learning will obliterate our current need to render asunder that poor word "other." Whether as adjective, pronoun, or noun, whether burdened with italics or initial capital, other is simply other no matter how we deconstruct the text or strive to distance the one from the other in time and space. Others knowing others must eventually, if not sooner, face one another without masks as living, feeling, and communicating beings growing older together in a real world. I am grateful for what others have written here about themselves and their lives with others.

Contributors

Joan Ablon (Ph.D., University of Chicago) is a professor of medical anthropology at the University of California, San Francisco. Her research interests include the anthropology of health systems and stigmatized health conditions.

Warren L. d'Azevedo (Ph.D., Northwestern University) is professor emeritus at the University of Nevada, Reno. His research interests include ethnology and comparative art and religion in West Africa and the western United States.

William A. Douglass (Ph.D., University of Chicago) is director of the Basque Studies Program at the University of Nevada, Reno. His research interests center on European peasant societies and ethnic minority groups.

James W. Fernandez (Ph.D., Northwestern University) is a professor of anthropology at the University of Chicago. His research interests include studies of cultural symbolism and change, especially in the Western Mediterranean region.

Catherine S. Fowler (Ph.D., University of Pittsburgh) is a professor of anthropology at the University of Nevada, Reno. Her research interests include Native American languages and ethnography and ethnobiology.

Don D. Fowler (Ph.D., University of Pittsburgh) holds the Mamie Kleberg Chair in Anthropology and Historic Preservation at the University of Nevada, Reno. His research interests are in North American archaeology and the history of anthropology.

Donald L. Hardesty (Ph.D., University of Oregon) is a professor of anthropology at the University of Nevada, Reno. His research interests are in ecological anthropology and historical archaeology of frontier societies.

Simon Ottenberg (Ph.D., Northwestern University) is professor emeritus at the University of Washington. His research interests include social and political change, art, and ethnicity, especially in Africa.

M. Nazif Shahrani (Ph.D., University of Washington) is professor of Uralic and Altaic studies and anthropology at Indiana University. His research interests include social and political anthropology, religion, and cultural ecology in the Middle East and Central Asia.

Robert L. Winzeler (Ph.D., University of Chicago) is a professor of anthropology at the University of Nevada, Reno. His research interests include social change, psychological anthropology, and ethnicity in insular Southeast Asia.